The Intangible Economy

The volume highlights the evolution and significance of services in the global economy, including as a vehicle for development. It discusses the major pillars that hold the services infrastructure together, namely, its governance and financing mechanisms.Some of the chapters adopt more specific geographical or sectoral perspectives, including a regional study of the impact of services in economic integration in ASEAN; a country-level analysis of the role of services in economic and social upgrading in India; a look at industry-specific dynamics through the business process outsourcing model; and finally, a value chain view to understand how services are impacted on a granular or micro level by policies.

Deborah Elms is Founder and Executive Director of the Asian Trade Centre, Singapore. She is also a senior fellow in the Singapore Ministry of Trade and Industry's Trade Academy. Her research interests are negotiations and decision making and her current research involves the Trans-Pacific Partnership (TPP), Regional Comprehensive Economic Partnership (RCEP), ASEAN Economic Community (AEC) negotiations and global value chains.

Arian Hassani is currently based in Hong Kong where she covers J. P. Morgan's philanthropic activities across ASEAN and Australia, focusing on job creation and poverty alleviation. She has over 14 years of experience as an international development professional. Before joining J. P. Morgan, Arian managed Fung Global Institute's (FGI) research on Asian finance, supply chains, governance and sustainability.

Patrick Low is Visiting Professor and Director of the Asia Global Institute's Asia Global Fellows Programme at Hong Kong University. From 1997–2013, he was Chief Economist at the World Trade Organization and a senior research economist at the World Bank from 1990–94, where he worked on trade issues, trade and environment, fiscal policy and governance in customs administrations.

Development Trajectories in Global Value Chains

A feature of the current phase of globalization is the outsourcing of production tasks and services across borders, and increasing organization of production and trade through global value chains (GVCs), global commodity chains (GCCs), and global production networks (GPNs). With a large and growing literature on GVCs, GCCs, and GPNs, this series is distinguished by its focus on the implications of these new production systems for economic, social and regional development.

This series publishes a wide range of theoretical, methodological and empirical works, both research monographs and edited volumes, dealing with crucial issues of transformation in the global economy. How do GVCs change the ways in which lead and supplier firms shape regional and international economies? How do they affect local and regional development trajectories, and what implications do they have for workers and their communities? How is the organization of value chains changing and how are these emerging forms contested as more traditional structures of North-South trade are complemented and transformed by emerging South-South lead firms, investments, and trading links? How does the large-scale entry of women into value chain production impact on gender relations? What opportunities and limits do GVCs create for economic and social upgrading and innovation? In what ways are GVCs changing the nature of work and the role of labour in the global economy? And how might the increasing focus on logistics management, financialization, or social standards and compliance portend important developments in the structure of regional economies?

The series includes contributions from many disciplines and interdisciplinary fields and approaches related to GVC analysis, including GCCs and GPNs, and is particularly focused on theoretically innovative and informed works that are grounded in the empirics of development related to these approaches. through their focus on the changing organizational forms, governance systems, and production relations, volumes in this series contribute to on-going conversations about theories of development and development policy in the contemporary era of globalization.

Series editors

The Intangible Economy

How Services Shape Global Production and Consumption

Edited by
Deborah K. Elms
Arian Hassani
Patrick Low

CAMBRIDGE
UNIVERSITY PRESS

CAMBRIDGE
UNIVERSITY PRESS

University Printing House, Cambridge CB2 8BS, United Kingdom
One Liberty Plaza, 20th Floor, New York, NY 10006, USA
477 Williamstown Road, Port Melbourne, vic 3207, Australia
4843/24, 2nd Floor, Ansari Road, Daryaganj, Delhi – 110002, India
79 Anson Road, #06–04/06, Singapore 079906

Cambridge University Press is part of the University of Cambridge.

It furthers the University's mission by disseminating knowledge in the pursuit of education, learning and research at the highest international levels of excellence.

www.cambridge.org
Information on this title: www.cambridge.org/ 9781108416153

First published 2017

Printed in India by Shree Maitrey Printech Pvt. Ltd., Noida

A catalogue record for this publication is available from the British Library

Library of Congress Cataloging-in-Publication Data
Names: Elms, Deborah Kay, editor. | Hassani, Arian, editor. | Low, Patrick, 1949- editor.
Title: The intangible economy: how services shape global production and consumption / edited by Deborah K. Elms, Arian Hassani, Patrick Low.
Description: Delhi: Cambridge University Press, 2017. | Includes bibliographical references and index.
Identifiers: LCCN 2016059504 | ISBN 9781108416153 (hardback :alk. paper)
Subjects: LCSH: Service industries–Government policy. | Service industries–Economic aspects. | Globalization--Economic aspects.
Classification: LCC HD9980.6 .I58 2017 | DDC 338.4--dc23 LC record available at https://lccn.loc.gov/2016059504

ISBN 978-1-108-40265-1 Paperback

CONTENTS

LIST OF FIGURES, TABLES AND BOXES

FIGURES

TABLES

BOXES

ACKNOWLEDGEMENTS

Most of the chapters in this volume originated from presentations and discussions at a Singapore Dialogue on Services held in June 2014. The Dialogue was organized jointly by the Temasek Foundation Centre for Trade and Negotiations (TFCTN) and the Fung Global Institute of Hong Kong. In addition to the presenters, the Dialogue was attended by senior government officials from the Asia region.

The editors wish to express their gratitude to TFCTN for funding the event and to the contributors – both those who attended the Dialogue and those who contributed chapters subsequently – for their willingness to contribute to the volume and their patience and cooperation as the volume was prepared for publication.

The editors would also like to express their gratitude to Cambridge University Press, India for their support. In particular, Dhiraj Pandey, Qudsiya Ahmed and Aditya Majumdar who were helpful and supportive throughout the process of preparation for publication.

Finally, we would like to thank the anonymous referees whose comments helped to make this volume a better product.

Deborah K. Elms
Arian Hassani
Patrick Low

1

Introduction

Deborah K. Elms, Arian Hassani and Patrick Low

The literature on global value chains (GVCs) has been growing fast over the past decade. It is diffused and has to deal with a rapidly changing world. The authors contributing to this collection of essays consider contemporary challenges and opportunities facing business and government, which in different ways determine the location, configuration and operation of GVCs. The role of services in GVCs is at the centre of the analysis. Through that prism, the chapters consider the extent to which services can act as a catalyst for fuller GVC participation to promote development, growth and jobs.

In what follows, chapter 2 by Low and Hassani focuses on the role of services in the global economy. It begins with a historical discussion of the distinguishing features of services, and considers some of the reasons for past neglect of the contribution of services to the economy, including their perceived incapacity to contribute to productivity growth. Attention is also paid to definitional challenges, measurability and data issues. Certain shortcomings in these domains have resulted in misleading analysis of the importance of services, especially in trade.

In chapter 3, Findlay discusses the challenges of making services work for development. He argues that there are some common principles among goods and services for the development and design of successful reform packages. However, a number of differences between reforms aimed at goods and those targeting services require closer attention. Political economy considerations related to local political interests may influence attitudes to foreign entry in services markets. If impediments to services affect costs, rather than profits, reform could have significant employment effects. If protection is higher in services markets than in goods markets, domestic services providers will be more severely affected. Where services suppliers are subject to universal services obligations – for example in telecommunications or public transport – the ability to finance these obligations may constitute an additional source of resistance to change.

Abrenica (chapter 4) discusses the challenges facing East Asian economies in surpassing the middle-income trap. Only a handful of these economies have attained developed country status, while a good number seem to be caught in a pit of relative economic stagnation. In mainstream literature, a huge part of the East Asian success story in attaining middle income status is attributed to the use of trade to promote domestic growth and overcome development hurdles. While the author does not deny that the realities of the present global ecosystem and the development challenges they present are different from the 1980s, she observes that many still see the East Asian model relevant insofar as it offers an escape path that combines trade with the right mix of domestic policies. The chapter considers how middle-income countries might escape the trap by leveraging their participation in GVCs. However, policy needs to give full play to the development of services as an enabler of trade.

In chapter 5, Stephenson and Pfister seek to clarify the discussion of governance in GVCs, including in the realm of services. They argue that the debate has been obscured by a lack of definitional clarity as to the meaning of the word 'governance'. The authors set out a typology of GVC governance in three different categories. First, industrial policy frameworks look at the governance of GVCs from the firm perspective. Second, national policy frameworks consider governance from an individual country perspective. Finally, in a global trading system framework, the focus is on the World Trade Organization (WTO) and major preferential trade agreements. Stephenson and Pfister maintain that governance considerations at the firm level are the most straightforward to comprehend. For the other levels of analysis, they lay out several recommendations to remedy governance gaps, urging the WTO and the international community to step up efforts in multilateral leadership, ensuring that any gains captured through more efficient GVC governance are beneficial for development and inclusive growth.

Pasadilla (chapter 6) looks at how financial services enable GVCs. She notes that no globally-accepted framework has been developed in this domain. The chapter seeks to demystify various structures and incarnations of supply chain finance by applying two lenses. One is structured trade finance and the other involves specific bank financing instruments that link suppliers and buyers in a supply chain relationship. The author argues that in order to facilitate supply chain financing for small and medium-sized enterprises (which are significant sources of revenue and job creation in developed and developing countries), there is a need to shift more broadly toward asset-based lending practices instead of balance sheet-based ones. This will require the reform of legal and regulatory frameworks in many economies, especially to facilitate financing for movable assets.

Chapter 7 (Tijaja) looks at the role of services in GVCs in the Association of South East Asian Nations (ASEAN). She observes that as trade, investment and GVCs have proliferated in the region, services have accounted for the largest share of direct investment inflows to the region in recent years. A number of ASEAN economies are seeking to overcome the middle-income trap and move up value chains, while others are seeking entry points for participating in GVCs. In all of these cases, services will feature more prominently in national as well as region-based agendas. The author argues that ASEAN's challenge is to further advance the region's understanding of services in order to shape a strategy, not only in the narrow terms of services integration, but also as an integral part of the region's development agenda. Beyond regional integration, future efforts should be informed by trends in e-commerce, additive/digital manufacturing, and data analytics, all of which have considerable services components where continuous innovation is a necessary element.

Nathan, Sarkar and Mehta (chapter 8) examine lessons from a 2004 decision by Airtel, an Indian telecommunications company, to outsource its entire information technology (IT) services requirement to a foreign company – International Business Machines Corporation (IBM) – rather than to one of several Indian IT majors, given the strong positioning of the latter companies in global outsourced IT services. The explanation is provided by taking a close look at the role of Indian IT companies in different segments of the IT services production network, with special attention to declining margins resulting from substantial increases in salaries. The authors argue that Airtel's decision hinged on IBM's stronger end-to-end service provision experience. Since that time, Indian IT companies have focused increasingly on developing end-to-end services and software products to remain globally competitive, while companies in the United States and elsewhere have been integrating low-end tasks (traditionally dominated by Indian IT majors) to provide fully managed services. This convergence between the US and Indian IT majors has significant implications for the role of services in India's economic development trajectory, which will necessitate addressing policies that promote human capital development, innovation and competitiveness.

In chapter 9, Mukherjee and Rawat examine how the outsourcing of business processes, also referred to as BPO, has enabled many businesses to improve the efficiency and effectiveness of their operations. Businesses have leveraged BPO to make their operations more scalable, flexible, resilient and cost effective, while delivering better service and value to their customers. Globally, the BPO industry has also created millions of jobs in low-cost countries, acting as a key enabler of economic transformation and opening up channels into the global services market. The authors argue that governments seeking to leverage the economic development potential of the BPO sector must adopt a planned approach to build capacity and market their value proposition. This requires that they enhance and mature their service delivery capacities and competitiveness, reduce capital and operational costs, and create business linkages with buyers of BPO services from target countries.

Cheung and Sit (chapter 10) consider the relationship between services and manufacturing activities in GVCs and examine the role of various policies in shaping value chain arrangements. Services are generally more highly regulated by governments than goods. Policies can impact costs and supply chain configurations in ways that are sometimes less than fully appreciated by policymakers and by business. They can add unnecessary costs if they are poorly designed or administered. The chapter identifies some of these policy influences, making reference to illustrations from case studies conducted by authors and their colleagues. The authors then explore approaches adopted in Singapore and Thailand, which have different economic structures and policy backdrops, in an attempt to set out government best practices for enhancing value addition of services in manufacturing GVCs.

2

Contextualizing Services in the World Economy

Patrick Low and Arian Hassani[1]

Introduction

Services are increasingly accorded a prominence in economic analysis and policy deliberation that they were long denied. This fresh focus is taking hold in tandem with the growing importance of services as a source of value in the global economy. The neglect of services can be explained largely in terms of western classical precepts, concerns about the sources of growth, traditional statistical conventions and the sparseness of data. Deep economic change is propelling their growing importance. Before analysing what is bringing about this change, it is worth taking a brief look at the growing contribution of services to gross domestic product (GDP) in different economies. Table 2.1 reports services shares in GDP for all income groups, geographical groupings and some individual economies. The table demonstrates two main things. The first is that worldwide, services are the most important source of value in the global economy, and by extension generate the greatest number of jobs and, on average, the most growth. The second is that services are consistently growing their share.

Table 2.1: Share of services in GDP by income group, region and selected countries (%)

Economy	1980	1990	2000	2013
World	n/a	n/a	67	70
High-income	n/a	n/a	70	74
Middle-income	39	44	50	55

Contd.

1 The contributors undertook this work while they were at the Fung Global Institute.

Low-income	n/a	41	45	46
East Asia and Pacific	n/a	n/a	n/a	n/a
Europe and Central Asia	n/a	n/a	n/a	n/a
Latin America and the Caribbean	n/a	n/a	n/a	n/a
Middle East and North Africa	n/a	n/a	n/a	n/a
North America	n/a	n/a	n/a	n/a
OECD	n/a	n/a	71	74
Sub-Saharan Africa	n/a	n/a	n/a	n/a
Bangladesh	48	47	53	56
Brazil	45	53	68	70
China	22	32	40	47
Hong Kong	n/a	n/a	88	93
Japan	58	60	67	73
Norway	58	63	7	59
Singapore	62	67	65	75
United Kingdom	n/a	67	72	79
Uzbekistan	n/a	34	43	48
United States	n/a	n/a	76	78

Source: World Bank, World Development Indicators (2015)

What about the preponderance of services in trade? The picture is quite different when contrasted with services in GDP. Historically, it has always been reported that services represent a small share of total exports. According to the WTO using traditional data, services were in the range 18.4 per cent (2011) and 23.4 per cent (2008) between 2008 and 2014 as a share of total merchandise imports (WTO, various years). These numbers are limited to services flows recorded separately, and in gross terms, in balance-of-payments statistics. When measured in a non-traditional way, in value-added terms consistent with the approach for measuring overall GDP, the share of services in merchandise trade was estimated at 45 per cent in 2008. That is an enormous difference and shows how poorly our understanding of the contribution of services to the economy has been because of the difficulties of extracting the appropriate data. We will revert to this issue in due course.

The rest of the chapter is organized as follows. Section 2 examines some of the reasons why services have been considered less important than they deserve over the years. Section 3 will seek to explain some of the statistical challenges encountered in dealing with services. Section 4 will explore aspects of services in national and global settings. It will consider how services are defined, whether it makes sense to attempt a definition of services based on their economic functions, and the issue of services and tradability.

The traditional neglect of services

Classical economic thought

The roots of economic reflection on services can be traced back to the classical thinkers. Adam Smith wrote in *The Wealth of Nations* that: '[T]he labour of a menial servant ... adds to the value of nothing ... services generally perish in the very instant of their performance, and seldom leave any trace or value behind' (Smith, 1776).

In essence, the issue turned on a distinction between productive and unproductive labour. Unproductive labour did not produce anything that contributed to accumulation in the cycle of production. A product that did not form part of a subsequent production process, nor embody value through accumulation, was unproductive. Services for consumption fitted into that category. Even today, with technological progress, many services are not storable and require instantaneous use, although contemporary reasoning would not relegate them to worthlessness.

In the classical framework, though, value tended to be attached to labour that made material commodities. Labour producing non-storable products was unproductive and such labour did not contribute to growth. This notion of value was not refuted by subsequent classical economists like Ricardo, but underwent modifications a generation or two later in the nineteenth century with influences from socialist thought, most notably from Marx.

Marx distinguished between the use value and the exchange value of a commodity, arguing that capitalist actors were only interested in the surplus value that could be realized upon the sale of a commodity rather than the mere use of it (Marx, 1867). As such, Marx concluded that productive labour is that which produces capital. If selling a good or a service produced capital, then the labour that would go into the production of this good or service would be 'productive' in nature. Marx did not place emphasis on physical accumulation when attributing value; rather, he underscored the importance of re-sale value of goods or services.

Needless to say, the role of services has evolved significantly since then, and the notion of productivity, in its multifaceted incarnations, has continued to be an important element in this evolution.

The Baumol cost disease

In the 1960s, Baumol and Bowen (1966), Baumol (1967) and Fuchs (1968) drew attention to what they viewed as an intrinsic lack of productivity associated with the services sector. These authors observed that labour productivity in the manufacturing sector grew much faster than in services industries, where it might not grow at all. These were labour-intensive services or relied heavily on human interaction, such as teaching and nursing.

Baumol and others argued that because productivity gains are primarily driven by technological innovation, over time services would become more expensive on a per unit basis. They were less amenable to technological advances than the manufacturing or retail sectors, for example. A key feature of the model was that wage levels were driven by those activities that generated productivity gains, thus raising wages inefficiently in some service industries. The market would not drive out the costly and unproductive service industries because they were considered socially essential and often supported by governments. Yet as economies became richer, those same service sectors would expand, aggravating the problem of low productivity growth.

In the wake of the technological integration of the knowledge economy in the late 1980s and early 1990s, along with more careful distinctions among categories of services and a re-thinking of the sources of productivity growth, fears regarding a cost disease trap receded. Baumol (1988, 1993), along with many others, contributed to this re-assessment of services in the economy. Francois and Hoekman (2010) reviewed a significant body of research that had been developing since the mid-1980s, suggesting that 'there is increasing evidence that services liberalization is a major potential source of gains in economic performance, including productivity in manufacturing and the coordination of activities both between and within firms' (Francois and Hoekman, 2010).

Manufacturing and neglect of services

Some recent commentaries and academic work on the implications of trade on jobs have pointed to massive job reductions in manufacturing employment (see, for example, Acemoglu *et al.*, 2016; Scott, 2015; Morley, 2006). The losses have mostly been attributed to trade with emerging economies, as opposed to productivity growth. The main point to be made here about this literature is that little or nothing is said about job opportunities in services, which have been growing as part of the process of adjustment to new competitive forces.

Similarly, in public policy discussions following the 2008 global financial crisis and its knock-on effects in the real economy, policymakers in advanced and emerging economies have tended to focus on increasing investment and net exports in manufacturing. Any consideration of services is frequently absent despite the fact that job expansion has been observable in services sectors, both in the context of manufacturing activities and in the wider economy.

This neglect is partly attributable to the statistical challenges of identifying and measuring services in production (see Section 3 below). Other factors on both the production and consumption side raising the economic footprint of services activities have also received less attention than deserved. A part of the explanation for this may be rooted in an embedded sub-consciousness that sees services as the poor cousin of manufacturing and perhaps other sources of value in the economy at large.

Services and productivity

The notion that services were characterized by low productivity took a narrower sectoral view than would be warranted today and additionally, was more prominent before the digital economy became what it is today. How, then, are services contributing to productivity growth? A major part of the story has to do with the advancement of technological innovation in the services sector; however, another, and arguably more policy-significant, component of the discussion relates to an evolution in the way productivity is perceived and understood. Productivity is a complex and multifaceted notion, and what follows only scratches the surface to illustrate some of the issues upon which clarity is required in order to make precise claims about changes in productivity.

A traditional measure of productivity, defined as output per working hour, is a single factor productivity measure that relates output to labour. The same approach could be used with labour and capital, although measuring the value of capital is harder than estimating hours worked by the labour force. These are relatively straightforward measures, but do not capture all sources of increased efficiency. The notion of total factor productivity (TFP) was developed in an effort to capture other sources of growth, particularly those emanating from services.

TFP is a multifactor measure that accounts for effects in total output not caused by labour and/or capital inputs, including technology, organizational efficiency, networks, institutions, and much more. TFP is not determined through a direct measure; rather, it is residual – what remains once labour and capital contributions to growth are accounted for. This has led many policymakers to assume that TFP represents the aggregate efficiency with which labour and capital inputs are utilized, a concept that at its surface seemed more aligned with the characteristic needs and drivers of the services sector.

As Krugman noted (1994), and as many other scholars, including Felipe (2008), have echoed, TFP by itself does not have a useful or meaningful purpose. In laymen's terms, Felipe draws attention to the 'cake problem,' where he draws an analogy between assessing the importance of a cake's individual ingredients to the size (or taste) of the baked cake, and analysing the individual contributions of labour, capital and TFP to the size of the economy (Felipe, 2008). It seems pointless to conclude that 40 per cent of a cake's size (or taste) is due to flour, 30 per cent due to butter, and so on, until a remaining 10 per cent is due to the cook's own skills. The cake tastes the way it does because of the interaction of the cook's skills, ingredients, cooking conditions, tools and utensils. Focusing productivity-augmenting policy efforts solely on TFP outcomes does not make sense.

What does this mean for policymakers? Improving productivity, especially in the services sector, requires a thorough understanding of an economy's specific dynamics including structural conditions, security, savings rates, educational outcomes (and returns to education), labour force development/training, rule of law, technological development and innovation, sustainability and all of the other factors that lead to prosperous economies.

The challenges of data

Identifying and pricing the product

The value of services has always been difficult to estimate. There are several explanations for this. Apart from the analytical neglect of services in the past, they are statistically elusive for at least three reasons. First, they are hard to count because of their intangibility and this can make transactions more difficult to observe and record.

Second, often services are attached or incorporated in other products and so their value can be mis-specified as part of those products. This is far less likely to happen where statistics are collected on a value-added basis, as with GDP accounts. Even then, however, in the absence of arm's length transactions – that is, when the services are supplied in-house as inputs into other products – their value will typically be recorded in the cost or price of the final product into which they were incorporated. The same is true of goods entering production via in-house supply in a production process, but this would seem to be a much more infrequent occurrence than in the case of services.

Third, services by their nature are customized. A dentist, for example, will not be selling the identical product to every patient – the composition of each offering will usually be different, according to need. Goods, on the other hand, are more often produced to standard specifications. Observing real as opposed to actual prices, and accurate price-quantity relationships, are fraught with difficulty. In practice, ways are found around this. Service suppliers, for example, will often price in terms of delivery time. Identifying the real nature of the underlying products is nigh impossible when costs are expressed in hours and a good deal of heterogeneity is overlooked.

Value-added versus gross measurement

As noted previously, when services exports are measured in gross terms rather than net or value-added terms, they appear to represent a much smaller share of trade because they are typically classified as part of the product to whose value they contributed as inputs. This is arguably the single most important insight occasioned by the switch to estimating trade in value-added rather than gross terms. The estimated share of services in exports jumps from less than one-quarter of trade to around one-half. This is still an under-estimate for the reasons spelled out below.

Strictly speaking, this under-counting of the services share only occurs when the exported product is a good. If it is a service, then the nature of the service input is not recorded correctly. The problem in this case is one of classification only, not of an under-estimation of the overall contribution of services. A final point here is that whether the value chain in question is for goods or for services, even national GDP data will not fully specify the correct sources of value-added unless an arm's-length transaction has been recorded. This difficulty arises when inputs are supplied in-house, which is more likely to be the case with services than with physical inputs.

What can be characterized as a statistical problem has far-reaching ramifications for the way we see the world. The rise of international value chains – as a result predominantly of advances in information and transport technology – has significantly changed patterns and the composition of trade over the years. Up the two-thirds of trade now consists of intermediate products, many of which enter the production of exports. If these are not netted out through a value-added calculation, intermediate imports are incorrectly attributed to a country's export basket be they goods or services.

The only way to avoid this is to use an aggregated input-output matrix of the global economy that makes it possible to trace the origin and destination of all traded products. Essentially, what this does is to treat trade flows in the same way as purely domestic economic activity – that is, in value-added terms that net out the imports in a country's exports. Work of this nature is quite recent. It has been undertaken most notably by Institute of Developing Economies – Japan External Trade Organization (IDE-JETRO) (IDE-JETRO and WTO, 2011), the University of Groningen (Timmer, 2012), the Organisation for Economic Co-operation and Development (OECD) and WTO (OECD-WTO, 2012). Detailed explanations and some applications of the results of this work are reported in Elms and Low (2013).

These calculations are complex and time-consuming. They require the standardization and summation of national input-output matrices and for this reason existing databases do not include all countries. Increasingly, individual economies will be able to rely on firm-level data to make the necessary value-added estimates.

The consequences of expressing trade flows in value-added rather than gross terms are far-reaching, and emphasize the misleading nature of traditional trade measures. We have already noted the severe under-counting of the services' contribution to trade using gross flows. Second, bilateral trade balances can look quite different when the numbers tell us what the actual contribution of each jurisdiction is in a multicountry value chain. The IDE-JETRO/WTO (2011) study referred to above estimated that 2005 trade data recorded in gross terms over-stated China's current account surplus with the United States by 50 per cent. In other words, the true size of China's trade surplus with the United States was reduced by half when the import content of China's exports was allocated correctly to the countries where that value was generated. Value-added calculations do not change a country's aggregate trade balance. They only shuffle around the bilateral balances that sum to the total balance.

Third, because origins of added value are wrongly identified in gross trade flows, so too is their technology content. Several product-level studies undertaken in recent years have highlighted this point, including those on the iPod (Dedrick *et al.*, 2009), the iPhone (Xing and Detert, 2010), the iPad (Linden *et al.*, 2011) and the Nokia 95(Ali-Yrkkö *et al.*, 2011). In each case, these products were assembled in China and the gross trade data suggested that all the value of these relatively high tech products came from China. In reality, China's added value to these items was in single-digit percentage shares and consisted largely of assembly.

A fourth consequence is that gross trade data fails to demonstrate the nature of interdependency through trade relationships. A note by OECD-WTO (2012) on the iPhone 4, for example, shows that 90 per cent of the export value of this item that gross trade flows would have attributed to China actually came from Taiwan, Germany, Korea, the United States and a range of other countries. These numbers reveal a degree of trade interdependency entirely missing when everything is assumed to come from China merely because China was the last point of manufacture.

Services in national and global settings

Defining services

No straightforward definition of services has gained wide acceptance. Many definitions turn on product characteristics. In the WTO's General Agreement on Trade in Services (GATS), services are defined in terms of the manner in which they are delivered. Other attempts have been made to characterize services in terms of their economic functions. The most straightforward approach is to rely on a single specific characteristic of services – namely intangibility. This would seem to be the only characteristic of services that distinguishes them clearly from goods.

Other characteristics of services have attracted attention as distinguishing features, but these either do not apply to all services or they are not unique to services in a comparison with goods. These features include their storability, the question whether physical proximity is required between consumers and producers and their lack of homogeneity. These will be considered briefly in turn.

Services are non-storable if they must be produced and consumed simultaneously. This was the feature of services that led classical thinkers to argue that services embodied no value, since value was associated with accumulation. An example of a non-storable service might be live music. Concert-goers consume the music a band is making as it is made. But music can also be stored by multiple means and listened to repeatedly at any time. One may argue, of course, that a recording is not the same product as a live performance, in which case the products in question may not be 'like', or 'identical'. But they are no doubt highly substitutable.

Another frequently cited example is a haircut. Production and consumption are simultaneous and there is no medium through which a haircut can be produced and stored for later consumption. The hairdresser example also demonstrates the second feature of some services transactions, namely the need for close proximity between the provider and the customer. The physical presence constraint is often but not always linked to simultaneity of production and consumption. The haircut illustrates this, where not only must the haircut be consumed as it is produced, it also requires physical proximity for the transaction to occur.

Unlike intangibility, neither instantaneous production and consumption, nor the need for physical proximity, uniquely defines services. Moreover, digital technology, along with other technologies, has lessened the imperative for these transactional requirements over time. Information and communications technology and the internet have taken out these historical constraints on doing business to a significant degree. Besides the fact that these constraints do not beset all services, they can be found in some cases involving goods, weakening any suggestion that these transactional characteristics are unique to some services. Take the example of highly perishable food that does not travel or keep. The diners will need to be very close to the chefs to enjoy the product.

The final characteristic mentioned above that is often linked with services is the heterogeneous nature of products entering markets. While we often associate manufacturing, mining and food production with rather homogeneous mass output bearing identical or near identical characteristics, services are often differentiated and customized.

But differences and similarities among product categories are a matter of degree. If one thinks of personal offerings such as medical, dentistry or surgery services, these will often be quite different and unstandardized among patients. On the other hand, low-priced tourism packages are likely to vary much less.

Similarly with goods, cars may come off the production line as identical, but they are then customized in a variety of ways and can no longer be seen as perfect substitutes. Uniformity is a matter of degree, as well as a matter of the extent of disaggregation applied to product categories. While services may tend to be more customized than goods, this cannot be usefully seen as a binary distinction. Moreover, pricing practices commonly encountered in service supply, such as charging by the hour, will have a smoothing effect on actual differences in the market place.

The functions of services in production

So far the discussion has been about what makes goods and services different. A relative lack of familiarity with services, for all the reasons discussed above, makes it worthwhile to consider whether more can be said about the functions of services in production. One way encountered in the literature of distinguishing between functions is in terms of 'embodied' and 'embedded' services. It is not entirely clear, at least to this author, where this distinction originated.

Embodied services are defined in Drake-Brockman and Stephenson (2012) as those entering manufacturing, such as transport, communications and financial services. Embedded services contribute to the sale of a good, such as retail and after-sales service. The distinction is not entirely clear or complete. Some services, such as back-office functions, management and administration may be both embodied and embedded. Moreover, if the definitions only cover services entering manufacturing value chains, a gap opens up when it comes to services in services – that is, when services are inputs along value chains whose final output is a service and not a good.

Even if definitional distinctions that distinguish among services more directly in terms of what they actually bring to production, trade and consumption could provide a better take on sources of value, such distinctions are elusive. No functional definition has been developed and so services are not classified in this manner in established nomenclatures, such as the UN's Central Product Classification (2015). Some input services have been referred to as the 'glue' that holds value chains together, making their particular configuration and operation possible. Such services have also been characterized as 'producer services' and include transport, communications, financial services, distribution and business services.

These services could arguably be considered indispensable in one form or another across practically all value chains, whether the final product is a good or a service. Their demand is derived and this is a major reason why it has become increasingly futile to draw sharp distinctions between goods and services. The fact that the demand for so many services is driven from the input side is also one reason for challenging the assumption that there is a feasible development path that allows countries to skip manufacturing and go straight from the primary to the tertiary sector.

This does not help us greatly with the definitional question. Is there anything useful or revealing about a function-based categorization of services? Ultimately, one could argue that all services inputs, whether into manufacturing or some other sector, are producer services. This would suggest a certain futility in any attempt to develop a functional categorization, even if we know that services are a source of great variety in terms of product characteristics.

Service inputs and tradability

A last point worth making about what distinguishes goods and services concerns tradability. Traditionally, many services have been considered non-tradable, whereas this is regarded as far less frequent in the case of goods. Many services supplied as products for final consumption are indeed non-tradable. Take, for example, restaurants, hairdressers, or real-time live entertainment. The only way these can be traded is if factors of production cross frontiers so that the supplier of the services changes jurisdiction rather than the service itself. Allowing for product and factor flows across frontiers makes almost everything tradable, at least in a temporally neutral sense – that is, before the sunk costs of investment have been incurred. In other words, the two means of trading services – through delivery across jurisdictions or through a commercial presence – are by no means perfect substitutes.

When it comes to services that are inputs into production, however, almost all of these are tradable as long as the final product that they are part of is also tradable. Take the example of cleaning services in a shoe factory that exports footwear. Those cleaning services are highly location-specific if taken alone. But a reckoning of the sources of value that make up the shoes that are exported will include the service of keeping the factory clean where the shoes are produced, and so the cleaning services are tradable. Other examples are labelling and packaging services, which by themselves cannot be traded, but as part of the value of the product that is traded, they are indeed traded. What these examples point to is the fact that any services entering the production of a traded good or service are traded. The same logic applies to goods, but it is less surprising because many a physical component entering production could also be traded independently.

The realization that services are tradable across frontiers to a much greater degree than commonly assumed has implications for perceptions of comparative advantage and is relevant when it comes to specialization choices. Supplier decisions about what to bundle together in a product offering will be influenced by a range of market-related factors. But government policy can also exert a significant influence on these decisions. Good reasons may well exist for taking a different regulatory stance with various components of a bundled offering. Nevertheless, there remains a sense in which the absence of policy neutrality can affect the composition of a bundle in ways that are not necessarily optimal from both a social and private perspective.

Summary and conclusion

This chapter has briefly reviewed a range of issues pertinent to an understating of the role of services in the economy. The starting point is recognition of the historical neglect to which services has been subjected, partly on account of the traditions of classical economic thought. Later on, a widespread view of services was that they contributed little to productivity and would therefore become a growing drag on economic growth. Both of these perspectives have been greatly modified in more recent times. Moreover, services generate an increasing share of GDP, a share that grows bigger as economies expand and become more sophisticated. Services are also a larger share of trade than originally appreciated, and in all likelihood make up at least half of cross-border product trade.

A further challenge traditionally confronting services is the challenge of measurement. Services are invisible, frequently customized and not readily priced with the same accuracy as goods. The multiplicity of service activities and their importance in both production and trade has been highlighted by the recent breakthrough in measuring international trade in value-added rather than gross terms, just as GDP is measured. Much remains to be done to improve measurement and data collection.

A good deal has been written about how to define services in terms of their characteristics, particularly in relation to goods. The only truly differentiating characteristic between all services and all goods is that services are intangible. Other characteristics of services, such as the need for physical proximity in transactions, the lack of storability and a lack of product homogeneity are mostly a matter of degree, or do not matter significantly in substantive terms. It is the intangibility that complicates identification and challenges measurement the most.

Despite efforts to define services in terms of their multiple functions as inputs in production, this does not seem to be a very fruitful or a useful endeavour from an analytical perspective. Nevertheless, the absence of an internationally agreed nomenclature for services sometimes hinders clarity. An important consequence of treating services as components of value-added in production in their own right is that it provides an insight into the bundles of goods and services that frequently make up third-party transactions in the economy. Identifying the sources of value in this way leads to the realization that all services inputs on value chains producing exported products are themselves part of traded value. In other words, all services entering production are in principle tradable. This has implications for views on the sources of competitiveness as well as for the potential impact of policy.

References

Acemoglu, Daron, Davind Aurtor, David Dorn, Gordon H. Hanson and Brendan Price. 2016. 'Import Competition and the Great U.S. Employment Sag of the 2000s', *Journal of Labor Economics* 34 (S1): S141–S198. Chicago: University of Chicago Press.

Ali-Yrkkö, Jyrki, Petri Rouvinen, Timo Seppäl and Pekka Ylä-Anttil. 2011. 'Who Captures Value in Global Supply Chains? Case Nokia N95 Smartphone', *Journal of Industry, Competition and Trade* 11 (3): 263–78.

Baumol, William J. 1967. 'Macroeconomics of Unbalanced Growth', *American Economic Review* 57 (3): 415–26.

———. 1988. 'Productivity Policy and the Service Sector', in *Managing the Service Economy: Prospects and Problems*, edited by Robert P. Inman, 301–18. Cambridge: Cambridge University Press.

———. September 1993. 'Health Care, Education and the Cost Disease: A Looming Crisis for Public Choice', *Public Choice* 71 (1): 17–28.

Baumol, William J. and William G. Bowen. 1966. *Performing Arts—The Economic Dilemma: A Study of Problems Common to Theater, Opera, Music, and Dance*. New York: The Twentieth Century Fund.

Canada-United States Free Trade Agreement (CUSTA). 1988. Available at: http://www.international.gc.ca/trade-agreements-accords-commerciaux/assets/pdfs/cusfta-e.pdf.

Dedrick, Jason, Kenneth L. Kraemer and Greg Linden. 2009. 'Who Profits from Innovation in Global Value Chains? A Study of the iPod and Notebook PCs', *Industrial and Corporate Change* 19 (1): 81–116.

Drake-Brockman, Jane and Sherry Stephenson. 2012. 'Implications for Twenty-First Century Trade and Development of the Emergence of Services Value Chains'. Available at: http://www.ictsd.org/downloads/2012/11/implications-for-21st-century-trade-and-development-of-the-emergence-of-services-value-chains.pdf.

Elms, Debbie and Patrick Low (eds.). 2013. *Global Value Chains in a Changing World.* Geneva: World Trade Organization.

Felipe, Jesus. 2008. 'What Policy Makers Should Know about Total Factor Productivity', *Malaysian Journal of Economic Studies* 45 (1): 1–19.

Francois, Joseph F. and Bernard Hoekman. September 2010. 'Services Trade and Policy', *Economic Literature* 48 (3): 642–92.

Fuchs, Victor, R. 1968. *The Service Economy*. New York: Columbia University Press.

IDE-JETRO and WTO. 2011. *Trade Patterns and Global Value Chains in East Asia: From Trade in Goods to Trade in Tasks.* Geneva: World Trade Organization.

Krugman, Paul. November/December 1994. 'The Myth of Asia's Miracle', *Foreign Affairs* 73 (6): 62–78.

Linden, Greg, Kenneth L. Kraemer and Jason Dedrick. March 2011. 'Who Captures Value in the Apple iPad?', unpublished mimeo.

Low, Patrick. 2013. 'The Role of Services in Global Value Chains', in *Global Value Chains in a Changing World*, edited by Deborah K. Elms and Patrick Low. Geneva: World Trade Organization.

Marx, Karl. 1867. *Capital*, Volume 1, Chapter 1, Section 3. Available at: https://www.marxists.org/archive/marx/works/download/pdf/Capital-Volume-I.pdf.

Morley, Robert. 2006. 'The Death of American Manufacturing', *The Trumpet.* February.

OECD-WTO Joint Note. 2012. 'Trade in Value-Added: Concepts, Methodologies and Challenges', Mimeo. Available at: https://www.wto.org/english/res_e/statis_e/miwi_e/miwi_articles_e.htm.

Scott, Robert E. August 2015. 'Manufacturing Job Loss: Trade, Not Productivity, Is the Culprit', *Issue Brief #402*. Economic Policy Institute.

Smith, Adam. 1776. 'An Inquiry into the Nature and Causes of the Wealth of Nations', in *Library of Economics and Liberty*, Book II.3.1 *Of the Accumulation of Capital, or of Productive and Unproductive Labour*, edited by Edwin Cannan. 1904. Groningen, Netherlands: University of Groningen. Available at: http://www.econlib.org/library/Smith/smWN8.html.

Timmer, Marcel. 2012. 'The World Input-Output Database (WIOD): Contents, Sources and Methods', *WIOD Working Paper Number 10*. Available at: http://www.wiod.org/publications/papers/wiod10.pdf.

United Nations Central Product Classification, Version 2.1. 2015. Available at: http://unstats.un.org/unsd/cr/downloads/CPCv2.1_complete%28PDF%29_English.pdf.

World Trade Organization. Various years. *International Trade Statistics*. Geneva: World Trade Organization.

Xing, Yuqing and Neal Detert. 2010. 'How the iPhone Widens the United States Trade Deficit with the People's Republic of China', *ADBI Working Paper Series No. 257*. Tokyo: Asian Development Bank Institute.

3

Services and Development

Priorities for Reform

Christopher Findlay

Introduction

The relationship between economic development and the role of the service sector has attracted much attention. The first point of focus is the relationship between development and the size of the sector. There is a positive relationship between per capita income and the share of services in GDP and between per capita income and the share of services in employment. In developed economies, these shares can be very high. For example, these shares in output are around 90 per cent in Hong Kong and Macau, and nearly 80 per cent in the United States. Even in developing countries, the services share of GDP is relatively high, for example, around 50 per cent in Bangladesh and 40 per cent in Vietnam, and can be larger than manufacturing.

Analysts have also paid attention to positive connections between services and other aspects of development. For example, the Asian Development Bank (ADB) stressed a linkage between female participation in the workforce and a reduction in poverty rates (2012). The reduction in poverty is associated with the employment effects of services sector growth. Economies with higher service sector shares also have higher female participation rates in their workforces.

More recently, researchers have given greater attention to the intersectoral significance of services, and the role of services in facilitating the development of the competitiveness of other sectors of the economy. This role is especially important with a greater focus on GVCs in the world economy (OECD, 2013). Participation in GVCs is seen to depend on the presence of high-performing service sectors (OECD, 2013). A further consequence of this contribution of services is a greater connectivity to markets and thereby to making globalization more inclusive, i.e., delivering a wider distribution of benefits to citizens.

In addition, services are attracting more attention as they have become more tradable. Their tradability, discussed in more detail below, is adding to the contributions services make to economic development. Participating in services trade and investment increases productivity through, for example, gains from trade and consequences of competition. However, as also discussed further below, there is a growing body of evidence of the impediments to trade and investment in services and of the value of reforms. Given the number of sectors and the complexity of policies involved, it is difficult to set and implement a pathway for services reform.

The aim of this chapter is to present a discussion of these challenges and some of the responses in making services work even better for development.

The next section returns briefly to the nature of services and the origins of the sector's growth. Then, the chapter offers a review of the drivers of the greater tradability of services and why tradability matters, followed by a discussion of the nature and extent of the impediments to tradability. Next, a section highlights the design of strategies for reform with a focus on four key policy points. The conclusion makes a point about successful implementation of reform.

Nature of services and their output share

understanding the nature of services and their origins adds to the value of a framework for designing a strategy for services reform.

Services were once compiled as a list of intangibles in national accounts – wholesale and retail, transport, communications, finance, business services, community services and personal services, for example. As discussed by Findlay (1990), a more analytical approach was proposed by Hill (1977) who argued that services were the result of transactions between economic organizations that had the effect of adding value to goods belonging to other people or those people themselves.

Production and consumption of services can take place simultaneously, unlike the production of goods. Services remain a value-adding activity that uses labour and capital as inputs, and the different intensities involved in different sectors lead to a scope for gains from trade. While the outputs of goods production processes can be stored as inventories, what is accumulated in the case of services production is the capacity to provide the services. This feature determines the structure of costs, as, for example, there is more likely a relatively high level of fixed costs and lower marginal costs (but not always).

Such a situation has consequences for the nature of competitive behaviour in these markets.

While transactions of a services-type can take place within organizations, for example, from machinery repairs or transport, once the transaction is derived from an external contract, it becomes part of the measured and identified 'service sector.' This phenomenon requires the act of contracting out, which involves a cost. However, as this cost is reduced as a result of greater confidence in the use of markets and the enforcement of contracts, the use of services transactions increases. There may be some loss due to the advantages associated with in-house familiarity, but new technologies, the importance of scale economies, the gains from specialization and the benefits from competition can all provide offsetting benefits, leading to the emergence of more and more services firms.

Bhagwati (1984) discussed the process that leads to services splintering off from goods. He argued that services generated in this way will be 'technologically progressive,' especially given drivers of scale and specialization. This is an important observation in the context of concerns of some scholars that productivity growth is more difficult in the services sector because it requires human interaction. Bhagwati also identified the possibility of situations in which technological change makes it possible for the provision of the services to be 'disembodied' from the provider and turned into a good. He used the example of recordings instead of live concert performances or university lectures. Bhagwati suggested that this 'disembodied' change occurs mainly in final services and that the process leaves behind a more labour-intensive and unproductive set of activities in the services sector.

The splintering process that occurs in service sectors is subject to the same drivers as those behind the growth of global value chains in goods production. Firms are deciding what to do in-house and what to contract out, as they do with respect to services activities. The same variables are relevant to the decisions. The global value chain emerges when some value adding activities are located offshore. The same international relocation can occur with respect to services inputs. Services production itself can be devolved into a series of activities that are located across economies, that is, services are associated with their global value chains. In addition, these processes are not independent since the growth of the service sector facilitates the emergence of global value chains in goods, and the latter creates new markets for services providers.

The splintering process alongside the positive income elasticity of demand for many personal services has led to a changing structure of the economy and rising shares of services in output and employment. Many authors have examined this process. Katouzian (1970), for example, considered three types of services. Old services were those involving domestic activities, such as cooking and cleaning, which he expected to decline in number as industrialization occurred given that demand for labour would rise as durable consumer goods replaced these tasks. Second, there are services that are complementary to industrialization, such as transport and storage. Finally, new services are those set to increase with income in the later stages of development, such as tourism and health. The advancement of complementary and new services contributed to the growth of the service sector overall, especially once old services had disappeared (which was likely to happen early in this process).

Buera and Kaboski (2012) stressed the connection between skill accumulation and service sector growth. As development occurred, workers acquired higher levels of skills, which tended to be specialized. The emergence of markets allowed workers to offer those skills in value-adding activities and the costs of market compared to in-house procurement fell. Rising incomes would lead to greater demand for these skilled services, raising the return to the acquisition of skills and thus leading to even greater purchases of services in the market.

Eichengreen and Gupta (2011) distinguished among three groups of services. The first was called traditional services and included activities such as retail and wholesale trade, transport and storage. Another group was modern services, including financial, computer, business, legal, and communications services. Eichengreen and Gupta called the third group a hybrid; mainly consumed by households, such as education, health, hotels, restaurants, and personal services. They found two waves of growth of the services sector. The first wave occurred even at low income levels and involved traditional services. The second wave was more likely to be focused on modern and hybrid services. There was variation in the rates of growth and the starting income levels across economies, and one significant factor that makes the second wave more apparent is openness to trade.

Eichengreen and Gupta compared their categories to those of Katouzian – their modern services were not so evident at the time of Katouzian's paper – and they argued that Katouzian's complementary services had become their traditional services, and that his new services are their hybrids. They were, therefore, mapping in quantitative terms the evolution that Katouzian envisaged in 1970.

As a result of the splintering process, the rest of the economy procures a rising share of value added from outside of the enterprise (or household). But the extent to which this occurs depends on the stage of development and other features of the economy. Recent work by the OECD and the WTO has demonstrated the significance of services for other sectors of the economy. Figure 3.1 shows the services share of gross exports in 2009 from domestic and foreign sources; that is, services exported in their own right as well as embodied in the exports of goods. The range of values is of interest. As expected, there are differences between high and low-income economies, but even economies with similarly high incomes have significantly different levels of service activity in exports. Policy conditions might be one explanation for this variation, in addition to economic structure, whose contribution to this variation is discussed below.

Figure 3.1: Services content of gross exports, 2009 and 1995

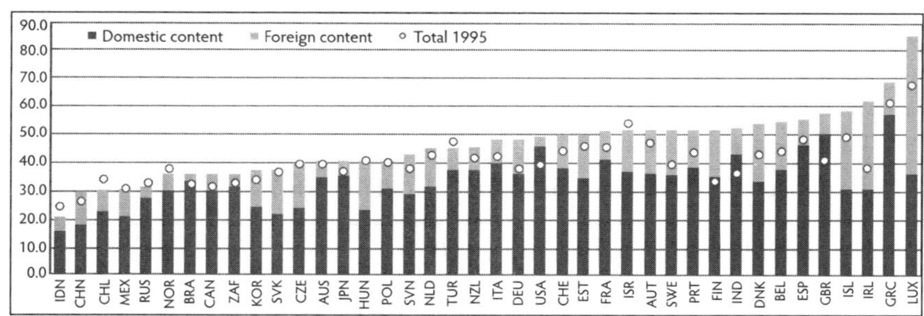

Source: http://www.oecd.org/industry/ind/measuringtradeinvalue-addedanoecd-tojoint-initiative.htm

Tradability of services

There is growing scope for international transactions in services and the WTO's GATS categorizes the options in terms of its 'modes of supply.'[1]

- From the territory of one member into the territory of any other member (Mode 1: cross-border trade), for example, services are provided through the internet or the postal service
- In the territory of one member to the service consumer of any other member (Mode 2: consumption abroad), for instance, international tourism or education
- By a service supplier of one member through commercial presence in the territory of any other member (Mode 3: commercial presence), such as services provided through a business established offshore

1 http://www.wto.org/english/tratop_e/serv_e/cbt_course_e/c1s3p1_e.htm.

- By a service supplier of one member through the presence of natural persons of a member in the territory of any other member (Mode 4: presence of natural persons), for instance, a university lecturer travels to another country to teach

The ability to trade services in each of the four modes is increasing with lower costs associated with the movement of people and digital information. The measurement of the activity within each mode remains an issue. An assessment is shown in Table 3.1. These transactions are embodied in the value added data highlighted in Figure 3.1. (Note that transactions as a result of commercial presence become part of 'domestic services' in those data.)

Table 3.1: Relative importance of mode of supplies in international services transactions

Cross-border supply (BOP[2])	35%
Consumption abroad (BOP travel)	10-15%
Commercial presence (Foreign affiliates)	50%
Presence of natural persons (BOP compensation)	1-2%

Source: Maurer, Magdeleine, and d'Andrea, (2006).

Trade and investment in services add to the contribution of services to the development process. Abrenica, Findlay and Lim (2009) argue that low-income economies can gain from services trade and investment liberalization, and that in the process, low-income households gain as well, through the following mechanisms:

- The introduction of foreign investment adds to capacity, lowers domestic prices and creates new services. Poor households, in particular, can gain as consumers of these services and Abrenica *et al.* (2009) refer to research that suggests the income effects for those households are more significant than for the average (in the case of financial development, for example, or access to information and communications technology).
- Trade and investment add to competition and productivity in other sectors, reducing transport markets and the cost of intermediate inputs. The impact of reform on the transport and logistics sectors for agriculture is an example. Most of the benefits of lower transport costs can be passed back to farmers since the final retail price can now be determined by world markets, leading to very significant changes in workers' incomes.

2 Balance of payments.

- Poor households may also gain through the labour market effects of foreign investment, adding to capacity and the demand for labour.
- Transactions in other modes offer access to services at lower costs and provide complementary inputs, enhancing productivity in various service sectors.

While these benefits are associated with international transactions, there are significant impediments to their execution, especially in modes 3 and 4 of those listed above. For example, there may be rules that limit the extent to which foreign investors can enter a market (e.g., through a licensing system), or rules on the ways in which foreign firms can enter a market (e.g., only as a joint venture, limits on services that can be provided or limits on location in which they can be provided). There may be rules that limit the ability of professionals to supply their services in another country (e.g., through lack of recognition of their qualifications or limits on the scope of services they can provide). The challenge is that these sorts of regulatory measures are widespread and also show a great level of diversity. They are in turn difficult to measure and therefore assess and compare across countries. A measure of that type would permit an assessment of the degree to which trade and investment in service was restricted in general and how that varied across economies. New work has made some progress on this problem.

The OECD has recently provided a new picture of the extent of the impediments to trade and investment and their variation by sector. As the OECD (2014) explains, its Services Trade Restrictiveness Index (STRI) is derived from a regulatory database across 40 countries and 18 sectors. The database is used to compile indices of restrictions across five categories with values from zero to one. A score of zero means the sector in the country concerned is completely open to trade and investment, while a score of one signified complete closure. Figure 3.2 contains summary data across the sectors, showing high, low and average index scores. The OECD stresses that the large gap between the average score and the maximum score of one should not be mis-interpreted as suggesting that services markets are largely open; 'they are not … a sector score above 0.1 is significant and scores between 0.2 and 0.3 represent quite significant restrictions on international trade' (OECD, 2014).

Figure 3.2: OECD STRI minimum, maximum and average scores

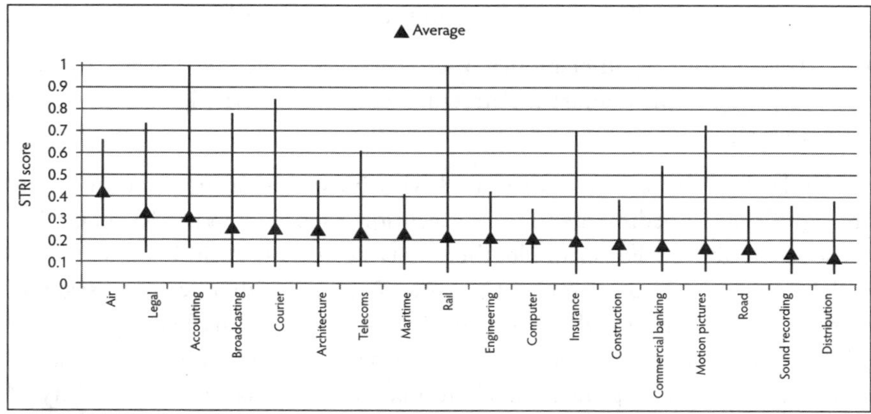

Source: OECD (2014)

Another form of a restrictiveness index was released by the World Bank based on a different framework and applied to information collected from a variety of sources, including respondents to a business survey.[3] He and Findlay (2014) used these index values to examine the drivers of the services' share of gross exports (using the trade in value-added data from the OECD/WTO project). They found that reducing the level of restrictions by this measure had a significant effect on the measured extent of services in gross exports. By examining the impact of reform on the various origins of services in exporters, they interpreted their results to imply that the policy effect of a reduced level of restrictiveness operated mainly through its effects on the scope for foreign firms to enter and establish a base in the economy from which exports were occurring.

The OECD also makes some observations about the impact of the reform of the policy measures included in the calculations of its index (OECD, 2014). OCED researchers conducted an experiment in which index values were reduced by five basis points for air transport, legal services, banking and insurance. They reported findings of a greater effect on services exports than on imports. Such an outcome could follow from the impact of services policies being mainly behind the border and thereby affecting the costs of all firms established in the economy (a similar channel to that identified by He and Findlay, 2014). It might also follow from effects on competition and consequent incentives to search out new markets, including exports.

A question that is important for the welfare effects of restrictions is whether

3 http://iresearch.worldbank.org/servicetrade/aboutData.htm.

they add to profits of those protected or whether they add to costs and therefore add to welfare effects. The OECD reports results in which higher STRI values raise the profit margins of domestic firms but lower those for foreign affiliates, suggesting that those from offshore who are able to establish in the face of the restrictions incur higher costs in doing so.

There are significant relationships between restrictiveness measures and the performance of markets. For example, the OECD (2014) reports that higher degrees of restrictiveness in telecommunications services are associated with lower rates of internet access. Further it found that better service quality in that sector contributed to improved export performance. Greater telecom density is associated with a greater degree of two way trade in electronics and also higher export prices. The OECD also found that lower degrees of restrictiveness in legal services, courier and distribution services were associated with lower costs of delivered intermediate inputs in electronics and lower consumer prices. In banking, they found that higher degrees of restrictiveness were associated with less access to credit in the private sector, higher net interest margins and greater operating expense as a proportion of interest income.

Applying a restrictiveness index from a similar methodology to that of the OECD but specific to liner shipping, Bertho, Borchert and Mattoo (2014) found that costs were higher due to restrictions, especially those on foreign investment, by between 24 per cent and 50 per cent, with some cases not observable since trade maybe inhibited completely. These higher shipping costs in turn reduce trade volumes by up to 46 per cent.

Services reforms will also complement policy initiatives in other areas. For example, the benefits of a large infrastructure investment programme could be distributed more widely if accompanied by reform to support the provision of services using those facilities in competitive markets. Otherwise the facility owners gather the gains from the additional capacity. The importance of competition was stressed in the case studies reviewed by Dee (2013) and Findlay (2013). Reforms in gas, electricity and rail sectors illustrate the value of setting a priority to introduce competition to these sectors rather than seeking to shift to private ownership in the first stages of reform.

Reform strategies for improving service opportunities

The methodology used to compile the OECD STRI values[4] illustrates the

4 http://www.oecd.org/tad/services-trade/methodology-services-trade-restrictiveness-index.htm.

complexity of measures that apply to services. Services can face a wide range of barriers, including horizontal measures related to foreign equity shares, the presence of statutory monopolies, rules on the movement of people, public procurement processes or administrative processes. In addition, there are specific measures to consider for some services, including licensing arrangements for professionals, barriers to competition in telecommunications, air transport regulations, network access arrangements in rail transport, the role of designated postal operators in courier services and various issues in banking and insurance. This list of items also provides an indication of the range of agencies likely to be involved in reform in services, even within one sector. The design and implementation of a package of reform in this context will be a challenge for policymakers. Given constraints on resources and different experiences in managing services reform, policymakers will be keen to identify priorities for action. This is the topic of the discussion of this section, with a view to deriving a series of policy suggestions or implications.

Services become increasingly important as development advances, especially since their contribution interacts with development. Development itself drives a larger services sector, while services support the next stage of growth. Markets are critical in this two way interaction, so appropriate institutions must be built to support and maintain confidence in contracting and the use of markets. This is the first policy implication.

Reform is fundamentally about competition and the conditions of entry for all providers. Services can contribute better to development when reforms lead to changes that exploit their tradability across all modes of supply. It is critical that services are delivered through rules that ease obstacles to establishment. However, significant barriers to trade and to investment remain. There are substantial gains in such cases from reforms to remove these impediments; although the removal of barriers will have implications for both domestic and foreign providers. The second key policy point is that the development of competition should be the priority in any reform programme.

Third, international commitments can play a part in sustaining policy reform domestically. Such promises can limit backsliding and provide confidence to investors. Commitments to trading partners can be scheduled whenever the policy environment is complex and/or multidimensional. The use of a negative list approach to negotiations, which highlights only areas where commitments do not apply, helps keep the provision of services open in new markets, including sectors that are not currently conceived or operating. However, evidence shows that often commitments made in trade agreements are less liberal than actual policy. The OECD (2014) reports, for instance, that GATS commitments are consistently more restrictive than actual policy, and in many cases by a number of basis points in terms of the STRI. As a result, governments should, at a minimum, engage to remove the 'water' in the commitments, which would have no effect on current policy since promises would be bound to actual current levels.

Finally, with respect to the policy agenda, there is the question of deciding on sectoral priorities for reform. It is important to pay attention to:

- *The height of barriers:* Dee (2013) not only refers to the height of barriers, but also to their effects on costs and profits. Greater welfare effects come from dealing with higher barriers that have greater effects on costs rather than profits. Priorities will vary by economy, and a benefit of the OECD and World Bank indices is to provide some guidance on the height of barriers. Further empirical work on barriers' impacts on costs and profits could be valuable.
- *The size of the sector:* As development takes place, the relevance of particular services will vary over time. The studies examined here refer to the relative importance of different types of services at the various stages of growth since sector size (current and expected) will also be an important determinant of welfare gains. In addition, it will be worth paying attention to using reforms to develop new markets. Most commonly used examples in this respect relate to internet access where, for example, developing markets to share capacity that is already available but could be used for different purposes. Uber's taxi service serves as a topical case and there are other instances of contracting out parcel transport to drivers of otherwise empty cars on a desired route.[5]
- *The sector's role as a facilitator of competitiveness in other areas:* Dee also points out that the impact of reform varies according to the structure of economies. She observes that those involved in or seeking to be involved in global value chains will benefit from reforms that support their competitiveness. Some guidance on the most useful areas of focus is available from the trade in value added (TiVA) data. Figure 3.3 shows TiVA shares of particular sectors in manufactured exports. As might be expected, transport and distribution sectors account for significant elements of the total share, in addition to finance and business sectors. Telecommunications and business services are also expected to be important. In fact, business services are

5 https://www.uber.com/ and http://www.anyvan.com/.

attracting greater attention. Jensen (2013) argues that developing Asian economies, which have relatively small business services sectors, could benefit from the reduction of impediments to trade in the short term and from investment in educational attainment that adds to the pool of skilled labour in the longer term.

Policymakers can develop a manageable portfolio for reform. A focus on value chains suggests that rather than working through services reforms sector-by-sector or one-by-one, it might be more helpful to take a value chain view of the problem. Officials will need to identify the inputs that are critical to the competitiveness of a host at the current and next prospective points in the value chain. Case studies of important chains and consultations with businesses involved in their operations might also lead to the identification of a more limited and well-defined – but critical – set of services reforms that will enhance the operation of the supply chain. Note, however, that businesses involved in these chains have mixed incentives to reveal information about the nature of impediments, but they are more likely to do so when barriers are cost-increasing rather than rent-creating.

Figure 3.3: Services' share of value added in manufactured exports

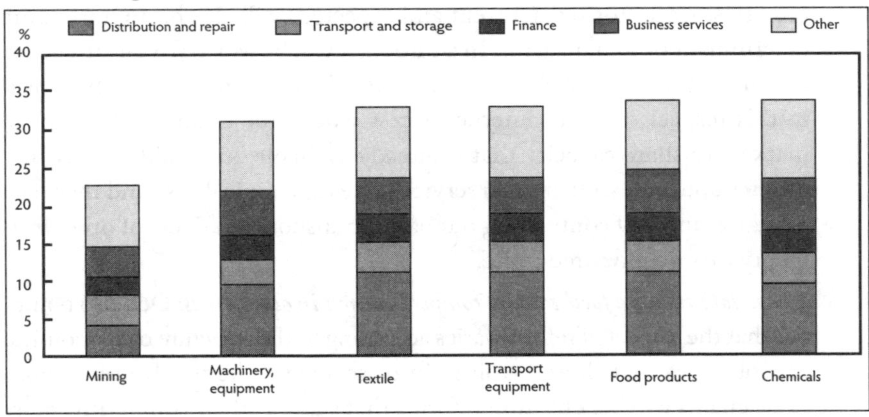

Source: OECD (2013)

Conclusion

Finally, it is important to think through the implementation of reform packages. There are some common principles among goods and services for the development and design of successful packages, such as the importance of knowing the costs of the current regimes, having access to independent and transparent processes of policy evaluation, recognizing that structural change 'never ends,' taking advantage of technological changes and running experiments (Findlay 2013). However, there are also a number of differences between reforms aimed at goods and those targeting services.

- Dee and Findlay (2008) have argued that, unlike for tariff reform, there will be divided positions on foreign entry in services markets among local political interests because employment and output can both increase following policy reform. Worker groups may then support reform, though some domestic firms may fail and their owners will resist change. There are other sources of resistance from regulatory bodies and their related interest groups.
- Dee (2013) also observes that if services impediments affect costs, rather than profits, then reform could have significant employment effects. Strong economic growth ameliorates this effect and, as she says, to some extent 'services reforms provide their own reward, in terms of stimulating activity' (26).
- There is also the concern that when services reform removes significant discrimination against foreign competitors, domestic providers could lose out. A package of measures across sectors can alleviate that concern by raising the competitiveness of domestic providers, benefiting both current and potential domestic entrants. Dee also suggests that foreign entrants tend to focus on their niches or segments, which may differ from those of local firms. As a result, domestic service providers may face less significant losses.
- The ability to finance universal service obligations can be a source of resistance to change. For example, those obligations are often implemented within a monopolized market, where profits made in one are used to subsidize services in another. That monopoly position may be the result of regulation applied to limit competitive entry. In that situation, cross subsidies between consumer groups can be sustained. Deregulation makes that more difficult to do. These obligations should then be transferred to directly-applied policy instruments rather than be met through market regulation (Findlay, 2013).

Overall, it is necessary, though not sufficient, for successful reform to mobilize the winners from the reform process. The most politically effective allies are likely to be other enterprises, which are services consumers, including in the services sector itself. The best approach may be to create or enhance institutional arrangements in which they can present their views on reform, for example, through a transparent and independent policy review process that invites their submissions, or a sectoral organization that puts the parties together, such as the various services roundtables and dialogues that now operate in some economies. Setting up these institutions would be an important contribution to making services work better for development.

References

Abrenica, Joy, Christopher Findlay and Aik Hoe Lim. 2009. 'Future of Trade in Services for Developing Countries', in *Trade and Poverty Reduction in the Asia-Pacific Region Case Studies and Lessons from Low-income Communities*, edited by Andrew Stoler, Jim Redden and Lee Ann Jackson. Cambridge: Cambridge University Press.

ADB. 2012. *Asian Development Outlook 2012: Services and Asia's Future Growth*. Manila: ADB.

Bertho, Fabien, Ingo Borchert and Aaditya Mattoo. 2014. 'The Trade Reducing Effects of Restrictions on Liner Shipping', *Policy Research Working Paper 6921*. Washington: World Bank.

Bhagwati, Jagdhish N. 1984. '*Splintering* and Disembodiment of *Services* and Developing Nations', *The World Economy* 7 (2) (June): 133–144.

Buera, Francisco and Joseph Kaboski. 2012. 'The Rise of the Service Economy', *American Economic Review* 102 (6): 2540–69.

Dee, Philippa. 2013. 'Measuring and Modelling Regulatory Restrictions in Services', Chapter 1 in *Priorities and Pathways in Services Reform – Part I: Quantitative Studies*. Singapore: World Scientific.

Dee, Philippa and Christopher Findlay. 2008. Services: 'A Deal-maker in the Doha Round?', in *Monitoring International Trade Policy: A New Agenda for Reviving the Doha Round*, edited by B. Blonigen. London: Centre for Economic Policy Research.

Eichengreen, Barry and Poonam Gupta. 2011. 'The Two Waves of Service Sector Growth', *Oxford Economic Papers* 65: 96–123.

Findlay, Christopher. 1990. 'Trade in Services in the Asia Pacific Region', *Asian-Pacific Economic Literature* 4 (2): 3–20.

———. 2013. 'Overview', Chapter 1 in *Priorities and Pathways in Services Reform – Part II: Political Economy Studies*. Singapore: World Scientific.

He, Xiaobo and Christopher Findlay. 2014. 'Policy Restrictions and Services Performance: Evidence from 32 Countries', *Journal of International Commerce, Economics and Policy* 5 (1): 1–19.

Hill, T. P. 1977. 'On Goods and Services', *Review of Income and Wealth* 23 (4) (December): 315–38.

Jensen, Bradford. 2013. 'Overlooked Opportunity: Tradable Business Services, Developing Asia and Growth', *ADB Economics Working Paper Series, no. 236*. Manila: ADB.

Katouzian, M. A. 1970. 'The Development of the Service Sector: A New Approach', *Oxford Economic Papers* 22 (3): 362–82.

Maurer, Andreas, J. Joscelyn Magdeleine and Barbarad Andrea. 2006. 'International Trade in Services: GATS, Statistical Concepts and Future Challenges', paper presented to the 2006 'Conference of the International Association for Official Statistics (IAOS)', Ottawa, Canada.

OECD. 2013. *Interconnected Economies: Benefiting from Global Value Chains*. Paris: OECD.

———. 2014. *Services Trade Restrictiveness Index: Policy Brief.* Paris: OECD.

4

Gainfully Linking into Global Value Chains

A Middle-Income Country's Perspective

Maria Joy V. Abrenica

Introduction

The post-war miracle of the East Asian economies[1] has resurfaced in policy discussions, precipitated by observations that only a handful of middle-income countries (MICs) have attained developed country status, whilst a good number seem to be caught in a pit of relative economic stagnation – dubbed the 'middle income trap'.[2] A huge part of the East Asian story is ascribed to these economies' cunning ability to use trade to promote domestic growth and overcome development hurdles. Drawing from this model, it may be inferred that those trapped in the middle-income zone have failed to exploit trade enough to allow them passage to a higher income level. There is no denying that the realities of the present global ecosystem and the development challenges they present are different from the 1980s. However, many still see the East Asian model relevant insofar as it offers an escape path that combines trade with the right mix of domestic policies.

What makes the present development challenges different from when the Asian MICs were transitioning to high-income status is the increasing dominance of GVCs. Production processes have been spread across countries for decades, but they were not as fragmented and dispersed as one finds them now. Simple and complex networks have developed around value chains at an unprecedented pace. Since these value chains cover the full range of activities,

1 Refers to South Korea, Taiwan, Hong Kong and Singapore, sometimes referred to as the Four Asian Tigers

2 The existence of a 'middle-income trap' has been used to explain why a high proportion of those who successfully moved from low- to middle-income status in the 1960s have remained middle-income (or regressed to low-income in some cases). Apparently, the policies and strategies that propelled their initial growth have ceased to be effective, and they have yet to find new growth impetus.

from conception to final use, specializations have developed among tasks rather than goods. That includes services, which are increasingly important as sources of value in GVCs.

It has become impractical to recreate the value chain domestically without considerable costs and loss of opportunities to the host economy. As a consequence, the East Asian economic transformation of gradual, yet systematic build-up of productive capacity – from light manufacturing to heavy and, eventually, knowledge-intensive industries – seems archaic in a nearly borderless production system where tasks or activities, rather than goods, are the objects of trade. Productive capacities are being built through participation in dynamic, complex and overlapping international business networks, created through a maze of foreign direct investments (FDIs) and global sourcing, which make linking into GVCs a development imperative.

Yet, participation in GVCs is not a development panacea. Greater participation may lead to more exports, but not necessarily to higher income and employment. There are also attendant risks in participation, such as stifled technological learning as a result of being held up in low value-added tasks, or unequal market relationships and increased exposure to market volatilities and imported crises. Whether GVCs can provide an escape route to the middle-income trap depends on the country's capacity to manage these risks and use their participation to create jobs, raise incomes, and acquire technology.

This chapter deals with the predicament of MICs to leap out of the trap by leveraging their participation in GVCs. These economies have the wherewithal to join GVCs, but need to confront the difficult tasks of remaining part of and moving up the chain. Growth opportunities abound in GVCs, but for most middle-income-trapped economies, their participation has not translated into substantial creation of domestic value. So, how should a country structure its participation in GVCs to capture and optimize the benefits that would fuel its economic development? This chapter explores the prospects of participation and deflates some views on how a country could capture the most value from its participation.

Opportunities and challenges in GVCs

The middle-income label has been variably applied in different contexts. For present purposes, the term 'middle-income' will refer to an economy situated in the middle of the distribution of countries ranked by per capita income.[3] Since a country's income does not always reflect its level of development, the income definition is often supplemented by a characterization of economic structure (e.g., the proportion of the labour force in the primary sector) and quality of life (such as adult literacy, life expectancy and infant mortality). Thus, from a development perspective, middle-income status connotes attainment of some economic and social standards that are quite advanced for a developing economy, but short of the achievements of developed economies.

The MICs whose middle-income status has not budged since the 1960s and 1970s take on an additional dimension in development discourse as countries that are deemed to be stuck in the middle-income trap. They attract special attention and include countries like India, the Philippines, Indonesia and Thailand.

Given the realities of fragmented production and the ubiquity of global networks, the development literature has suggested that the only viable development path is through participation in GVCs, especially because they are perceived to offer an escape route from the middle-income trap. In that respect, it is critical to understand how MICs are faring in GVCs and what opportunities GVCs present to them.

At least three trends bode well for MICs. First, trade statistics are reflecting the income trends that fuelled optimism for global convergence. Just as income levels in developing economies pick up growth momentum, so do their trade flows. As shown in Table 4.1, the average annual GDP growth of developing economies, both in absolute and per capita terms, exceeds that of developed economies before the 2009 financial crisis and even more so afterwards. Trade in goods and services followed the same pattern as exports of developing economies grew by an average of 7 to 8 per cent per year before 2009 and as much as 14 per cent after the crisis, compared to only 6.3 and 5.5 per cent growth in developed economies, respectively.

3 The World Bank classifies economies based on their per capita gross national income (GNI), calculated using the World Bank Atlas method. Low-income countries (LICs) have GNI per capita of US$1,045 or less in 2013; low middle-income countries (LMICs), more than US$1,045, but less than US$4,125; upper middle-income countries (UMICs), US$4,125 or more, but less than US$12,746; and high-income countries (HICs), US$12,746 or more. Developing countries are those that have not reached HIC status.

Table 4.1: Income and trade performance since the 1990s, by income groups

	LIC	LMIC	UMIC	HIC
GDP growth (average annual %)				
1995–2009	4.90	4.30	4.31	3.81
2010–13	4.99	4.48	4.26	3.02
GDP per capita growth (average annual %)				
1995–2009	2.16	2.60	3.18	2.56
2010–13	2.61	2.84	2.76	1.05
Exports of goods and services growth (average annual %)				
1995–2009	8.11	7.31	7.11	6.28
2010–13	14.47	7.71	5.46	5.50

Source: Author's calculation based on World Bank databank

The second positive trend for MICs is the high correlation between the growth of gross exports and value added (VA) in exports, inasmuch as the latter translates into higher national income and employment. Presented in Table 4.2 are measures of correlation between changes in gross exports, VA, and services VA of exports. The statistics were computed on trade data from 58 countries covered by the OECD-WTO TiVA database.[4] Albeit small, the set includes countries representing all income classes, accounting for about 95 per cent of global trade. Apart from a positive and significant correlation between changes in gross exports and domestic VA, changes in gross exports are also positively and significantly correlated with changes in services VA. Additionally, the correlation between changes in domestic VA and services VA is nearly as tight as the correlation between changes in gross exports and domestic VA. This gives rise to expectation that domestic employment and incomes of developing countries are expanding with the growth of their exports.[5] However, changes in gross exports are not statistically correlated with changes in the proportion of domestic VA or services VA in gross exports. Thus, it is not surprising to

4 The most recent available data in the OECD-WTO database is for 2009, but that year was marred by financial crisis that limited the availability of trade finance, resulting in temporary shortening of the GVC. Any analysis using that year may be distorted by the cyclical changes made in response to the crisis.

5 This should not be taken to imply a causal direction from trade growth to income growth, or vice-versa. The most likely reality is a two way association.

find that even if both gross exports and domestic VA in exports increase, the share of domestic VA in gross exports may not increase and could even fall, depending on the relative changes in these two variables.

Table 4.2: Pairwise correlation of changes in gross exports, VA and services VA, 1995 and 2008

Change in	Gross exports	Domestic VA in gross exports	Services VA in gross exports	Share of domestic VA in gross export
Domestic VA in gross exports	0.9586*			
Services VA in gross exports	0.8269*	0.8673*		
Share of domestic VA in gross exports	-0.1114	0.1669	0.1640	
Share of services VA in gross exports	-0.1700	-0.0365	0.3988*	0.4898*

*Denotes significance at 1%

Source: Author's calculation based on OECD-WTO's TiVA database

Indeed, Table 4.3 shows that shares of domestic VA in gross exports are declining across all income classes, whilst the import content of exports is increasing. This trend mirrors the heightening fragmentation of production and the proliferation of outsourcing and offshoring activities. Similarly, shares of domestic services in the exports of low- and upper-middle income economies are falling, reflecting the growing volume of trade in intermediate services.[6] Consistent with the changes in their economic structure, high-income economies export, in relative terms, significantly more services than other economies.

6 The OECD estimates that 70 per cent of the world's imports of services are intermediate services.

Table 4.3: VA in exports of selected economies, 1995 and 2008

	High-income a/	**Upper middle-income b/**	**Low middle-income c/**	**Others d/**
Share of domestic VA in gross exports				
1995	73.44	79.85	78.72	75.91
2000	69.65	75.38	71.80	73.15
2005	69.15	72.99	69.65	70.75
2008	68.48	72.28	69.84	70.67
Share of domestic services VA in gross exports				
1995	31.18	29.25	26.57	21.26
2000	30.33	29.04	22.44	22.00
2005	31.71	26.53	23.14	20.24
2008	32.35	26.45	24.11	17.60

[a/] Australia, Austria, Belgium, Canada, Czech Republic, Denmark, Estonia, Finland, France, Germany, Greece, Iceland, Ireland, Israel, Italy, Japan, Luxembourg, Netherlands, New Zealand, Norway, Portugal, Slovak Republic, South Korea, Sweden, Switzerland, United Kingdom, United States, Brunei, Chinese Taipei, Hong Kong, Malta, Saudi Arabia and Singapore

[b/] Argentina, Brazil, Bulgaria, Chile, China, Hungary, Latvia, Lithuania, Malaysia, Mexico, Poland, Romania, Russia, South Africa and Turkey

[c/] India, Indonesia, the Philippines and Thailand

[d/] Cambodia, Vietnam and rest of the world

Source: Author's calculation based on OECD-WTO's TiVA database

The foregoing trends portend benefits from increased participation in GVCs, but how much of the benefits are actually seized by the MICs? Despite the growth differences between developing and developed countries, the former have barely gained economic prominence, neither in terms of income nor in terms of trade. Table 4.4 provides the evidence. As of 2013, LICs still accounted for less than 1 per cent of global income and exports, whilst low middle-income countries (LMICs) made up less than 6 per cent. HICs' share of global income and exports contracted, but not substantially – from 84 per cent of global income in 1995 to 74 per cent in 2013, and from 81 per cent to 73 per cent of total exports for the same period. Most of the shares lost by HICs were gained by UMICs, which now account for about one-fifth of global income and exports.

Table 4.4: Income and trade performance since the 1990s, by income groups[7]

	LIC	LMIC	UMIC	HIC
Share in total GDP (constant 2005 US$)				
1995	0.39	3.70	12.06	83.85
2009	0.54	5.12	17.17	77.17
2013	0.61	5.72	19.30	74.37
Share in total goods and services exports (constant 2005 US$)				
1995	0.31	4.18	14.12	81.39
2009	0.37	4.97	19.39	75.27
2013	0.41	5.26	21.26	73.07

Source: Author's calculation based on World Bank database

Regardless of whether exports are reckoned in gross or value-added terms, the benefits reverting to low and low-middle countries seem limited. The share of LMICs in the total value added created by GVCs improved marginally and is still less than 4 per cent as of 2008 (Table 4.5). HICs still have the dominant shares, even if these were reduced from 80 to 67 per cent of total value and from 84 per cent to 77 per cent of total services value. As in the distribution of exports, a big portion of the shares lost by HICs was captured by UMICs that now account for 21 per cent and 16 per cent of the total and services value, respectively.

Table 4.5: Distribution of VA and services VA in exports, 1995–2008

	High income 1/	Upper middle-income 1/	Low middle-income 1/	Others 1/
Share in total VA in gross exports				
1995	80.47	11.80	3.14	4.59
2000	77.00	13.60	3.26	6.14
2005	71.74	17.57	3.60	7.09
2008	66.56	20.81	3.97	8.66
Share in total services VA in gross exports				

Contd.

7 This follows the World Bank's classification based on GNI calculated using the World Bank Atlas method. LIC are those with a GNI per capita of US$1,045 or less in 2013; LMIC, more than US$1,045, but less than US$4,125; UMIC, US$4,125 or more, but less than US$12,746; and HIC, US$12,746 or more.

	High income 1/	Upper middle-income 1/	Low middle-income 1/	Others 1/
1995	84.17	9.87	2.52	3.44
2000	81.67	11.11	2.50	4.72
2005	79.39	12.84	3.17	4.61
2008	76.55	15.49	3.68	4.28

1/ See countries covered in Table 4.2

Source: Author's calculation based on OECD-WTO's TiVA database

Although HICs generate about two-thirds of total global VA, a handful of MICs have larger VA shares compared to their richer counterparts. In 2008, China ranked third and fourth in shares in total VA and services VA, respectively. Russia ranked eighth in total VA and tenth in services VA. India ranked thirteenth in total VA, just behind South Korea, and twelfth in services VA, two notches above South Korea.

Table 4.6: Countries with largest shares in VA and services VA in GVCs, 2008

	Total VA in GVCs		Total services VA in GVCs	
	Share	**Rank**	**Share**	**Rank**
United States	11.6	1	14.0	1
Germany	8.3	2	9.3	2
China	8.1	3	4.9	6
Japan	5.3	4	5.3	5
United Kingdom	4.5	5	6.6	3
France	4.2	6	5.5	4
Italy	4.0	7	4.7	7
Russia	3.7	8	2.6	10
Canada	3.2	9	2.8	9
Saudi Arabia	2.4	10	0.2	46

Source: Author's calculation based on OECD-WTO's TiVA database

Conceptually, a country gains from GVC participation if it leads to expanded domestic production and employment. This happens when a country produces more value added through its participation. Using this metric, Table 4.7 identifies countries that gained the most from GVC participation between

1995 and 2008. These countries experienced the largest increases in domestic VA in their exports, and consequently, the biggest jumps in their shares in total VA. Thus, as Vietnam's VA in its exports grew more than eight-fold during this period its share in global VA tripled, going from 0.1 to 0.3 per cent. Quite significantly, seven out of the top 10 gainers are developing countries. Among the LMICs, only India made it to the list, with its share in total VA improving from 0.75 to 1.75 per cent. In contrast, the shares of Thailand, Indonesia and the Philippines fell despite more than two-fold increases in domestic VA content in their exports. Specifically, Thailand's share slid from 1.02 to 0.98 per cent. Indonesia's share went from 0.99 to 0.95 per cent and the Philippines' share decreased from 0.36 to 0.28 per cent.

Table 4.7: Top gainers in GVC market share

Rank	Country	Income status	Domestic VA in export 2008 over 1995	Share in global VA, 2008 over 1995
1	Vietnam	LIC	3.02	8.31
2	China	UMIC	2.97	8.17
3	Lithuania	UMIC	2.82	7.77
4	India	LMIC	2.32	6.39
5	Latvia	UMIC	2.27	6.24
6	Romania	UMIC	2.17	5.98
7	Saudi Arabia	HIC	2.15	5.93
8	Slovakia	HIC	2.02	5.57
9	Estonia	HIC	2.00	5.52
10	Cambodia	LIC	1.98	5.46

Source: Author's calculation based on OECD-WTO's TIVA database

Maximizing gains in GVCs

Low middle-income countries appear to be losing their share of value in GVCs. How can such decline be avoided? This issue confounds policymakers in these countries, some of whom are still attuned to the East Asian experience of building national industries. There are several hypotheses concerning the factors that may affect the value that countries capture in GVCs. They relate to the nature of a country's participation, length of value chain and location in the chain. Each of these is considered below.

Forward or backward linkage?

The benefits a country derives from GVC participation depend on the nature of its participation. A country links up to GVCs in two ways: (1) by sourcing inputs abroad to be used in its exports (backward linkage); and (2) by providing inputs into exports of other countries (forward linkage). The participation index (Koopman *et al.*, 2011) is the sum of foreign VA in a country's exports and domestic VA used in exports of other countries, expressed as a proportion of a country's gross exports. The proposition is that the benefits to a country can be measured by the 'net value added' of its participation – that is, the difference between domestic VA incorporated into other countries' exports and foreign VA in a country's own exports (Banga, 2013). A country gains if it is creating and exporting more domestic VA than it is importing, or equivalently, if it has more forward than backward linkages. This means that a country is a net gainer if the ratio of its forward to backward linkages exceeds one and a loser if this ratio is less than one.

Table 4.8: GVC participation rate, by income group

	High income[1/]	**Upper middle income**[1/]	**Low middle income**[1/]	**Others**[1/]
Participation index				
1995	44.21	38.88	36.70	38.46
2000	51.58	46.72	46.78	47.53
2005	54.89	50.65	55.55	52.81
2008	55.77	51.29	56.14	53.44
Participation index, backward				
1995	26.24	20.15	21.28	18.05
2000	29.93	24.62	28.20	22.20
2005	30.47	27.01	30.36	22.37
2008	31.21	27.72	30.16	23.00
Participation index, forward				
1995	17.97	18.73	15.42	20.41
2000	21.66	22.10	18.58	25.33
2005	24.42	23.65	25.20	30.44

Contd.

	High income[1/]	Upper middle income[1/]	Low middle income[1/]	Others[1/]
2008	24.56	23.57	25.98	30.43
Ratio of forward to backward index				
1995	1.28	1.27	0.92	1.42
2000	1.49	1.18	0.88	1.42
2005	1.44	1.28	1.01	2.28
2008	1.42	1.31	1.00	2.49

[1/] See countries covered in Table 4.2

Source: Author's calculation based on OECD-WTO's TiVA database

Table 4.8 reports the significant increases in the participation rates of economies from all income classes between 1995 and 2008. Until 1995, the LMICs had lower participation rates than higher income groups, but they subsequently caught up and surpassed the UMICs. What differentiates the LMICs from other income classes is that the increase in their participation stems more from sourcing inputs from the value chain than supplying inputs to it. The opposite is true for UMICs and HICs. Thus, the forward to backward linkage ratio exceeds one and increases for these two income groups, whereas it is less than one for LMICs.

The nature of a country's participation in a value chain is determined by its resource endowments and economic structure. A small open economy tends to have higher backward linkage than an equally open but larger economy, since the former needs to source more inputs from the value chain. A country that exports primary inputs, in contrast, would be likely to have stronger forward than backward linkage, but a lower participation rate if domestic production were limited. Significantly, the three countries with the highest VA shares in 2008, namely the U.S. (11.57 per cent), Germany (8.32 per cent) and China (8.05 per cent), have different relative strengths of linkage. China and Germany have stronger backward linkage than forward, so their forward to backward ratios are 0.43 and 0.87, respectively. The opposite applies to the U.S., which has an index ratio of 2.03. Considering the previous discussion, it is clear that having stronger forward than backward linkage, or equivalently, exporting more than importing VA, is not necessarily optimal.

Shorter or longer chains?

Nor is it always beneficial to choose to engage in a longer value chain. This contradicts the view that the length of the value chain is an important determinant of the benefits that may be derived from GVC participation. Traditionally, longer chains have been viewed more favourably because their length is perceived to be correlated with their complexity, which, in turn, is associated with value. Arguably, a longer chain with many production stages, which gives rise to more fragmented production, creates more VA.

The complexity, value, and length of a value chain are naturally linked. High-tech industries tend to be more fragmented than low-tech ones. Thus, not surprisingly, estimates using the OECD intercountry input-output model reveal that the top five industries in terms of length of GVCs are radio, television and communication equipment, motor vehicles, basic metals, electrical machinery and other transport equipment, which are all considered 'high-tech industries'.[8] Generally, services have short value chains. Hence, the bottom five industries comprise real estate activities, education, mining and quarrying, renting of machinery and equipment, and wholesale and retail trade. Except for mining and quarrying, the rest are all services (OECD, 2012).[9]

Table 4.9 presents value chain length, measured by the number of production stages, for different income classes. Introduced by Fally (2011), this index has a base value of one if there is a single stage involved in production, and increases when inputs from the same or other industries are used.[10] It is decomposed further into stages according to the origin of inputs (foreign or domestic).

8 The model consists of 37 sectors based on two-digit International Standard Industrial Classification (ISIC) Rev. 3. Other industries classified as high-tech are: machinery and equipment, chemicals and non-metallic mineral products. Low-tech industries include: textiles, textile products, leather and footwear, wood and products of wood, pulp paper, paper products, printing and publishing, food products, beverages and tobacco, agriculture, hunting, forestry and fishing, mining and quarrying, manufacturing, NEC, recycling.

9 Exceptions to this trend are the textile, leather and footwear industries, which are considered low-tech, but have a longer value chain than other high-tech industries, such as chemicals and precision and optical instruments.

10 If the available data were at the firm level, the length of the chain would correspond to the number of plants or stages in the production of a good. Since the data is aggregated, the measure is just an index, estimated in the same way that backward linkage is computed in an input-output model.

Across all income classes, the average length of value chains has increased with declining domestic length and increasing foreign length. For example, the overall index for LMICs rose by about 3 per cent, or from 1.78 in 1995 to 1.84 in 2008, with a rise in the foreign index (from 0.25 to 0.33) compensating for the fall in the domestic index (from 1.53 to 1.51). The opposite changes in domestic and foreign indices are consistent with growing vertical specialization and outsourcing activities, as continuous innovations in production and organization allow for greater fragmentation.

Table 4.9: Measure of the number of production stages in gross exports, by income group

	High income1/	**Upper middle income**1/	**Low middle income**1/	**Others**1/
Total number of production stages				
1995	1.80	1.86	1.78	1.89
2000	1.84	1.90	1.82	1.95
2005	1.85	1.89	1.84	1.98
2008	1.89	1.92	1.84	1.96
Number of production stages, domestic				
1995	1.49	1.59	1.53	1.54
2000	1.49	1.58	1.52	1.51
2005	1.49	1.56	1.51	1.45
2008	1.50	1.56	1.51	1.40
Number of production sstages, international				
1995	0.31	0.26	0.25	0.36
2000	0.35	0.32	0.30	0.44
2005	0.36	0.34	0.33	0.52
2008	0.39	0.36	0.33	0.56

1/ See countries covered in Table 4.2

Source: Author's calculation based on OECD-WTO's TiVA database

The empirical evidence shows that all income classes are experiencing the same changes in the length of their value chains. More importantly, the lengths of the value chains across income classes are only marginally different. Hence, whilst a longer value chain may create more value, participating in one is not a recipe for gainful participation in GVC.

Table 4.10: Mapping VA in GVCs by sector and income class, 2008

	Value (US$M)	Share (per cent)			
		High income[1/]	Upper middle income[1/]	Low middle income[1/]	Others[1/]
Agriculture, hunting, forestry and fishing	305.6	52.9	32.2	5.7	9.2
Basic metals and fabricated metal products	853.5	64.9	29.9	3.1	2.1
Business services	725.6	86.4	5.8	7.2	0.7
Chemicals and non-metallic mineral products	1,601.4	71.2	21.1	3.9	3.9
Construction	25.6	55.8	44.1	0.1	-
Electrical and optical equipment	1,347.2	65.3	27.0	4.5	3.2
Electricity, gas and water supply	47.2	77.8	21.1	1.0	-
Financial intermediation	419.3	89.6	2.9	1.4	6.0
Food products, beverage and tobacco	576.7	62.1	21.7	8.5	7.6
Machinery and equipment	867.3	79.6	17.5	1.3	1.6
Manufacturing, recycling	309.2	54.6	31.3	9.7	4.5
Mining and quarrying	1,684.6	42.1	20.6	2.1	35.1
Other services	176.7	69.4	9.4	5.9	15.3

Contd.

	Value (US$M)	Share (per cent)			
		High income[1/]	Upper middle income[1/]	Low middle income[1/]	Others[1/]
Textile, textile products, leather and footwear	534.2	30.8	44.7	8.1	16.4
Transport and storage, post and telecommunication	841.4	79.3	14.0	3.5	3.2
Transport equipment	1,067.8	82.5	15.5	1.5	0.4
Wholesale and retail trade, hotels and restaurants	857.1	70.0	19.0	4.8	6.2
Wood, paper, paper products, printing and publishing	400.1	65.6	19.0	2.6	12.8
Total	12,640.6				

[1/] See countries covered in Table 4.2

Source: Author's calculation based on OECD-WTO's TIVA database

Downstream vs. upstream?

In many industries, the proliferation of GVCs was accompanied by a shift in value from manufacturing to managing and marketing activities, or those considered in the final stages of the value chain. More value is also being created in industries that are intensive in research and development (R&D) skills and advertising, rather than those intensive in physical capital and/or raw materials. The former is usually closer to final demand. These trends are fostering thinking that the optimal location in the chain is near the final stage, or in downstream activities.

An industry's location in the chain may be represented by an index of distance from final demand, introduced by Fally (2011) and Antras *et al.* (2012). The average index by income class is reported in Table 4.11. Contrary to what may be expected if the conjecture on value and distance were true, the average industry distance to final demand has increased in all income classes. However, it is difficult to conclude that the change from 1.89 in 1995 to 2.03 in 2008 for high-income economies, for example, represents a real shift of production upstream, especially since all indicators point to increasing specialization in services by these economies. The general increase in the index is nonetheless consistent with the lengthening of GVCs due to outsourcing. As the OECD (2012) explains, outsourcing of inputs shifts the value back to the supplier of intermediate inputs which, in turn, increases the distance of a country's exports from final demand. More importantly, however, skill-intensive activities are located both upstream and downstream relative to manufacturing or assembly of inputs. R&D and design are upstream, whilst marketing and customer services are considered downstream, which means that economies can seek to upgrade their value added by moving in either direction.

Table 4.11: Measure of distance of exports from final demand

	High income[1/]	**Upper middle income[1/]**	**Low middle income[1/]**	**Others[1/]**
1995	1.89	1.94	1.88	1.89
2000	1.97	2.00	1.99	1.97
2005	1.99	2.01	2.00	1.92
2008	2.03	2.00	2.00	1.87

[1/]See countries covered in Table 4.2

Source: Author's calculation using OECD-WTO's TiVA database

High-tech vs low-tech?

Most GVCs have evolved in high-tech industries where technology has allowed for greater fragmentation of production. The longer value chains in these industries have also opened up opportunities for developing countries to participate. As a result, the proportion of high-tech goods in the exports of MICs has grown and even exceeded that of the high-income group. As shown in Table 4.12, nearly half, or 48 per cent, of 2008 low middle-income country exports are classified as high-tech, as opposed to 46 per cent for the high-income group. More than half (51 per cent) of the domestic value of the exports of LMICs comes from these industries, compared to only 40 per cent for the high-income group.

Table 4.12: Share of high-tech industries in exports and domestic VA, 2008

	High Income[1/]	Upper Middle Income[1/]	Low Middle Income[1/]	Others[1/]
Share in total exports	**45.76**	**46.16**	**47.98**	**10.83**
Share in domestic VA	**39.64**	**37.15**	**51.16**	**8.75**

[1/]See countries covered in Table 4.2

Source: Author's calculation Using OECD-WTO's TiVA database

Understandably, most developing countries are targeting to expand the share of high-tech goods in their exports, with the expectation that operating in a dynamic environment would facilitate technological learning. Increasing exports inevitably requires increasing production. However, the high-tech exports of a country do not mirror its innovation capacity. As Table 4.13 confirms, the disparity in resources for innovation across income groups is still immense, notwithstanding the broad participation in GVCs.

Table 4.13: Resources for innovation by income groups, 2012

	HIC	UMIC	LMIC	LIC
Technicians in R&D (per million population)	1052.6	250.8	81.2	56.7
Researchers in R&D (per million population)	3611.7	1001.6	413.4	102.0
R&D expenditures (% of GDP)	1.7	0.7	0.3	0.3

Source: Author's calculation based on the World Bank's Development Indicators

Deficiency in innovation does not prevent participation in GVCs, but it is certainly a constraint to increasing the value of participation in the chain. In the chemical industry, for example, participants are distinguished by the level of specialization of the chemicals they handle. Basic chemicals are produced in large volumes and sold at low cost to mass markets, whilst specialty chemicals are produced in low volume and require substantial R&D and marketing investments. A low level of R&D does not prevent a country from joining the chain, but limits its ability to move to production of higher value, specialty chemicals.

Conclusion

None of the hypotheses considered above provide a straightforward recipe for gainful participation in GVCs. Incurring negative net VA, engaging in short value chains, locating upstream in the chain, or producing in traditional industries do not limit a country's ability to create more value. Put bluntly, the issues of forward versus backward linkage, long versus short chain, upstream versus downstream location in the chain and high-tech versus low-tech exports, are false dichotomies in terms of acquiring greater domestic VA.

A country's benefit from GVC participation, measured by its share in the value of GVCs, is not statistically related to the net value added of participation (ratio of forward to backward linkage), length of the chain (number of production stages), or distance of production from final demand. It is positively and significantly correlated, however, to backward participation, suggesting that accessing competitively priced imported inputs – rather than domestic inputs – enables a country to capture a larger share of the GVC value.

Table 4.14 : Correlation with share in total VA in GVCs

Indicators	
Ratio of forward to backward linkage	0.1376
Participation index, backward	0.6618*
Participation index, forward	0.1829*
Index of number of production stages	-0.1344
Ratio of domestic to international number of production stages	-0.4260*
Index of distance from final demand	-0.0718
Share of high-tech industries in gross exports	0.3303*
Share of domestic value added in gross exports	0.3535

*Denotes significance at 1%

Source: Author's calculation based on OECD-WTO's TiVA database.

The existence of a middle-income trap remains an issue that still needs to be resolved in the development literature. But whether or not countries are held up in a state of income immobility is perhaps less important. It is sufficient that attention has been drawn to the challenges these economies face, and the fact that the policies and conditions that propel them from LICs to MICs have ceased to be effective. Will their participation in GVCs provide them the growth impetus they need to escape the trap?

This chapter points to the opportunities and pitfalls of participating in GVCs through a simple analysis of trends and indicators. The imperative of GVCs is vertical specialization, rather than vertical integration. Hence, it does not matter if a country has more forward or backward linkages, integrated in a long or short value chain, undertaking activities upstream or downstream, or engaged in high-tech or traditional industries. Value that can be harnessed for domestic growth may still be created through participation in the chain. Thus, concerns about dependency on imports and producing only a segment of production have no place in a tightly interdependent environment.

Finally, what this chapter has not sought to explore is a differentiation among value chains in terms of scope for innovation and growth through enhanced productivity. This is a topic for further analysis.

References

Antras, Pol, Davin Chor, Thibault Fally and Russell Hillberry. 2012. 'Measuring the Upstreamness of Production and Trade Flows', *NBER Working Paper 17819*. Cambridge, Massachusetts: NBER.

Banga, Rashmi. 2013. 'Measuring Value in Global Value Chains', *UNCTAD Background Paper RVC-8*. Geneva, Switzerland: United Nations Conference on Trade and Development (UNTAD).

Cattaneo, Olivier, Gary Gereffi, Sébastien Miroudot and Daria Taglioni. 2013. 'Joining, Upgrading and Being Competitive in Global Value Chains: A Strategic Framework', *World Bank Policy Research Working Paper 6406*. Washington D.C.: World Bank.

Fally, Thibault. 2011. *On the Fragmentation of Production in the U.S.* Mimeo. Boulder: University of Colorado.

Koopman, R., W. Powers, Z. Wang and S. J. Wei. 2011. 'Give Credit Where Credit is Due: Tracing Value Added in Global Production Chains', *National Bureau of Economic Research Working Paper 16426*. Cambridge, Massachusetts.

OECD. 2012. *Mapping Global Value Chains*. OECD Working Party of the Trade Committee. Paris: OECD.

5

Who Governs Global Value Chains?

Sherry Stephenson and Anne-Katrin Pfister

Introduction

Much has been written on GVCs over the past few years. However, this literature has often gone in different directions, resulting in inconsistent analysis using different terminology. This has tended to muddy the waters. Authors have discussed the key concept of 'governance' in different contexts with alternate meanings in relation to the operation of GVCs, which has resulted in confusion for analysts and practitioners of trade policy.

Since the focus of authors has often been different, there has been no consensus around the notion of 'governance' of GVCs. Many economists have written about governance of value chains with what, in this chapter, we are going to call 'g'. Our definition covers industrial and national policy frameworks from the perspective of firms and individual countries.

Note that the term 'governance' is also being used to refer more broadly to the WTO, the entire global trading system, and its relationship to this new phenomenon. In this chapter we call the latter 'G', as it is more concerned with systemic issues.

The aim of this chapter is to bring some clarity and shed light on the various perspectives that have been used by economists in the GVC literature and to remedy terminological confusion when talking about governance with respect to GVCs. This should remove some of the misunderstandings that have been generated by discussing the same term with underlying reference to different contexts.

A typology of GVC governance

We propose to set out a typology of GVC governance in three different categories:

- industrial policy frameworks and the governance of GVCs from a firm perspective;
- national policy frameworks and governance of GVCs from an individual country perspective; and
- global trading system framework and governance of GVCs from the WTO perspective and/or that of major preferential trade agreements.

For the purpose of this chapter, governance of GVCs from the firm and individual country perspectives will be discussed with a small 'g' while governance of GVCs from the perspective of the multilateral trading system or multiparty trade agreements will be discussed with a capital 'G'. This is because in the first and second cases governance is used in a micro sense, applied to either firm behaviour or national government policy, while in the third case governance is used in a broader, systemic sense as affecting all economic actors in the world economy or in a regional economic grouping.

Figure 5.1 below sets out a typology of the different levels of governance relevant to GVCs, together with the objectives, challenges and policy analysis that are applicable at each level.

Figure 5.1: Typology of governance of GVCs

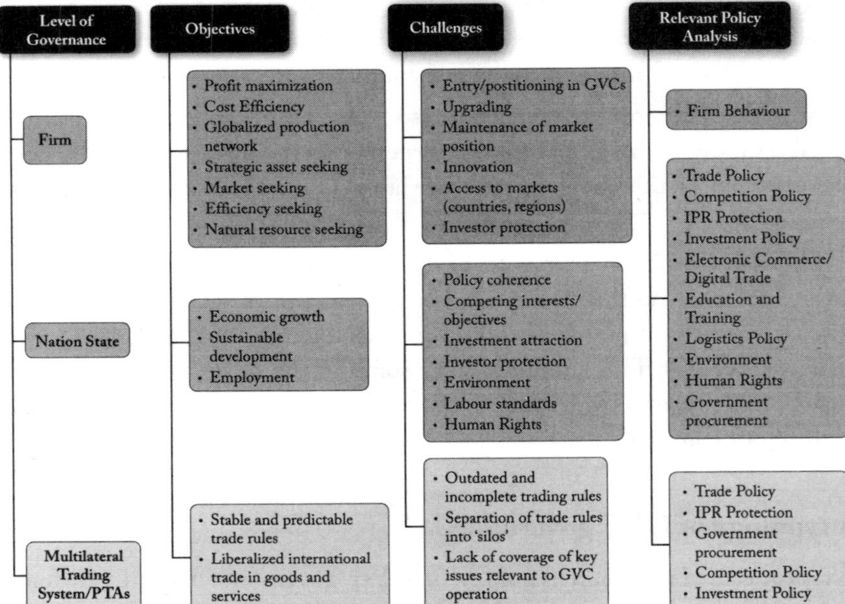

Looking at value chain operations according to this typology highlights differences in the motivation that drives the actors at all three levels of governance, as well as how and why this motivation might differ. For firms, the primary motivation is one of market power; how they position themselves in the value chains; how they interact vis-à-vis other firms; how they can maintain and/or gain dominance; and how they can keep control of the strategic assets, intellectual property and know-how that define the essence of the firm's activities, while directing the other firms in the production chain. Of course, firms are also concerned with how they can upgrade in the value chain and increase their percentage of the overall pie or VA. Thus, from a firm's point of view, the question of governance in a GVC setting is a zero-sum game; they win dominance and profits at the expense of other firms in the chain.

Nation-state governance is motivated either by efficiency or by a desire to influence the country's relative position in the value chain. Most nation-states wish to see their involvement in GVCs strengthened, and thus the efficiency motivation is the basis for a panoply of policies to allow firms to most efficiently access and compete in a value chain structure. Other nation-states are driven by the desire to influence their placement within the value chain, as well as the distribution of gains deriving from it, and attempt to do so through the adoption of more directed economic and other policies.

At the third level, the global trade system does not appear to have a specific motivation for its role in the governance of GVCs, as it is not an entity with a distinctive personality but rather a collection of government actors. The main body in the global trade system is the WTO, but it is only one of many actors at present, with greater or lesser influence.

A number of regional and bilateral trade agreements cover much of world merchandise trade flows, and thus an overlapping set of countries is beginning to be concerned with how the structure and rules of these trade agreements do (or do not) influence the operation of value chains at the regional level, as well as through the WTO. However, the discussion of governance of GVCs at the systemic level has barely begun; thus, the motivation at this level is cloudy.

Another consideration in a GVC typology is overlap between the three levels of governance. There would seem to be no overlap between the governance of GVCs at the level of the firm and that of the nation-state, as each actor has separate objectives (i.e., profit-making vs. non-profit operation), motivations, and areas of activity. With regard to overlap between the governance of GVCs at the level of the nation-state and that of the WTO/trade agreements within the global trading system, only a few policy areas would seem to be common to both at present, namely trade policy, investment policy, competition policy and government procurement.

In the sections below we discuss the main trends in this literature according to the three perspectives of governance: firms, nation-states and the multilateral trading system.

While there is a quite voluminous amount of industrial policy literature discussing firm behaviour, as well as a growing body of literature discussing how governments can and should create the best possible environment to facilitate the participation of their firms in GVCs, there is a real dearth of literature and views on how the global trading system should adapt – or not – to this phenomenon. Hence, the governance discussion has been more focused on 'g' rather than 'G'.

This chapter modestly aims both to clarify the ways in which the term 'governance' is being used with respect to GVCs and to suggest options and policies for moving forward at the third, or systemic level, for the governance of GVCs by the WTO.

Firm-level GVC governance concepts

An early approach to GVC governance from the firm perspective was developed by Gereffi (1994), who discussed governance of what he then called the 'global commodity chain'. His theory laid out how global buyers used explicit coordination to help create a highly competent supply-base upon which global-scale production and distribution systems could be built without direct ownership. He defined governance as the 'authority and power relationships that determine how financial, material and human resources are allocated and flow within a chain' (97). In this context, governance ensures that interactions between firms along a value chain exhibit some reflection of organization rather than being simply random. Gereffi distinguished between two ideal-typical governance structures: producer-driven and buyer-driven GVCs. In producer-driven chains, the key parameters were set by firms that controlled key product and process technologies, such as the car industry. In buyer-driven chains, retailers and brand-name firms set the key parameters by focusing on design and marketing, not by necessarily possessing any production facilities.

According to Ponte and Sturgeon (2014), the producer-driven variant is akin to the internal and external networks emanating from large multinational manufacturing firms, such as General Motors and IBM. Multinational firms have long been a focus of research and debate among scholars of the global economy (c.f. Hymer, 1976; Caves, 1996; Zanfei, 2000; Doz, Santos and Williamson, 2001). These scholars examined and debated the methods, timing and motivations of multinational companies' (MNCs) engagement with the global economy. Some scholars focused on the degree to which MNCs acted as conduits for the transfer of capabilities from developed to developing countries (Lall, 2000). The novel aspect of the 'global commodity chain' framework was the attention it paid to a set of firms that had been largely ignored in previous research: 'global buyers'.

The value chain governance debate shifted in the 1990s, when technology-intensive firms began engaging in extensive outsourcing and thus became more buyer-like, highlighting the need for a more nuanced and dynamic theory to help explain changes in the organization of global industries over time. These changes led to further developments of GVC governance frameworks from an industry perspective.

In their work on 'Governance in Global Value Chains', Humphrey and Schmitz (2001, 5) defined governance as 'the inter-firm relationships and institutional mechanisms through which non-market coordination of activities in the chain is achieved.' They used the term to 'express that some firms in the chain set and/or enforce the parameters under which others in the chain operate' (Humphrey and Schmitz, 2006, 2). Nonetheless, they acknowledged that different parts of the chain could be governed in different ways. This insight was especially relevant for the upgrading prospects of producers in developing countries (see further Humphrey and Schmitz, 2000 and next section).

One of the more important contributions to firm-level discussions of governance came from Gereffi, Humphrey and Sturgeon (2005). They developed a 'typology of value-chain governance' emerging from previous work by Gereffi and Korzeniewicz (1994) on 'global commodity chains' as well as increasingly available literature originating from GVC field research. The typology identified five basic types of value chain governance: markets, modular value chains, relational value chains, captive value chains and hierarchy (Gereffi, Humphrey and Sturgeon, 2005, 84).

Figure 5.2 below illustrates these five types of governance along the dual spectrums of explicit coordination and power asymmetry. Smaller arrows represent exchange based on price while the larger arrows embody thicker flows of information and control, regulated through explicit coordination.

Figure 5.2: Five GVC governance types at the firm level

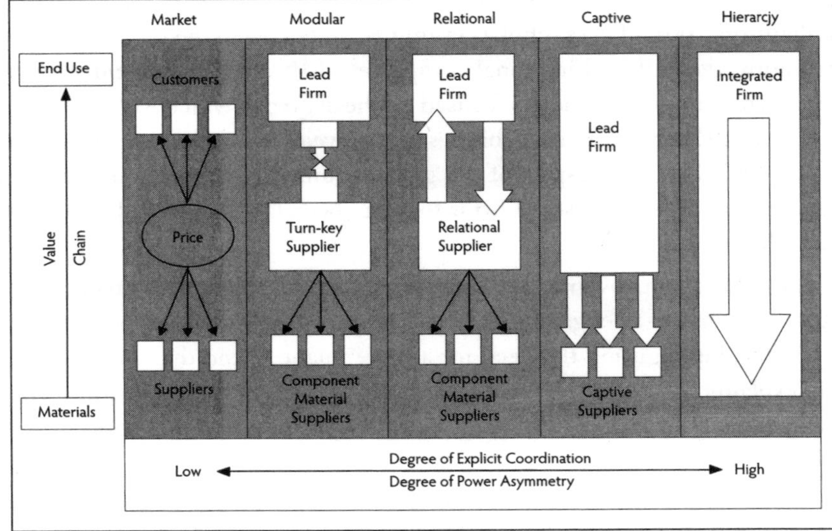

Source: Gereffi *et al* (2005), 89

To summarize, 'governance' in Gereffi's (1994) formulation refers to the role played by powerful firm-level actors, or chain 'drivers' (buyers or producers), while Gereffi, Humphrey and Sturgeon (2005) focus on the determinants of 'make-versus-buy' decisions in transactions and the characteristics of linkages among value chain activities.

Building on this foundation, more recent literature written from a firm perspective has tried to examine different types and linkages in firm governance in GVCs to determine how firms enter value chains, how they behave once they are inside a chain, and importantly, how they can upgrade along an existing value chain. MNCs drive most variants of firm governance in GVCs through their investment and outsourcing and offshoring activities (Dunning and Lundan, 2008; Aldonas, 2013). Smaller firms are drawn into GVCs through providing intermediate inputs or 'tasks' in the case of services (Low, 2013). A key question in this context is how the benefits are divided between MNCs and small and medium-sized enterprises (SMEs), which appear to be dependent upon where they are located in the chain and the governance structure. This can influence the type of benefits realized by both the firm and the host economy. Some authors have written that the political economy of value chain management by firms makes it difficult for upgrading to take place, given the role of the lead firm and the efficiencies in the chain that it drives (Gereffi and Sturgeon, 2013). This debate is still ongoing.

GVC governance from the country perspective

The second level of governance relevant to GVCs is that of the country or nation-state perspective. Many analysts have suggested that the GVC policy agenda is primarily a national or a domestic one. They underline the need for governments to create the best possible enabling environment to facilitate the insertion of their firms into GVCs. Relevant policies in this regard are numerous and touch on many areas. Trade policy, for instance, is a part of a broader package in the GVC area; it is viewed as a necessary but not sufficient component of national GVC governance. The cost of protectionist measures undertaken in a globalized context is higher than appreciated because such policies impact not only on final goods but also on intermediate inputs that now represent more than half of the imports of OECD countries. The World Bank/World Economic Forum's 'Enabling Trade' report (2013) underscored the need to adopt a holistic approach to removing logistics barriers to trade in goods and key national-level infrastructure services, such as transport and telecommunications, in order to allow value chains to operate efficiently.

Yet while open markets are viewed by many as an essential component in a government's policy arsenal, they will not be effective without the human capital base necessary to provide the quality inputs to be fed into supply chains. Other policies are vital. Several authors have emphasized the need for governments to attribute greater importance to their relative competitiveness in services given the important role these play in GVCs (Low, 2013; Drake-Brockman and Stephenson, 2012). Fostering a competitive services industry depends on creating and nurturing a cluster of talent and expertise. Key ingredients in services development are education policy and innovation policy. In this context, government intervention through positive support measures to develop higher education learning centres as well as vocational institutions can have an across-the-board economic impact. Government support to encourage compliance with international services standards and quality assurance processes can be extremely important, especially in developing countries.

Given the links between investment and GVCs, the national government stance on investment is also viewed as an essential factor in the policy mix. It is generally acknowledged that the investment decisions of MNCs, through their outsourcing and offshoring activities, are driving the operation of GVCs worldwide. Thus, multinational firms will look globally for a welcoming investment climate. Governments can take a multitude of actions in order to make their countries more attractive destinations for investors. These actions are linked to investment entry, promotion, investor protection, the adequate use of incentives (transparent for domestic as well as foreign investors) and further considerations regarding linkages and spill-over effects for the country. A country's participation in preferential trade agreements and the rule of law in the country are also decisive factors for MNCs' investment decisions.

A solid institutional environment is also important to create a solid national framework for the operation of GVCs. This includes strong government institutions with a minimum of corruption as well as effective intellectual property enforcement mechanisms and avenues for legal recourse in the case of disputes.

Stephenson and Drake-Brockman (2014) proposed a framework of eight factors that play a role in determining competitiveness, particularly in the sphere of services, and thus impact the ability of firms to participate in GVCs. This framework draws on firm-level evidence emerging from business associations in the Asia-Pacific Economic Cooperation (APEC) region, and on empirical results from several developing country case studies undertaken by the World Bank and the African Union Commission. Key factors include:

- Endowments, especially human capital (talent, education, skills, ideas, culture of customer focus) (see also Chanda and Pasadilla, 2011)
- Investment in intangible assets (corporate intellectual property, e.g., copyright, business methodologies, brands)
- Enabling digital infrastructure (see APEC Policy Support Unit, 2012)
- Quality of institutions (see Goswami, Mattoo and Sáez, 2011)
- Efficiency of domestic regulation (see McCredie and Findlay, 2011)
- Connectedness with the international markets – logistics (see Stephenson, 2014)
- Services business stakeholder consultations (see ITC, 2014)
- Policy focus, or putting services explicitly in national planning strategies

This framework highlights many policy variables relevant to the determination of competitiveness related to GVC governance at the national level, and indicates the broad scope of policies within the purview of governments that enables them to do much to create and/or enhance the opportunities for participation of their firms in global and regional supply chains. From this perspective, openness of an economy's own policies affecting trade and investment (inwards and outwards) is an important national policy ingredient, but must be complemented by domestic policies to create strong competition, judicial and intellectual property (IP) frameworks and a qualified human capital base.

Logistics are critical for supply chain performance in linking global operations and transiting goods across borders. Especially when goods may cross borders several times, all aspects of border management, automation in customs clearance procedures, efficient port operations and cargo handlers, and the quality of transportation services are key. Firms also need mutual recognition and interoperability of standards to create more seamless regulation across markets. Regulatory simplicity and efficiency, including predictability and coherence, are also key components of the national GVC governance framework for firms to be able to join and prosper in GVCs.

Several institutions as well as national governments have become involved in developing 'tool kits' for participation in GVCs to help government officials understand and better apply the various policies available at the national level for this objective. The Inter-American Development Bank (IADB) has studied GVCs in Latin America and published a volume with suggestions to governments in the region on how to improve their inclusion in GVC operations (Blyde, 2014). The United Nations Conference on Trade and Development (UNCTAD) and the International Trade Centre (ITC) provide policy advice to member governments on their participation in GVCs. The Canadian Trade Commissioner Service published a guide on linking SMEs into chains (2010). The World Bank has put online a comprehensive series of six modules to help officials diagnose the 'readiness' of individual countries and the ability of their firms to take advantage of GVC opportunities and to provide information and policy tools to leverage GVC participation for development.[1] These modules are applied as part of the technical assistance offered by the World Bank in its programmes with member countries.

It is worth noting that the idea of promoting GVCs through open policies, a welcoming stance to FDI and measures designed to promote international competitiveness is not a universally accepted view at present. There is debate in some governments about who captures the value in the value chain, what types of value chains are most suitable to bring about developmental benefits,

1 See The World Bank Open Learning, *Global Value Chains: The Basics,* at https://olc.worldbank.org/content/global-value-chains-basics.

and even whether or not participating in GVCs is a desirable goal (Draper and Freytag, 2014).

National-level concerns include equity, an unequal distribution of gains among participants in the value chain, and difficulty deriving benefits from innovation when upgrading within the chain may be impeded by lead firms (usually MNCs). The different types of gains to be derived from various kinds of value chains also generate worries, especially for countries heavily engaged in resource extraction or countries with firms involved in labour-intensive, assembly-driven GVCs. Anxieties abound over entrapment in a situation of poor comparative advantage or a middle-income trap, or the 'race to the bottom,' especially with respect to MNC behaviour (Draper and Freytag, 2014).

According to this line of reasoning, GVC governance at the national level should be directed not at policies designed to embrace FDI and open markets, but rather to the adoption of the newer version of 'industrial policies' based on targeted intervention that would allow governments to 'manage' FDI inflows into sectors of their choice and to strategically protect imports in favour of certain national industries that would be the object of 'deliberative targeted promotional efforts' (Draper and Freytag, 2014). Joseph Stiglitz, Dani Rodrik and Justin Lin are three of the most well-known and outspoken proponents of an active interventionist industrial policy, and their arguments have met a favourable resonance in many quarters (Stiglitz and Lin, 2013). In this context, GVC governance consists of adopting appropriate policy tools to promote specific skills, relevant technologies and markets, and develop public-private partnerships to generate investment and derive synergies for upgrading investment and innovation (Singh, 2014).

Thus, at the national level, governments have different underlying philosophies and areas of policy focus. However, the relevant question for these actors remains the type of governance (and resulting policies) they should adopt in relation to GVCs.

The evolving understanding of GVCs in an international trade context

GVCs have evolved in terms of the way that economists understand them in the context of international trade. While a good early working definition for a GVC can be taken as:

> the full range of activities which are required to bring a product or service from conception, through the different phases of production (involving a combination of physical transformation and the input of various producer services), delivery to final consumers, and final disposal after use (Kaplinsky and Morris, 2000, 4)

It is clear that this definition does not involve international trade.

In 2001, Arndt and Kierzkowski brought in the international dimension by using the term 'fragmentation' to describe the geographical separation of different parts of a production process.

With the development of databases that linked national input-output tables, economists such as Grossman and Rossi-Hansberg (2006) moved away from an 'old' paradigm of trade theory 'which conceptualizes the production process as generating finished goods from bundles of inputs combined at a single plant' in a single location to conceptualizing the production process in terms of component tasks, a 'new paradigm' (Grossman and Rossi-Hansberg, 2006, 7).

Baldwin (2006) has written extensively about GVCs from an international trade perspective. He describes a 'first unbundling' between production and consumption that took place in the second half of the nineteenth century (1850–1914) and from the 1960s onwards. This was followed by a 'second unbundling' that started in the mid-1980s, when the production process itself was split across countries both geographically (offshoring) and organizationally (outsourcing). Both of Baldwin´s 'unbundlings' were in part technology-enabled, with the first unbundling driven by the industrial revolution and the second unbundling driven by the information and communications technology (ICT) revolution (Baldwin, 2013).

Over the past few years there have been further developments of international databases that allow us to better understand the VA from trade contributed by each of the producers in a supply chain through examining the backward and forward linkages in value terms. New trade-in-value-added databases such as those published by the OECD/WTO (2013), among others, can now distinguish the position of countries in relation to their participation in supply chains overall and in individual sectors, and thus their involvement in globalized patterns of production sharing.

GVC governance from the global trading system perspective

While national governments wrestle with the appropriate governance structure for supply chains, at the global level the 162 member WTO has remained occupied with its Doha Development Agenda. The multilateral emphasis on twentieth century issues (mostly tariffs and agriculture) into the first two decades of the twenty-first century has left space for regional trade agreements to fill pent-up desires for rule-making on new issues. Baldwin argued that a 'supply chain governance gap' is being filled by piecemeal and uncoordinated developments in deep regional trade agreements that discipline behind-the-border regulatory issues as well as bilateral investment treaties (Baldwin, 2011; WTO 2011 World Trade Report). Ambitious mega-regional negotiating initiatives have also been launched, and emerging and other developing economies continue to carry out autonomous reforms. Such rule-making initiatives, both large and small, have all recently been concerned with 'Governance' of value chains with a 'G' for the systemic level.

This level differs significantly from the other two levels of GVC governance discussed above. No longer focused on a single actor, either a firm or a government, this level addresses decisions that affect trade and investment flows between two or more trading partners, as well as the trading system as a whole. The governance questions raised at this level, and particularly for the WTO, have been little explored.

Figure 5.1 on the typology of GVC governance presented earlier in the chapter highlights some of the challenges that the WTO faces when trying to deal with a world of GVCs. Putting aside the difficulty of reaching agreement among a very diverse membership of countries with differing priorities, the WTO at present is characterized by the following:

- *Outdated trading rules*: The WTO came into existence two decades ago with the transformation of the General Agreement on Tariffs and Trade (GATT) in 1995. Many of the trade issues that have become important for the global trading system – including rules relevant to GVCs – have come to the forefront since then, especially in the services area. Yet the WTO has not been able to find a way to 'modernize' its current rules. The Doha Development Round is in its thirteenth year but has not made much headway in the area of 'rules' negotiations for either goods or services.
- *Silos for existing WTO rules*: The current structure of WTO rules creates separate 'silos', with nearly complete segregation between rules for goods, services and intellectual property rights (IPR). But firms in the twenty-first century global trading system do not operate in that manner. Rather, they carry out integrated activities covering goods and services

in their investment and trade. The WTO has not been able to address this dichotomy between its structure and how international trade is being conducted, though several trade policy experts have called for these silos to be broken down and the rules better integrated (Low, 2013).

- *Lack of WTO coverage of key issues*: WTO rules do not include many key issues at present that are relevant, and even vital, to GVC operations. A complex set of policies is needed to address GVC governance at the national level, but the WTO does not have many arrows in its quiver to target all relevant aspects of GVC operations at the multilateral level. Other than trade policy and IPR protection, many vital issues for GVC operation have not yet been brought under WTO competence. Figure 5.1 highlights the importance of including rules on investment, competition policy and e-commerce/digital trade, as well as aspects of regulatory cooperation for logistics. The missing element of investment at the WTO is an especially glaring gap, as it is more and more evident that investment decisions lead trade flows and are a key determinant for GVC participation (UNCTAD, 2013).

Additionally, the WTO has two characteristics at present that limit its ability to fill the governance gap at the systemic level in dealing with a world characterized by GVCs. First, the negotiating mind-set of WTO members leaves few opportunities in the WTO's normal functioning to simply 'discuss' issues as opposed to 'negotiate' them. One of the main objectives of the WTO is to reach negotiated, binding sets of rules for world trade. However, this often blocks the ability of WTO members to sit back and take time to reflect on new issues, as well as to try new ways of doing things. Second, no processes within the WTO exist to allow members to look at issues and policies on a cross-cutting basis in order to evaluate their impact on trade flows, trade costs and investment decisions (Hoekman, 2014). But GVCs by their nature operate in a cross-cutting manner, concerned with trade and investment as well as the impact of differences in regulation across national jurisdictions, since all affect the ability of firms to engage in supply chain activities.

The lack of a cross-cutting discussion forum impedes the WTO in helping its members obtain information about the aims and effects of regulatory policies and thereby reach a better understanding of the interactions between these policies and how they impact trade flows and patterns. Hoekman (2014) refers to this as the lack of a 'knowledge platform' function within the WTO and cites this as a reason why business appears to be less engaged in and supportive of the WTO than in the past. He suggests the creation of a platform or various platforms, animated by private sector input and functioning on a product or sectorial basis, to allow the WTO to look across the various policy silos that all have an impact on supply chain trade. Such a discussion platform would also help prepare WTO members over time for negotiating new agreements to cover those areas where its competence is currently lacking.

The WTO should – in principal – have an advantage over national governments in adopting a supply chain focus, as it is the one body that can combine the assessment of the policies of various members and address the multicountry spill-overs in a single setting.

Remedying the current governance gap for GVCs at the WTO level is challenging, but can be approached in two ways: (1) through a focus on changes in process; and (2) through a focus on changes in, or additions to, WTO rules. The former can be viewed as relevant in a short-term context with steps that, if adopted successfully, could help pave the way to the latter in the medium and long term. The discussion below will be divided between these two. Another section will discuss a proposal to establish a 'GVC Platform' that would provide some of the analytical basis to help in bringing about these reforms.

Focus on changes in WTO processes (a short-term agenda)

Incorporating a supply chain perspective into trade discussions in all of the WTO's regular working bodies, as well as into the preparation of the WTO annual reports and into the trade policy review reports, would be a fairly straightforward process change that would help shape the understanding of GVC operations through consistent treatment of this issue. Private sector firms should nourish discussions in some WTO forums to help officials grasp how investment and trade are being conducted in the real world. These private sector representatives would share experiences on how they actually carry out value chain operations. Various suggestions as to how private sector input might be incorporated into the WTO are being considered in the E15 Initiative in the Expert Group on the Functioning of the Multilateral Trade System.

The recent OECD/WTO TiVA is an extremely useful tool with expanded coverage and analysis. The implications of looking at trade on a value-added basis alongside gross trade flows should be reported on an annual basis and discussed regularly in WTO meetings and in the various WTO working committees and bodies. This process change would again allow for greater familiarization with the value chain understanding of global trade and how this picture differs from one drawn with traditional trade statistics. It should be noted that the WTO Secretariat is already thinking in this direction and has put further emphasis into reflecting the reality of today's international trade through a new series of statistical profiles on GVCs by country that it began publishing in January 2016, based on statistics from the TiVA database.[2]

A work programme on GVCs, similar to the work programme on e-commerce, should be created within the WTO to focus discussions and break down silos. Such a step would involve more of a process than a rule change, and would allow for the impacts and implications of value chains to be better understood in a non-negotiating, non-threatening context. The trade policy and development implications of analyses undertaken within or synthesized by the GVC platform (see below) could be discussed under this work programme with a holistic view of GVCs and their impacts. These discussions would help to make developing countries more aware of how to better understand and define their objectives vis-à-vis the operation of GVCs.

The existing 'Aid for Trade' (AfT) Agenda could be re-oriented toward addressing those measures and constraints that impede the ability of least developed countries (LDCs) to increase their participation in GVCs. Many of the relevant policies regarding the ability of countries to participate in GVCs involve regulatory and infrastructure improvement and could be addressed under AfT programmes.

Focus on expansion of existing WTO areas of competence and changes to WTO negotiating approaches (a medium- to long-term agenda)

A major step toward bringing about a systemic focus on GVCs at the WTO level or in trade agreements would be to eliminate silos in the treatment of goods and services through a dedicated overhaul of existing rules on the one hand and to complete key missing disciplines most relevant to GVCs on the other. Ideally, multilateral negotiation should create new, comprehensive rules for investment, competition policy and e-commerce and digital trade. These may

2 The WTO has released statistical profiles on GVCs for 61 economies so far. These profiles bring together a set of indicators on trade taking place within GVCs. These profiles provide insights into the value-added content of exports, the interconnection between economies within GVCs and the role of the services industry in exports. Other indicators related to GVCs include trade in intermediate goods, trade facilitation and foreign direct investment. See www.wto.org/english/news_e/news16_e/stat_28jan16_e.htm.

both be daunting challenges, however, given the difficulties that the Doha Round has faced in engaging WTO members to negotiate on existing trade issues.

An alternative path to a multilateral overhaul of trade rules would be the negotiation of plurilateral agreements or critical mass agreements in areas to address these missing disciplines and substantively expand existing WTO competence. Hoekman (2014) notes that plurilateral agreements consist of a subset of WTO members agreeing to new commitments without extending the benefits to non-signatories, while critical mass agreements also cover new commitments but extend these benefits to non-signatories. As an example of each, a member might drop tariffs on pencils to zero in a plurilateral agreement – but only members of the plurilateral get this benefit. If pencil tariffs are dropped to zero in a critical mass deal, the benefit is automatically granted to every WTO member without reciprocity from those who are not part of the arrangement.

However, the distinction between the two seems somewhat less important in practice for GVC issues given that many of the regulatory disciplines that would be negotiated in plurilateral agreements would most likely have to be applied on a most-favoured-nation (MFN) basis as it is quite impractical for governments to apply different sets of regulations to different trading partners.

A set of plurilateral or critical mass agreements in core GVC-related areas, applied by WTO members accounting for the large majority of trade in goods and services, would go a long way towards addressing gaps in existing WTO competencies related to GVCs. One challenge is how to get new agreements incorporated into the WTO. Currently the incorporation of a discriminatory plurilateral agreement into the WTO requires consensus among all members, which is an almost impossible bar to meet. Passage would likely be easier if a non-discriminatory critical mass agreement were involved.

Hufbauer and Schott (2012) suggest relaxing the consensus requirement and adopting a requirement that a deal can proceed if it includes 'substantial coverage' of world trade or production (with a percentage to be determined, but presumably close to at least two-thirds of either or both). This reform could go a long way towards allowing the WTO to become an organization that is both more relevant and responsive to the needs and concerns of a majority of its members in particular areas, and has been advocated by several well-known trade economists (c.f. World Economic Forum, 2012; Lawrence, 2013).

A practical problem remains with this approach, however, in that excluded parties would still have resort to dispute settlement proceedings if there were discriminatory elements in the outcome. It is unlikely that agreement would ever be reached to deny a subset of members their right to dispute settlement. More generally, it is likely that many parties would resist what they would see as a potentially dominant situation of larger trading nations, with unpredictable consequences for the less powerful in future circumstances where they could find themselves on the wrong side of an argument.

Lastly, the standard GATT/WTO approach of negotiating separately on goods and services should be put aside in the next round of multilateral trade negotiations (if and when this occurs), and the areas relevant to the operation of a given GVC should be treated under a holistic approach. Adopting a 'supply chain approach' (Nakatomi, 2013) to multilateral trade negotiations might mean negotiating disciplines for goods, services and investment with respect to a cluster of productive activities associated with particular supply chains rather than with specific sectors, as has sometimes been done in the past such as in the Information Technology Agreement or the recently begun Environmental Goods Agreement negotiations. Negotiating in 'clusters' has not yet been attempted in the WTO, but this might arguably be the best route for approaching a world characterized by GVCs. A holistic negotiating approach will eventually lead to an integration of trade rules, whether this be on a horizontal basis (for all goods and services and investment) or on a cluster basis (for a cluster of goods and services and investment associated with a particular family of value chain chains) so that the distinction between these areas eventually disappears both on paper and in the thinking of trade negotiators and government officials.

Creation of a GVC platform to focus on the trade and developmental aspects of supply chain operation

The establishment of an external GVC platform could complement the steps described above within the WTO. Such a platform, inspired in part by the suggestion of Hoekman and Mattoo (2013) and Hoekman (2014) of 'knowledge platforms' under a slightly different focus, would have the objective of increasing the understanding of the trade and development aspects of GVC operation for government officials and the trade policy community. The platform would be focused on the trade and development aspects of GVCs. It would serve the purpose of fostering greater transparency of information and enhanced understanding of GVCs, and help highlight the interdependence between regulatory policies that impact GVC performance and operation. It would also help clarify the developmental consequences of participating – or not participating – in GVCs and the types of impacts that different types of supply chains might deliver. A GVC platform would bring together relevant work carried out at the WTO or in outside bodies, so that analysts could draw out the trade policy and developmental implications of various aspects of GVCs.

While such a platform could be established within the WTO, it would be easier and more convenient to do this outside the WTO, but with the possibility for feed-in into WTO discussions and deliberations. The GVC platform could foster better dialogue among governments and officials through new mechanisms such as online chats and question-and-answer sessions with experts. It should also offer a roster of GVC experts to provide technical assistance when requested and disseminate analysis to assist governments in understanding the opportunities, challenges, relevant policy responses and potential impact of GVCs both for individual economies as well as for the global trading system.

The GVC platform should serve as a virtual place for exchanging ideas and information and making available existing analyses on the trade policy and developmental implications of the functioning of GVCs. To the extent that resources were made available, it would also engage researchers to carry out analyses of particular interest. Such a platform should carry out four functions, namely to:

- create a repository for research and policy work that examines trade policy and developmental implications of GVCs;
- provide information and summary analyses of such research and policy work to the various WTO bodies upon request and to the broader trade policy community to facilitate discussion of GVCs and relevant trade policy and developmental implications;
- offer a virtual forum for discussion and question-and-answer sessions on GVCs for all interested officials and policymakers; and
- constitute a network of worldwide analysts with expertise in the trade policy and developmental implications of GVCs.[3]

3 In line with this recommendation and since the completion of this chapter, it is of note that a new Research Centre for Global Value Chains (RCGVC) has been established in Beijing, China, under the initiative of the Chinese Government. It will be dedicated to research and analysis of GVCs from a developmental perspective and will enjoy the institutional collaboration of many international organizations, think tanks and universities from around the world in this effort. It began operations in January 2016 and will issue its first report during the course of 2016

Conclusion and recommendations

This chapter has reviewed the notion of 'governance' and how it has been used in various contexts in relation to GVCs. We have tried to show that the interpretation and meaning of governance differs depending upon the context in which the term has been employed, leading to potential confusion for trade policy analysis.

While the role of firms in GVC governance is fairly obvious, governments need to be aware of the double role government plays in both the 'g' and the 'G' GVC governance space. Governments carry out national-level policies designed to influence the participation and positioning of their firms in GVCs, and simultaneously work with other governments to design and implement trade rules at the systemic level in the WTO and in bilateral, plurilateral and mega-regional trade agreements. These agreements also impact the ability of national firms to trade and invest in an increasingly GVC-dominated world.

The current supply chain 'G' governance gap at the systemic level is in great need of improvement. The following steps could help to close the gap:

- Explicitly incorporating a supply chain or GVC perspective into trade discussions at the WTO and all WTO reports.
- Publishing the OECD/WTO TiVA on a regular basis alongside gross trade statistics, with expanded coverage and analysis.
- Creating a work programme on GVCs within the WTO, similar to the work programme on e-commerce.
- Establishing a GVC platform outside the WTO, to increase understanding of GVC operations and implications for trade policies and development among government officials and the trade policy community.
- Finding more effective avenues for coordinating the AfT agenda with trade objectives involving GVCs.
- Completing key missing disciplines at the WTO level relevant to GVC operations either through multilateral negotiations of new rules on investment, competition policy and e-commerce and digital trade, or through a series of plurilateral or critical mass agreements addressing each of these key issues individually, and bringing them into the WTO through a relaxation of the current 'consensus' requirement.
- Using a different negotiating approach for the next round of multilateral trade negotiations, where disciplines for goods, services and investment are negotiated in a holistic manner by creating clusters of productive activities

associated with particular supply chains (a 'cluster' approach), gradually leading to the integration of goods, services and investment in a horizontal manner under a single set of trade disciplines. Such a 'cluster' approach could, for example, focus on the operation of the respective supply chains for certain specific industries, such as automobiles, electronics, tourism or processed agricultural goods, which would be the object of sectoral agreement. In these, governments would address all relevant issues of services, goods, investment and data flows relevant to the operation of the supply chain for that particular industry from a holistic perspective, reconciling the views of officials deciding within their 'g' (national interest) with those targeting the interest of the 'G' (global, systemic interest). The objective would be to identify all barriers or bottlenecks impeding the flow of the supply chain in order to liberalize and bind this openness. Under this approach, governments would address the complexity of today's trade as a whole, and achieving efficiency in logistics and trade facilitation would be as important in this GVC context as the reduction of border barriers. This is one of the possible ways of thinking about how to apply a GVC focus to trade negotiations, but it is by no means the only option.

At the latest WTO Ministerial Conference, which took place in Nairobi, Kenya, in December 2015, little progress was achieved on thinking about a GVC perspective in trade. Neither GVCs, nor services or investment came up for discussion in the context of the ministerial meeting, whose outcome focused primarily on new disciplines for export credits, food aid and public stockholding for essential food supplies.

The real challenge of the WTO 10th Ministerial Conference however was to try and overcome divergences on the future of the Doha Development Agenda (DDA) and on how to proceed in future trade negotiations. This did not prove to be possible and the WTO membership remained divided, as is evident in the final Declaration, where Para 30 states:

> While many Members reaffirm the Doha Development Agenda........, Other Members do not reaffirm the Doha mandates, as they believe **new approaches are necessary to achieve meaningful outcomes in multilateral negotiations** (bold added).

Exactly what these new approaches might be were not specified and have not yet been discussed. However, it is no secret that some WTO members have expressed a desire to incorporate a GVC approach into future negotiations.

This may however take a longer period of time to achieve. As it is unclear at present whether the Doha Round will be concluded in the future, it may well be the case that plurilateral initiatives such as the expanded Information Technology Agreement (ITA-II), the Trade in Services Agreement (TiSA) and the Environmental Goods Agreement (EGA), among others, will provide the vehicles for like-minded countries to move trade liberalization forward at the multilateral level, provided the outcomes of such initiatives are then granted to all WTO members on an MFN basis (as is the case for the ITA-II).

Although the WTO is still the first best option for the negotiation of global trade disciplines that apply to all countries regardless of size, economic weight or share in trade, in the current economic environment and with the inconclusive outcome of the WTO 10th Ministerial Conference (MC10), it is necessary to recognize the reality that WTO members are choosing to move at different speeds and with differing degrees of commitment on trade issues. Thus, it would also be important for members of regional, plurilateral and mega-regional trade initiatives to take the opportunity to design these trade agreements in a more holistic manner and to incorporate disciplines that foster the operation of GVCs. Many provisions in the recently-concluded Trans-Pacific Partnership (TPP) Agreement have been included or deepened to facilitate the operation of supply chains and ensure the free flow of investment, as well as services and data among members, all key to integrated production networks. These agreements may help prod the WTO by paving the way and showing more sceptical WTO members that it is not only possible but beneficial to think of trade in an integrated manner.

If the WTO does not modernize its approach to trade in the near future to address the systemic challenge posed by GVCs, it will find itself increasingly marginalized and ineffective in terms of its governance function. Instead of just showing the way forward, the deep preferential trade agreements (PTAs) will 'de facto' fill this governance gap to constitute the normative framework for the majority of world trade and investment. Without the WTO stepping up to the task, the 'G' governance vacuum for GVCs at the multilateral level will continue to grow and will be filled from other quarters in a less inclusive manner. And the developmental outcomes of a more fragmented governance system run a high risk of being less favourable for countries outside these alternative trade frameworks.

References

Aldonas, Grant. 2013. 'Trade Policy in a Global Age'. E15 Initiative. Geneva: ICTSD and World Economic Forum. Available at: http://www.ictsd.org/sites/default/files/research/E15_GVCs_Aldonas_FINAL.pdf.

APEC Policy Support Unit. 2012. 'APEC's Bogor Goals Progress Report'. Singapore: APEC Secretariat. Available at: http://www.apec.org/About-Us/About-APEC/Achievements-and-Bfits/~/media/Files/AboutUs/AchievementsBenefits/20120822_APECsBogorGoalsProgressReport.ashx.

APEC Second Senior Officials' Meeting. 2014. *APEC Strategic Blueprint for Promoting Global Value Chains Development and Cooperation Through Asia-Pacific Partnership*. Qingdao: APEC. Available at: http://mddb.apec.org/Documents/2014/SOM/SOM2/14_som2_049anx04.pdf.

Arndt, Sven and Henryk Kierzkowski. 2001. 'Introduction' to *Fragmentation: New Production Patterns in the World Economy*, 1–16. Oxford: Oxford University Press.

ASEAN Secretariat and UNCTAD. 2014. *ASEAN Investment Report 2013-2014: FDI Development and Regional Value Chains*. Jakarta: ASEAN Secretariat. Available at: http://www.asean.org/images/pdf/2014_upload/AIR%202013-2014%20FINAL.pdf.

Baldwin, Richard. 2006. 'Globalisation: The Great Unbundling(s)', *Globalisation Challenges for Europe and Finland*. Helsinki: Economic Council of Finland. Available at: http://www2.dse.unibo.it/naghavi/baldwin.pdf.

———. 2011. '21st Century Regionalism: Filling the Gap between 21st Century Trade and 20th Century Trade Rules'. Social Science Research Network (SSRN). Available at: http://ssrn.com/abstract=1869845.

———. 2013. Global Supply Chains: Why They Emerged, Why They Matter, and Where They are Going', in *Global Value Chains in a Changing World*, edited by Deborah Elms and Patrick Low, 13–60. Geneva: WTO.

Blyde, Juan S. 2014. *Synchronized Factories: Latin America and the Caribbean in the Era of Global Value Chains*. Washington, DC: Springer.

Canadian Trade Commissioner Service. 2010. *Linking In to Global Value Chains: A Guide for Small and Medium-Sized Enterprises*. Ottawa: Foreign Affairs and International Trade Canada. Available at: www.tradecommissioner.gc.ca/eng/gvc-guide.jsp.

Caves, Richard. 1996. *Multinational Enterprise and Economic Analysis*, second edition. Cambridge: Cambridge University Press.

Chanda, Rupa and Gloria Pasadilla. 2011. 'Employment and People-Movement Impacts of Services Trade Liberalization', paper presented at the PECC/ADBI (Pacific Economic Cooperation Council/Asian Development Bank Institute) 'Conference on Services Trade: New Approaches for the 21st Century', Hong Kong.

Doz, Yves, Jose Santos and Peter Williamson. 2001. *From Global to Metanational: How Companies Win in the Knowledge Economy*. Boston: Harvard Business School Press.

Drake-Brockman, Jane and Sherry M. Stephenson. 2012. *Implications for 21st Century Trade and Development of the Emergence of Services Value Chains*. Geneva: ICTSD. Available at: http://ictsd.org/downloads/2012/11/implications-for-21st-century-trade-and-development-of-the-emergence-of-services-value-chains.pdf.

Draper, Peter and Andreas Freytag. 2014. *Who Captures the Value in the Global Value Chain? Implications for the World Trade Organization*. E15 Initiative. Geneva: ICTSD and World Economic Forum. Available at: http://www.ictsd.org/sites/default/files/research/E15_GVCs_Draper%20Freytag_FINAL.pdf.

Dunning, John H. and Sarianna M. Lundan. 2008. *Multinational Enterprises and the Global Economy*, second edition. Northampton, MA: Edward Elgar Publishing.

Gereffi, Gary. 1994. 'The Organisation of Buyer-driven Global Commodity Chains: How U.S. Retailers Shape Overseas Production Networks', in *Commodity Chains and Global Capitalism*, edited by Gary Gereffi and Miguel Korzeniewicz, 95–122. Westport, CT: Praeger.

Gereffi, Gary and Timothy Sturgeon. 2013. 'Global Value Chain-Oriented Industrial Policy: The Role of Emerging Economies', in *Global Value Chains in a Changing World*, edited by Deborah K. Elms and Patrick Low, 329–60. Geneva: WTO.

Gereffi, Gary, John Humphrey and Timothy Sturgeon. 2005. 'The Governance of Global Value Chains', *Review of International Political Economy* 12 (1): 78–104.

Gereffi, Gary and Miguel Korzeniewicz (eds.). 1994. *Commodity Chains and Global Capitalism*. Westport, CT: Praeger.

Goswami, Arti, Aaditya Mattoo and Sebastián Sáez. 2011. 'Exporting Services: A Developing-Country Perspective', in *Exporting Services: A Developing Country Perspective*, edited by Arti Goswami, Aaditya Mattoo and Sebastián Sáez, 1–24. Washington, DC: World Bank.

Grossman, Gene and Esteban Rossi-Hansberg. 2006. 'Trading Tasks: A Simple Theory of Offshoring', *NBER Working Paper* 12721. Available at: http://www.nber.org/papers/w12721.pdf.

Hoekman, Bernard. 2014. 'Supply Chains, Mega-Regionals and Multilateralism: A Road Map for the WTO', *EUI-RSCAS Working Paper* 2014/27. Available at: http://cadmus.eui.eu/bitstream/handle/1814/30198/RSCAS_2014_27_Rev2.pdf.

Hoekman, Bernard and Aaditya Mattoo. 2013. 'Liberalizing Trade in Services: Lessons from Regional and WTO Negotiations', *International Negotiation* 18 (1): 131–51.

Hufbauer, Gary and Jeffrey Schott. 2012. 'Will the World Trade Organization Enjoy a Bright Future?', *Peterson Institute for International Economics Policy Brief* 12-11. Available at: http://www.iie.com/publications/pb/pb12-11.pdf.

Humphrey, John, Raphael Kaplinsky and Prasad Saraph. 1998. *Corporate Restructuring:*

Crompton Greaves and the Challenge of Globalization. New Delhi: SAGE Publications.

Humphrey, John and Hubert Schmitz. 2000. 'Governance and Upgrading: Linking Industrial Cluster and Global Value Chain Research', in *The Value of Value Chains*, edited by Gereffi, Gary and Kaplinsky, Raphael, *Institute of Development Studies Bulletin* 32 (3): 19-29. Brighton: Institute of Development Studies, University of Sussex.

———. 2001. 'Governance in Global Value Chains', *Institute of Development Studies Bulletin* 32 (3). Available at: https://www.ids.ac.uk/files/dmfile/humphreyschmitz32.3.pdf.

Hymer, Stephen. 1976. *The International Operations of National Firms: A Study of Direct Foreign Investment*. Cambridge, MA: MIT Press.

ITC. 2014. *Creating Coalitions of Services Industries*. Geneva: ITC. Available at: http://www.intracen.org/uploadedFiles/intracenorg/Content/Publications/Creating%20Coalitions%20of%20Services%20Industries%20-%20final%20Low-res.pdf.

Kaplinsky, Raphael and Mike Morris. 2000. *A Handbook for Value Chain Research*. Ottawa: International Development Research Centre. Available at: http://www.ids.ac.uk/ids/global/pdfs/ValuechainHBRKMMNov2001.pdf.

Lall, Sanjaya. 2000. 'The Technological Structure and Performance of Developing Country Manufactured Exports, 1985–98', *Oxford Development Studies* 28 (3): 337–69.

Lawrence, Robert. 2013. *When the Immovable Object Meets the Unstoppable Force: Multilateralism, Regionalism and Deeper Integration*. E15 Initiative. Geneva: ICTSD and World Economic Forum. Available at: http://e15initiative.org/wp-content/uploads/2014/11/E15_RTA_Lawrence_FINAL.pdf.

Low, Patrick. 2013. 'Services and Value Along Supply Chains', *Fung Global Institute Issue Brief 2013/01*. Available at: http://www.fungglobalinstitute.org/en/wp-content/uploads/IB%20Real%20Sector%20-%20S%26V%20Along%20Supply%20Chains_ONLINE.pdf.

Low, Patrick and Julia Tijaja. 2013. *Global Value Chains and Industrial Policies*. E15 Initiative. Geneva: ICTSD and World Economic Forum. Available at: http://www.ictsd.org/sites/default/files/research/E15_GVCs_Low%20Tijaja_FINAL.pdf.

McCredie, Andrew and Christopher Findlay. 2011. 'Determinants of Competitiveness and Factors affecting Productivity in Services', paper presented at the PECC/ADBI Conference on 'Services Trade: New Approaches for the 21st Century', Hong Kong.

Nakatomi, Michitaka. 2013. 'Global Value Chain Governance in the Era of Mega FTAs and a Proposal of an International Supply-chain Agreement'. VOX

– CEPR's Policy Portal. Available at: http://www.voxeu.org/article/it-time-international-supply-chain-agreement.

OECD. 2013. *Interconnected Economies: Benefiting from Global Value Chains*. Paris: OECD. Available at: http://www.oecd.org/sti/ind/interconnected-economies-GVCs-synthesis.pdf.

OECD and WTO. 2013. *OECD-WTO Database on Trade in Value-Added FAQs: Background Note*. Available at: Paris: OECD. http://www.oecd.org/sti/ind/TIVA_FAQ_Final.pdf.

OECD, WTO and World Bank. 2014. 'Global Value Chains: Challenges, Opportunities, and Implications for Policy', report prepared for submission to the 'G20 Trade Ministers Meeting', Sydney, Australia, 19 July 2014. Available at: http://www.oecd.org/tad/gvc_report_g20_july_2014.pdf.

Ponte, Stefano and Timothy Sturgeon. 2014. 'Explaining Governance in Global Value Chains: A Modular Theory-building Effort', *Review of International Political Economy* 21 (1): 195–223.

Singh, Harsha. 2014. 'Reinvigorating Manufacturing through Industrial Policy and the WTO'. Background paper prepared for E15 Expert Group on Reinvigorating Industrial Policy. E15 Initiative. Geneva: ICTSD and World Economic Forum.

Stephenson, Sherry. 2014. *Global Value Chains: The New Reality of International Trade*. E15 Initiative. Geneva: ICTSD and World Economic Forum. Available at: http://www.ictsd.org/sites/default/files/research/E15_GVCs_BP_Stephenson_FINAL.pdf.

Stephenson, Sherry and Jane Drake-Brockman. 2014. 'Services Trade Dimension of Global Value Chains: Policy Implications for Commonwealth Developing Countries and Small States', *Commonwealth Trade Policy Discussion Papers 2014/04*. London: Commonwealth Secretariat.

Stephenson, Sherry and Carolyne Tumuhimbise. 2016. *Services Exports for Growth and Development: Case Studies from Africa*. Addis Ababa: African Union Commission. Available at: http://www.au.int/en/trade-services-case-studies-africa.

Stiglitz, Joseph E. and Justin. Y. Lin (eds.). 2013. *The Industrial Policy Revolution I: The Role of Government Beyond Ideology*. London: Palgrave Macmillan.

UNCTAD. 2013. *World Investment Report 2013: Global Value Chains: Investment and Trade for Development*. New York and Geneva: United Nations. Available at: http://unctad.org/en/PublicationsLibrary/wir2013_en.pdf.

World Bank Open Learning. *Global Value Chains: The Basics*. Available at: https://olc.worldbank.org/content/global-value-chains-basics.

World Economic Forum. 2012. *The Shifting Geography of Global Value Chains: Implications for Developing Countries and Trade Policy*. Geneva: World Economic Forum. Available at: http://www3.weforum.org/docs/WEF_GAC_GlobalTradeSystem_Report_2012.pdf.

World Economic Forum, Bain & Company and the World Bank. 2013. *Enabling Trade: Valuing Growth Opportunities*. Geneva: World Economic Forum. Available at: http://www3.weforum.org/docs/WEF_SCT_EnablingTrade_Report_2013.pdf.

WTO. 2011. 'The Rise of Global Value Chains', in *World Trade Report 2011: The WTO and preferential trade agreements: From co-existence to coherence*. Geneva: WTO. Available at: https://www.wto.org/english/res_e/booksp_e/world_trade_report14_e.pdf.

———. 2014. 'The Rise of Global Value Chains', in *World Trade Report 2014: Trade and development: recent trends and the role of the WTO*, edited by WTO, 78–127. Geneva: WTO. Available at: https://www.wto.org/english/res_e/booksp_e/world_trade_report14_e.pdf.

Zanfei, Antonello. 2000. 'Transnational Firms and the Changing Organization of Innovative Activities', *Cambridge Journal of Economics* 24 (5): 515–42.

6

Supply Chain Finance[1]

Gloria O. Pasadilla

Introduction

The trade landscape has dramatically shifted over the past decades. Not only has global trade volume exploded, but the manner of production has also changed tremendously. The fragmentation of production among different jurisdictions has been greatly facilitated in recent years by a decline in transportation and communication costs, as well as technological advances. Global supply chains have become pervasive in many industries.

For efficient global supply chains, various services are important. Services, like information technology, research and development, human capital management, data analytics, inventory management and logistics, all have to be properly coordinated in an orchestra-like fashion. Financial services are keys to the operation of all supply chains. They can be likened to an invisible glue in global supply chain operations. Problems in financial services can bring global supply chain activity to a halt. For example, a study by the WTO shows that sudden financial constraints resulting from the global financial crisis contributed to the plunge in trade volumes during that period (Auboin and Engemann, 2013). Therefore, there is a need to look closely at financial services that underpin the smooth functioning of supply chains.

There is no globally-accepted definition of supply chain finance; however, this chapter considers two ways to understand supply chain finance and the various regulatory issues that can impact the availability of supply chain financing (SCF). First, SCF can be thought of as financing for the supply chain. Second, SCF

1 This chapter is an abridged version of 2014 Asia-Pacific Economic Cooperation (APEC) Policy Support Unit (PSU) Issues Paper No. 8 entitled 'Regulatory Issues Affecting Trade and Supply Chain Finance'. It has been printed with permission of the APEC Secretariat Policy Support Unit.

can also refer to modalities associated with a specific banking instrument to connect buyers and suppliers in the supply chain.

The next section tackles the first meaning of SCF – the financing of supply chains – as something akin to structured trade financing. This section explains the credit origination process and various factors that financial institutions consider in financing different stages of the supply chain.

The third section of the chapter discusses the other meaning of supply chain finance – that is, modalities involving a bank financing instrument to connect suppliers and buyers in a supply chain relationship. Supply chain finance takes on various forms, including buyer-centric, supplier-centric, or even multiple buyer and seller SCF. However, this chapter discusses in detail only the most widely used of these forms, namely the SCF that is anchored to a major buyer. The section explains how the process operates, its growing acceptance by more companies with global supply chains, and the challenges that affect its further growth and development, including:

- KYC, CDD and AML processes;
- Basel III regulations; and
- cross-border data flow restrictions.

Finally, the chapter argues that in order to facilitate supply chain financing for SMEs, which are significant sources of revenue and job creation in developed and developing countries, there is a need to improve the regulatory environment for asset-based lending practices.

Financing supply chains

Supply chain finance and the real economy

The financing of supply chains typically involves various complications and risks associated with different stages in supply chains. The term '*structured trade finance*',[2] is used here to refer to tailor-made solutions designed for specific supply chains and transactions within the chain.

2 As noted earlier, structured trade finance had been in use for decades – long before the term *supply chain finance* existed. But the idea of financing the supply chain faces similar issues to structured trade financing in the sense that at each step of the supply chain, varying risks exist that need to be taken into account and mitigated for financing purposes.

To illustrate, Box 6.1 gives a hypothetical example of financing a supply chain for a steel company that needs to make advance payments to a supplier of iron ore (its raw material) to ensure that it has sufficient raw material to meet its delivery obligations to its client (the buyer). To protect its advance payment, the steel company requires insurance from the iron ore supplier. On the other side of the transaction, the steel company exports steel to its buyers abroad on open account terms,[3] which means that payment will come after a period of time, say 90 to 120 days.

This example illustrates the steel company's need for financing because not only is it squeezed on the production side (due to the advance payment requirement), but it is also under pressure to provide trade credit to the buyer on the sale side. A financial institution (FI) can solve the steel company's financing needs, allowing it to focus on the company's core business (steel manufacturing), whilst mitigating its own risks through transaction structuring. In the example, it structures financing by providing the steel company the advance payment for the iron ore supplier in exchange for the steel company assigning[4] to the FI the insurance for non-delivery (in the form of standby letters of credit or L/Cs), as well as the supply agreement with the supplier. In addition, it cuts the steel company's waiting time for its sales payments by purchasing the company's accounts receivables (A/R). This structured financing deal illustrates how supply chain finance facilitates production, international trade and the movement of goods, all of which contribute to the growth of the real economy.

The steel company needs an assured supply of iron ores to be able to deliver steel to buyers. The iron ore supplier wants advance payment but will, in turn, provide a performance guarantee. The FI proposed the structured solution as follows:

---

3 'Open account terms' is a payment option that may or may not involve credit. Typically, though, under an open account, the supplier agrees to ship the goods without immediately being paid; hence, it can be considered akin to the supplier providing trade credits to the buyer.

4 To assign a security is to transfer the ownership of a right of action with regard to the security (Cenzon, 2014). In case of non-performance by the iron ore supplier, the FI can directly take appropriate action and collect payment from the institution that provided the guarantee.

Box 6.1: Example of SCF as structured trade finance

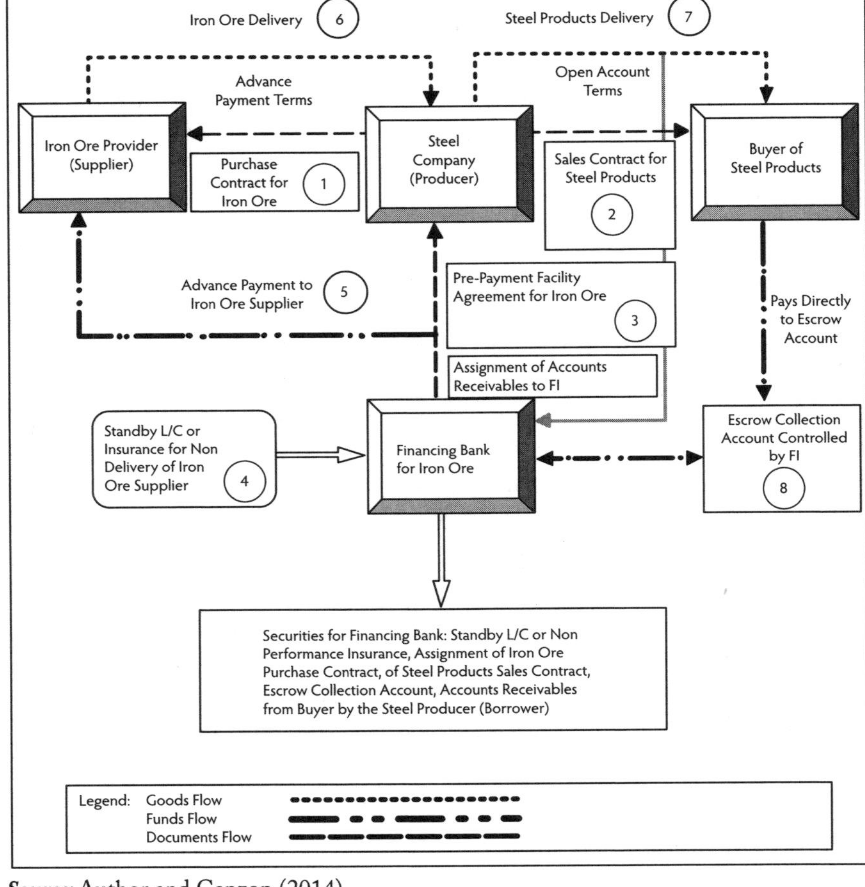

Source: Author and Cenzon (2014)

As shown in Box 6.1, the steel producer is a large company that is constrained by financing pressures from the production side, the sale side, or a combination of both. Oftentimes, similar trade transactions affecting SMEs also take place. For example, a small shoe manufacturer may need to make an advance payment for leather materials, and may try to secure financing using a purchase order from a highly-rated foreign buyer of shoes. FIs can structure advance payment financing using similar instruments to those in Box 6.1 such as insurance, guarantees, or purchase of receivables.

World Bank enterprise surveys have shown that SMEs consider access to finance as the biggest obstacle to their business ahead of tax, customs, trade regulations, political instability and corruption (see Figure 6.3 in Pasadilla, 2014). Helping SMEs access SCF should be, and is, a priority development goal for most governments because SME growth is critical for inclusive growth.

FIs are important players in helping SMEs participate in global trade, but most of these institutions are not development institutions, nor are they long arms of the government. Rather, they are in the business of making profits from providing financial services that include lending and, very importantly, risk mitigation. What are their considerations in providing supply chain finance? What type of risks do they face and what different risk-mitigating mechanisms do they employ? Understanding these elements is key to improving regulatory and legal environments that facilitate supply chain financing.

Supply chain finance: The creditor's perspective

FIs are no strangers to risk. For every simple loan they make, they face the risk of debtor's default. The risk in SCF is multiplied several-fold because of the number of actors in the chain and the complexity of the transactions involved at each step.[5] To illustrate, Box 6.2 provides details of the steel transactions shown in Box 6.1, highlighting the different types of risks the creditor (FI) faces along the supply chain, starting from the iron ore supplier to transport, to the steel mill company, storage in the warehouse and finally, sale to the buyers. The iron ore supplier might not deliver the right quantity or the right quality (performance risk). Something can go wrong in transporting the raw materials from the iron ore supplier to the steel mill (transportation risk). The steel mill can fold up (credit risk), or not deliver according to the buyer's specifications (performance risk). The warehouse facility may not have the capacity to maintain the quality of the inventory. The warehouse operator or collateral management companies may participate in fraud, leading to inventory losses. The buyer may default or refuse to accept the shipment of steel. On top of all of these risks are other macroeconomic risks, such as interest rate or exchange rate fluctuations, along with political risks like a *coup d'état* that may prevent goods from leaving the port.

---

5 Anything that can go wrong in the supply chain is essentially a risk to the FI. For cross-border transactions, risk is automatically increased and amplified. The structure of the financing solution can minimize or eliminate most of the anticipated risks in the supply chain.

Box 6.2: Risk spectrum in SCF

Possible mitigants	General risks	Supply chain	Risks along the supply chain	Possible mitigants
		Iron ore supplier	· Quality of supplier · Off-specification	· Look at track record · Make L/C payment with specified conditions · Performance guarantee
· Political risk insurance · Transport insurance · Hedging	· Political risk attecting payment · Transportation risk · Price risk	Steel manufacture	· Steel mill production risk · Steel mill credit risk	· Look at track record and balance sheet of
		Warehouse	· Losses, theft, reputation of warehouse	· Fidelity insurance
		Buyer	· Buyer's credit risk	· Credit risk insurance

Source: Author and Cenzon (2014)

To minimize potential losses from supply chain financing, FIs use various risk mitigation techniques and instruments. They check for credit risk by examining firm balance sheets, as well as historical export performance. They assess the quality of the product to determine if it is market-grade quality, especially in the case of exchange-traded commodities. They use various types of insurance to cover different risks (such as buyer credit risk, fidelity risk transport risk) and guarantees and other credit enhancements, both to protect the FI's own lent money and to be able to obtain approval within the FI's credit committee structure. If the risks are too high and too difficult to mitigate because of the absence of financial instruments or appropriate laws and institutions, then FIs can withdraw from financing certain types of transactions from certain types of creditors, in certain types of economies. Usually, the rejected transactions are those from SMEs and developing economies. One result can be financial exclusion, particularly of many potential borrowers from emerging economies.

Besides financial exclusion, another important element to note is that, normally, the higher the level of risk the FI takes on, the higher the cost of financing to the borrower. This is why in economies that have more developed physical and financial infrastructure for supply chains, the cost of financing tends to be lower and more inclusive for SMEs. Conversely, in economies where credit infrastructures are weak, with inadequate warehousing and collateral management capacity, or where asset-based lending is not widely practised, financing will be based mostly on the financial strength (i.e., balance sheet) of the borrower, thus excluding from financing many other companies (such as SMEs) with weak balance sheets but marketable goods and high growth potential. If, for example, FIs provide financing through asset-based lending, the cost is, nevertheless, much higher than otherwise can be obtained in other economies with more 'ideal' institutional infrastructure like a proper legal and regulatory framework.

Legal and regulatory issues: Survey of FIs

What is clear in the above discussion is that the legal and regulatory environment can either facilitate or hinder financing, especially SME financing. Unlike traditional balance sheet-based lending, the quality of the traded goods is primarily what is taken into consideration when granting financing.[6] Hence, the emphasis is on the enforceability of the security interest or the possibility to seize and re-sell the goods with relative ease and rapidity in the event of default. Understanding the creditors' perspective should help provide insights on the critical regulatory reforms related to asset-based lending that can help facilitate credit and SME access to finance.

To understand the perspective of the financial institutions, the PSU of the APEC Secretariat conducted a key informant survey and interviews of banks that operate within the APEC region (henceforth, the PSU-APFF (Asia Pacific Finance Forum)-ABA (ASEAN Bankers Association) survey).[7] The survey

6 This does not mean that balance sheet quality is no longer important. It remains vital but is supplemented by the traded goods as collateral. The importance of the traded goods in the credit and risk assessment varies: soft commodities and perishable exports involve a higher level of risk than other categories and may involve specialist structures.

7 With the cooperation of the member institutions of the APFF and ABA, the PSU sent out questionnaires to banks that operate in APEC member economies and conducted several phone interviews with global and regional banks that are active in trade financing.

itself is only indicative because of the few respondents,[8] but the insights are, nevertheless, in line with other survey results, particularly those carried out by the ADB and the International Chamber of Commerce (ICC).[9] Figure 6.1 shows the responses to the question on why banks reject certain trade finance proposals. The number in the graph corresponds to the average ratings given by respondents when asked to give a rating between one and five about the significance of the various possible reasons for rejecting a trade finance proposal.[10] The result shows that concern over credit risk has the highest average rating for significance, but financial crime risks came as a close second. Related to financial risk are CDD concerns, counterparty due diligence, concern over sanctioned economies and AML. Poor collateral quality, absence of cost-effective insurance, performance risk of anyone in the proponent's value chain, political risk, poor documentation and concern over the nature of transactions are likewise important reasons for rejecting loan applications. Concern over financial crime risk will be discussed more at length in the next section, but it is important to note the significant weight that banks appear to put on CDD and other compliance issues. Credit risk and poor collateral quality as reasons for rejection are not particularly surprising, but performance risk as a significant consideration is an interesting result, especially in light of Figure 6.3, which shows non-performance as one of the top reasons for trade disputes among United Nations Commission on International Trade Law (UNCITRAL) cases.[11]

---

8 In total, only 20 banks responded. They were based within ASEAN economies; Hong Kong, China and the U.S.A. Additionally, PSU staff conducted several interviews with six global and regional banks.

9 For example, see ICC (2014).

10 The most significant reasons for loan rejection are five and one was the least significant.

11 Based on PSU analysis of UNCITRAL cases; performance issues include non-delivery of goods, late delivery of goods and non-conformity of goods. Payment issues are related to delay, partial or non-payment for goods and/or services. L/Cs and documents issues generally concern non-compliant L/C documents, as well as lack of or discrepancies of information in documents, and the unwillingness or inability to amend the issues of non-compliance on the export side, and unwillingness to waive such discrepancies on the import side. Transport and charter party (contract between the owner of a vessel and the charterer of the vessel) issues are usually disputes revolving around charter party agreements, as well as who should be responsible for goods damaged or lost during shipment. 'Others' include disagreement in pricing mechanism, repudiation of warehouse lease, ownership claim to unpaid goods and post-purchase issues.

Figure 6.1: Reasons why loan applications get rejected

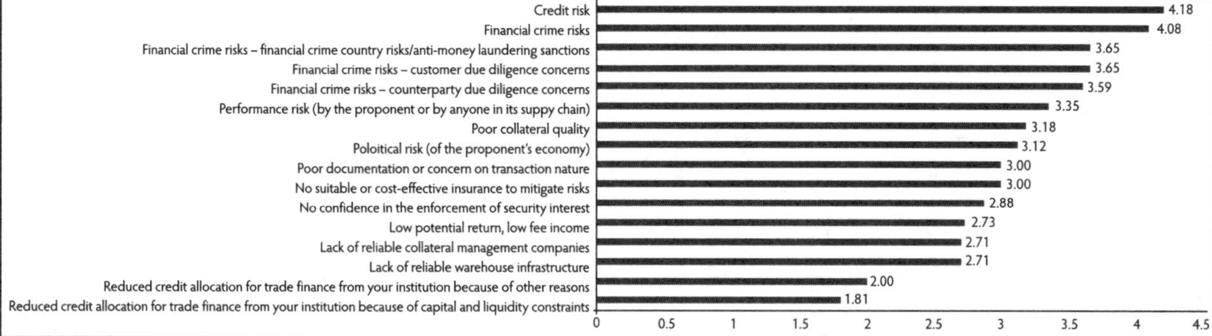

Source: APEC-PSU – Asia Pacific Finance Forum-ASEAN Bankers Association Survey (henceforward, PSU-APFF-ABA Survey)

Figure 6.2: Problems related to the transport of goods

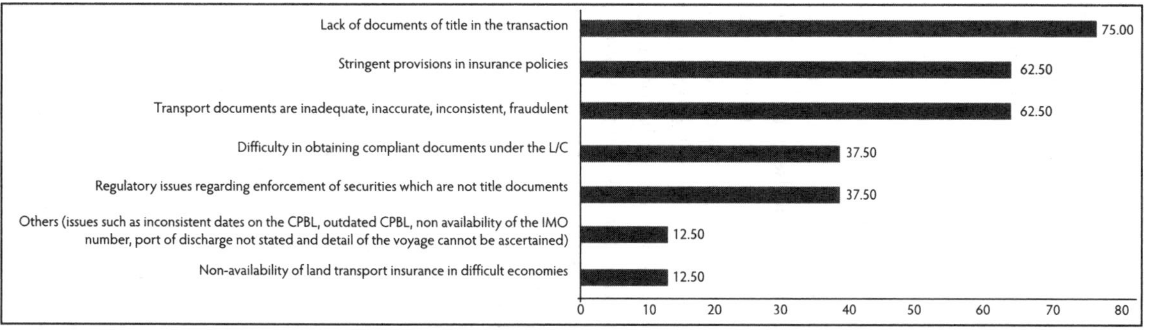

Note: CPBL = Charterparty bill of lading; IMO = International Maritime Organization Ship Identification Number
Source: PSU-APFF-ABA Survey

Figure 6.3: Reasons for trade disputes

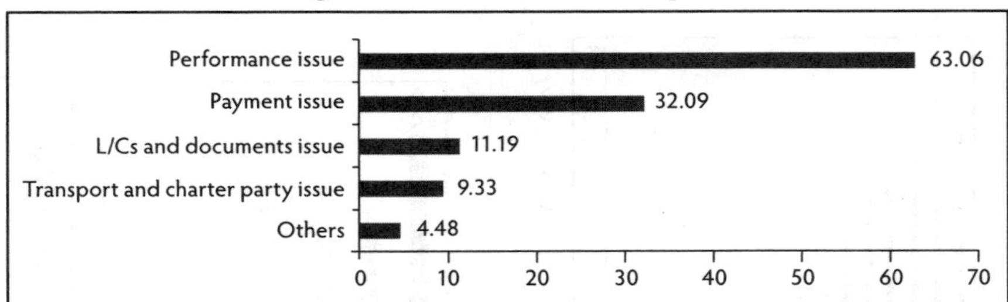

Note: Percentages do not sum to 100 per cent because each UNCITRAL case may involve multiple categories of issues and, in fact, may involve several issues within the same category.
Source: PSU compilation and analysis based on UNCITRAL database

When asked about problems encountered in transporting products from factory or farm to warehouse or port before customs clearance, 75 per cent of respondents cited the lack of document of title in the transaction, whilst more than 60 per cent mentioned stringent provisions in insurance policies or inadequate, inaccurate, inconsistent, or fraudulent transport documents. It is interesting to note here that since banks are primarily concerned with security, the lack of document title was indicated as the problem encountered by most (see Figure 6.2.).

When asked about problems with warehousing and storage, most respondents mentioned issues with low standards among collateral management companies (Figure 6.4.). This answer is tied with warehouse operators' insufficient fidelity insurance as the number one problem.[12] The unreliability of warehouse receipts, as well as the fact that they are not documents of title in some economies, can make it difficult for creditors to defend their lien[13] on the stored product, unless warehouse receipts are accompanied by a pledge. This issue was also cited by many. Banks also mentioned the problems of too few warehousing facilities, the absence of a harmonized legal framework across economies when dealing with collateral management companies and a lack of clear government regulations on standards and grading of commodities.

Box 6.3 shows a warehousing problem related to the losses of stocks of steel in a port in Qingdao, China, that could have been prevented if there were

12 An agreement where, for a designated sum of money, one party agrees to guarantee the loyalty and honesty of an agent, officer, or employee of an employer by promising to compensate the employer for losses incurred as a result of the disloyalty or dishonesty of such individuals (See Jeffrey and Phelps, 2005, *West's Encyclopedia of American Law, 2nd Edition*).

13 A *lien* is a type of security right given by the owner of a good to a creditor to secure debt payment or obligation to perform.

Figure 6.4: Challenges faced in warehousing

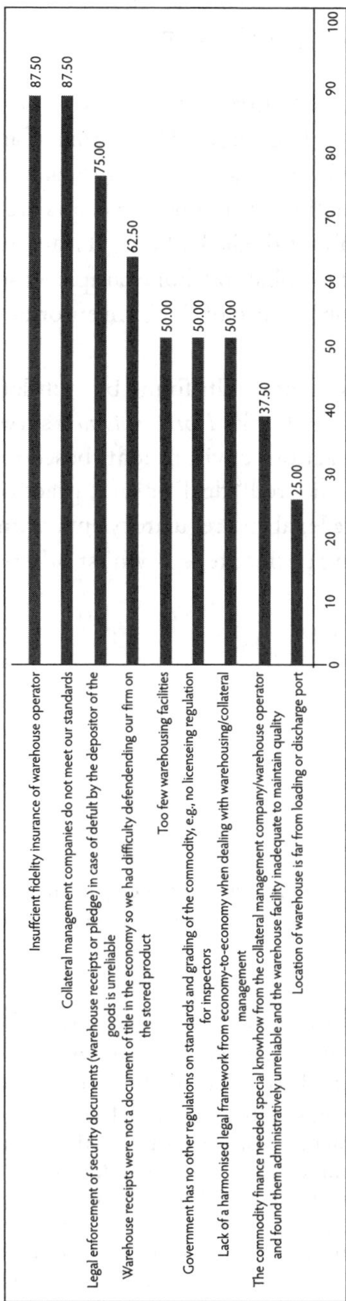

Source: PSU-APFF-ABA Survey

Figure 6.5: Challenges from the legal framework

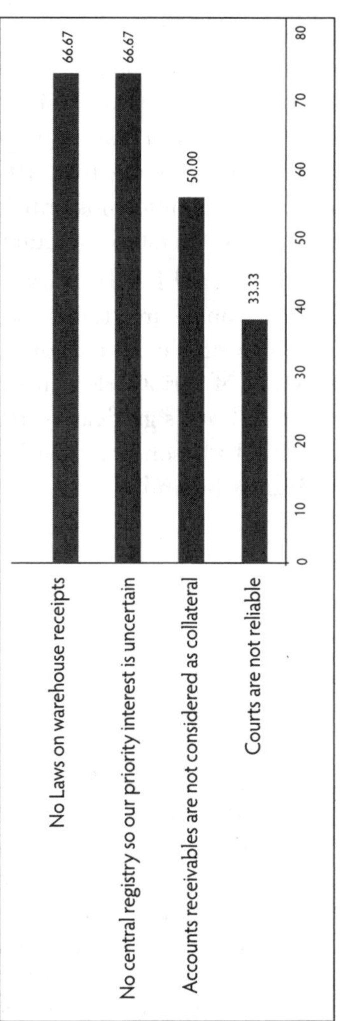

Source: PSU-APFF-ABA Survey

proper licencing standards for collateral management companies and warehouse operators, and if the regulatory framework required transparency in the lien priority over the commodity stocks.

On the legal and regulatory framework, most firms cited lack of a central registry for movable collateral that makes their lien priority[14] uncertain (Figure 6.5). Another common problem mentioned by companies was the lack of laws on warehouse receipts, since in many jurisdictions, warehouse receipts are not documents of title. Firms also complained about the lack of a legal framework that allows a wide scope for assets to be used as collateral. For example, in some economies, legal reform is only beginning on the use of A/R, inventories and invoices as collateral for obtaining loans.

The PSU-APFF-ABA survey confirms similar results found by multilateral institutions on secured transactions. The World Bank's *Doing Business* survey[15] shows the overall condition of secured transactions environments based on an assessment of various elements that are considered 'ideal' or 'best practice'.[16] Figure 6.6 shows significant variations in the legal and regulatory environment among APEC economies, with some having perfect tens,[17] whilst others lag significantly behind.[18]

---

14 Lien priority essentially specifies the order in which creditors get paid in case of bankruptcy, foreclosure, etc. A lien is said to have a priority if it gets paid first before the other lien.

15 See http://www.doingbusiness.org/.

16 See World Bank *Doing Business* for the set of questions on which the assessment is based.

17 The index corresponds to the positive answers to 10 questions that the *Doing Business* survey methodology deems to be major elements of a good, secured transactions environment.

18 Curiously, the US has a strong regulatory environment, but the survey has one negative assessment for the following question: 'Is a collateral registry in operation, that is unified geographically and by asset type, with an electronic database indexed by debtor's names'? This is why the United States received only 9 out of 10 points. The assessment of 'the lack of a centralized collateral registry' may be debatable, considering that the US does have a centralized registry per state, although not for the entire economy. Still, a centralized registry exists and considering the size of the US, the state-by-state registry might, in fact, be more efficient than one that is at the federal level.

Figure 6.6: Secured transactions environment in APEC

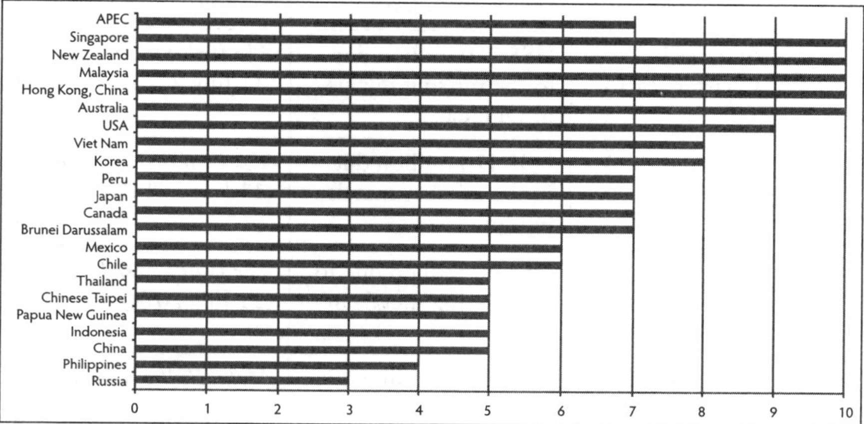

Source: PSU calculation from World Bank *Doing Business*

Box 6.3: Mystery of the missing metals in Qingdao

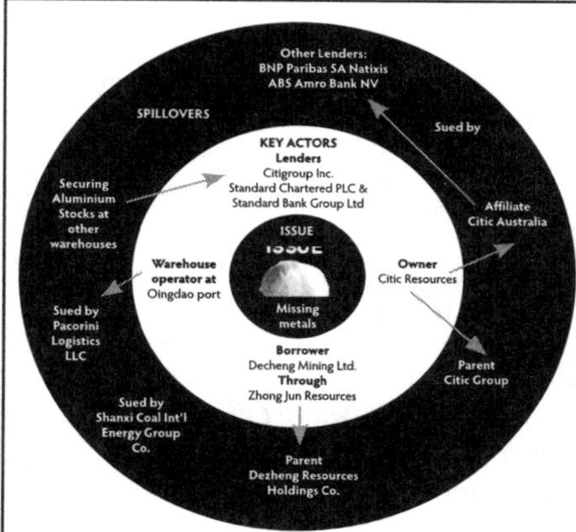

The case revolving around Qingdao metals came to public attention in June 2014 when a subsidiary of Citic Group, one of China's largest state-owned enterprises reported that approximately half of its alumina stockpiles could not be located. The missing alumina was stored in the port city of Qingdao and had been pledged by Decheng Mining Ltd. through Zhong Jun Resources, both subsidiaries of Dezheng Resources Holdings Co., in return for loans. As the probe expands, investigations have gone beyond locating the missing alumina to highlighting another serious problem, that is, the pledging of same assets using fake warehouse receipts to more than one lender to obtain multiple loans. The table below shows some of the disclosed exposure and related claims that have been made in response to this case:

Contd.

No.	Organization	Exposure/Claim	Source
1	Standard Chartered PLC	US$ 250 million due to the missing metals in Qingdao	*The Wall Street Journal* (11 July 2014)
2	Standard Bank Group Ltd.	US$ 170 million due to the missing metals in Qingdao	*The Wall Street Journal* (11 July 2014)
3	Citic Resources	US$ 50 million due to the missing metals in Qingdao	*The Wall Street Journal* (11 July 2014)
4	Shanxi Coal International	US$ 89.75 million plus interest against Citic Australia Commodity Trading (CACT) for undelivered aluminium ingots	*Metal Bulletin News Alert Service* (28 August 2014)
5	Shanxi Coal International	US$ 177 million in missed payments and interest against six companies, including Dezheng Resources Holdings Co. and Decheng Mining Ltd.	*The Wall Street Journal* (30 June 2014)
6	Pacorini Logistics LLC	US$ 58 million against Qingdao port's two subsidiaries over allegedly undelivered aluminium	*American Metal Market* (28 August 2014)
7	Citic Resources	US$ 108 million against Qingdao port over missing cargo	*Metal Bulletin News Alert Service* (18 August 2014)
8	ABN Amro	US$ 162,466 against Citic Australia for wrongful preservative measures of maritime claim against cargo whose pledge right is owned by ABN Amro	*Metal Bulletin News Alert Service* (18 August 2014)

Contd.

9	Citigroup	US$ 285 million of financing in return for metals stored in Qingdao and Penglai	*Reuters News* (1 August 2014)
10	Standard Chartered PLC	US$ 36 million as part of a US$ 40-million loan facility for Zhong Jun Resources	*American Metal Market* (22 July 2014)

The case in Box 6.3 illustrates the complex relationships involved in trade financing, particularly warehouse receipts financing in this case. Investigations into the alleged fraud are ongoing, and court cases have been lodged by defrauded creditors but, in fact, the impact of this incident had gone beyond the losses suffered by the banks. The first casualty has been the shattered confidence in China's warehousing and collateral management capacity. After the Qingdao Metals Case, some creditors shifted the location of their metal inventories to other warehouse locations in Hong Kong, China; Korea and Chinese Taipei. In particular, LME (London Metals Exchange) –licensed warehouses benefited from these transfers. A second consequence has been the pullback of warehouse receipts financing in China, and a tightening of credit. As is usually the case during tightened credit conditions, smaller traders are most adversely affected. In this case, the private traders will suffer a financing squeeze whilst the large state-owned traders sail through.

One set of lessons in the Qingdao case has been that there is a need for increased scrutiny and improved capacity and transparency in warehouse operations. These are a critical link in the supply chain, and need to be strengthened with a focus on the following core elements of a well-developed warehouse receipt system:

- *Importance of good reputation and track record for collateral management companies*: This can be facilitated by having a regulatory and supervisory agency that licenses and regularly audits collateral management companies.[19] As the Qingdao Metals Case showed, both the bank and the

19 Collateral management companies are not regulated in China, which gives rise to the possibility of collusion with borrowers to write multiple warehouse receipts. This is coupled with a lack of understanding of the important nature of warehouse receipt financing. Some creditors, particularly domestic ones, did not have proper entry requirements for their collateral management companies (CMCs), did not do proper due diligence on warehouses, did not understand the business and the operating cycle of the

borrower are highly reliant on the warehouse or collateral manager who, being more than a mere warehouse keeper, assumes the risk and control of the goods the moment he issues the warehouse receipt.

- *Availability of insurance*: The warehouse operator must insure the cargo, the premises, and staff-related risks. Insurance should help protect financing institutions from risks of theft, fraud, or negligence. The availability and growth of these types of insurance, the so-called fidelity insurance, needs to be encouraged and supported.
- *A proper legal and regulatory framework*: The growth of warehousing needs the proper legal and regulatory framework where warehouse receipts are recognized as movable collateral suitable for financing.
- *Collateral registry*: In view of this, warehouse receipts should, like other movable security interests, be registered in a collateral registry to prevent events such as multiple issuance of receipts from occurring.[20]

SCF connecting buyers and sellers

Supply chain finance is also understood, especially in the banking community, as a specific financing vehicle that supports a buyer-seller supply chain. Under this second definition, SCF is a tool for working capital management and an investment in strengthening a company's supply chain by providing its suppliers access to financing at lower costs.

The starting point in discussing supply chain finance is the fragmented production supply chain that the manufacturing business had become and the stark reality that a seamless supply chain is not always a reality, as it is sometimes neatly envisioned. Manufacturing faces major risks and disruption in supply chains from various sources, but the one event that drove the point home deeply was the earthquake and tsunami that hit Japan in 2011. This event highlighted how the failure of small but highly specialized firms to deliver supplies, due

borrowers and did not properly structure their loans. (Source: PSU e-mail correspondence with one interview respondent. PSU respects the confidentiality agreement with surveyed banks and interview respondents).

20 In the Qingdao case, part of the problem appeared to be linked with not having a centralized collateral registry. The security interests on inventory (of metals in the warehouse) are registered with China's Administration of Industry and Commerce (AIC). In contrast to the Credit Reference Centre of the People's Bank of China (CRC) that is very modern, the AIC is not a web-based national system. Under the AIC registry's unreformed registration system, it is difficult to spot multiple warehouse receipts.

to infrastructure destruction from the earthquake, could lead to the temporary shutdown of factories in other parts of the globe because essential parts and components from Japanese SME suppliers were missing.

The risks from various supply chain disruptions may require an inventory management model that moves away from physically vulnerable, strict, just-in-time supply chain models to ones where more inventory and work-in-progress are held. This strategy minimizes the supply chain disruption risk, but the downside is that inventories tie up working capital. To manage working capital, companies push for longer and longer terms of payment, or try to maximize days payable outstanding (DPO) from their suppliers. Because of their strategic dependence on specific buyers, suppliers are forced to agree to longer terms of payment, but the buyers' working capital management strategy merely shifts the burden to suppliers, leading to sometimes tense relationships between buyers and sellers. In some cases, especially during the global financial crisis, suppliers' working capital burden has threatened the stability of buyers' supply chains, because suppliers could not produce due to a lack of access to financing. Supply chain financing is one efficient solution that addresses the conflicting objectives of buyers and sellers. It provides a potentially win-win solution where both buyer and seller maximizee liquidity efficiency.[21]

Box 6.4 illustrates how buyer-led supply chain finance works. In a typical supply chain finance scheme, the buyer, usually a multinational company or one with investment-grade credit, partners up with a bank to structure the SCF facility and provide the funds. The buyer then gives the bank a list of its suppliers. The buyer and the bank both invite suppliers to participate in supply chain finance schemes.[22] Once set up, what supply chain finance entails is a buyer-seller-(supplier)-bank link up through a (digital) technology platform,[23] which provides visibility for transactions. Upon shipment of the goods, suppliers invoice the buyer stating agreed payment terms and send the information to the technology platform. The buyer, likewise, transmits the accounts payable file with approved invoices to the technology platform. With

21 The model where only the buyer is able to maximize its DPO is an inefficient way of raising financing because suppliers are forced to raise funds from FIs for working capital. However, suppliers' costs of funds are higher than those of big buyers, who typically enjoy an investment-grade rating. The higher cost of funds for suppliers is passed on to buyers through higher prices, which ultimately is absorbed by the final consumers.

22 This type of structure also allows the supplier to access financing without impacting their own banking relationships and facilities.

23 The platform may be proprietary to the bank or be managed by a third party.

supply chain finance, the supplier has an option to receive payment earlier, in as little as two days (depending on the structuring bank), if it opts to sell its receivables at a discount.[24] Thus, instead of waiting for the receivable to reach maturity, which can be as short as 30 days or as long as 120 days, the seller can manage its working capital with less need for a large bank credit line or working capital loan.

Box 6.4: Example of a buyer-led supply chain finance

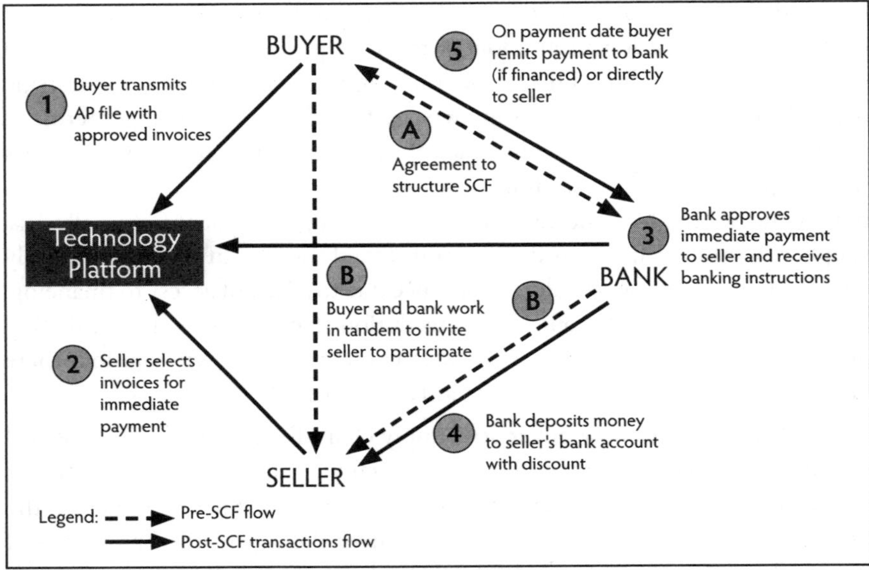

Source: Pricewaterhouse Coopers (2009) with author's adjustments

In SCF, banks provide funding to suppliers on the basis of their A/R. The transparency of the transactions that a technology platform allows enables banks to release funds to suppliers in a short period of time. Meanwhile, buyers only need to pay for the delivered goods upon maturity of the account payable, regardless of whether or not the supplier opted to submit its invoice or account receivable for discounting. If the supplier sold the account receivable, the buyer pays the bank directly; otherwise, it pays the seller directly.

Setting up the supply chain finance arrangement is the hardest part of the job. Part of the challenge in this phase is to get suppliers' buy-in; which, depending on the scope and complexity of the buyer's supply chain, can entail only several key suppliers or a multitude. Overall, it can take anywhere from

24 It can also use the A/R as collateral to obtain working capital loans.

six to 18 months to set up; but afterwards, actors in the supply chain finance programme greatly benefit from the stable relationships.

Advantages of SCF

Supply chain finance proved beneficial during the global financial crisis when companies, particularly SMEs, found it difficult to obtain financing from banks. Threatened by the potential bankruptcy of suppliers and possible destabilization of their supply chains, some multinational companies decided to use supply chain finance to obviate their suppliers' difficulties. Using the buyer's credit quality, banks provided funding to small suppliers through the purchase of their A/R. The cost of this financing was lower than it would have been had suppliers directly applied for a loan, because the bank premised the financing not on the suppliers' creditworthiness, but on the buyers'. After all, in the financing transaction via receivables purchase, the obligor is the buyer. Supply chain finance helped with the stability of supply chains and aided in improving buyer-supplier relationships.

By using supply chain finance, buyers can manage their working capital more efficiently by extending payment terms (or DPO) to suppliers without jeopardizing their strategic relationship with their suppliers and destabilizing the supply chain. A well-structured supply chain finance programme also helps improve the buyer's balance sheet because the payment is classified as a trade payable rather than a bank or capital market debt (Euromoney, 2012).

For the supplier, supply chain finance is a way to obtain cheaper funding because the bank cost is made on the back of the buyer's investment-grade rating, rather than on its own credit rating. If the supplier is an SME, its credit rating is usually below investment grade and thus, financing usually costs more.

Banks also benefit through the additional business created by supply chain finance. FI earns from the discount of the A/R, even as the transactions lower the overall credit risk of their portfolio, because big corporate clients (the ultimate obligor) tend to have lower non-payment risk. Spillovers into new SCF programmes can also follow as relatively large suppliers in the chain can also request the bank to structure another supply chain finance scheme with itself as the buyer. Electronic platforms enable greater visibility and transparency, which also serve to validate the invoices and receivables, thus limiting the possibility of funding fraudulent transactions.

Growth and development of supply chain finance

for some banks, supply chain finance has evolved from only being a side business of trade finance to being a main focus, with some banks' supply chain portfolios doubling or tripling over just three to four years. Supply chain finance programmes could grow to nearly US$2 trillion in five years and Asia is expected to lead the growth (Euromoney, 2012).

Government support for supply chain finance programmes is also growing. The United States, the United Kingdom and several other European economies have implemented, or are considering implementing, their own supply chain finance solutions, allowing government suppliers to be paid earlier and to obtain funding on the back of receivables from the government. For example, in the UK, a government procurement strategy offers a supply chain finance scheme to 4,500 community pharmacies. In this scheme, pharmacies get to be paid in full after just seven days instead of the usual eight weeks. They also receive a lower discount rate for their receivables, compared to what they might normally pay for a bank draft or credit line (J.P. Morgan, 2013).

Supply chain finance has also grown among non-bank and platform providers. Some leading supply chain finance arrangements might involve not just one bank, but multiple banks and not only one buyer but multiple buying entities in multiple economies. Each buyer might bring its own constellation of suppliers, all participating on a single integrated platform. GTNexus, Primerevenue and Demica provide examples of such technology platforms where financial institutions make use of existing platforms to effect payments.

A third-party supply chain finance platform, however, provides banks with less control over the onboarding[25] of suppliers where potential risks can emanate. For example, the buyer may return the products due to unacceptable quality, leaving banks with receivables that are worthless. One way to mitigate these risks is to ensure that buyers only invite very reliable suppliers, those with whom they have had long-term relationships, to participate in supply chain finance programmes. For buyers, third-party platforms with multibank participation helps diversify sources of liquidity, should their own bank lose its appetite for its own supply chain finance programme.

25 Onboarding generally involves several steps such as assessing suppliers, establishing credit process compliance, agreeing to legal terms and ensuring adherence to policies and regulations.

Challenges

Despite the many advantages from supply chain finance, the share of open account/supply chain finance in banks' trade finance portfolios is still relatively low at 20 per cent (ICC, 2014). One reason is its late-starter status, having been recognized as a strategy that makes good financial sense only in the beginning of the global financial crisis. However, bank awareness about SCF usefulness is growing. The other reasons for relatively low take-up consist of both internal and external challenges for banks and clients (or buyers).

One internal challenge for a buyer can be found in the 'traditional' corporate structure where different departments operate in silos. In structuring a supply chain finance programme, both procurement and treasury departments of multinationals have to cooperate, whereas they had previously operated on the basis of different – at times even competing – key performance indicators (KPIs). For example, treasury departments want payment terms to suppliers that are as long as possible, whilst procurement people prefer to have good supplier relationships and may balk at alienating suppliers with long payment terms (J.P. Morgan, 2013). Hence, implementing supply chain finance in corporations often requires long internal negotiations, especially between procurement and treasury departments. It also requires, to a certain extent, a change in culture and strong backing from the top of the organization.

The external challenges are those that banks face, particularly in view of the prevailing regulatory environment that is driving them toward very conservative lending practices. The next sections discuss some of the regulatory issues that appear to have major influences on bank lending decisions and, thus, impact on the growth of supply chain finance.

KYC, CDD, AML

A major factor causing the slow uptake of supply chain finance by more banks is the difficulty associated with the supplier onboarding process. Multinational corporations have suppliers from all over the world, usually from fast-growing emerging economies. Even if the buyer is the ultimate obligor and bears the credit risk; banks, reflecting an over-cautious stance, still follow through with a full KYC procedure for each supplier. A KYC procedure entails a thorough assessment of each company profile. This is not much of a problem for domestic suppliers, but for foreign suppliers, the KYC necessitates significant resources from banks,[26] because it requires that banks either be physically present in

26 Compliance cost has been cited by the ICC (2014) to reach as high as US$75,000 per counterparty.

each of the supplier's economies, or have the capacity to tap into good sources of information (ICC, 2014). However, not all economies and companies have the same level of control or proper systems to collect and store KYC-required data. Local banks, with which the buyer's bank has correspondent banking relationships, can assist in doing KYC checks, but the ultimate responsibility lies with the onboarding bank. KYC norms do not allow for outsourcing KYC procedures. Banks can send personnel directly to the different economies to do a first-hand KYC procedure, but this makes the process too expensive, especially if the suppliers are SMEs.

The multi-economy characteristic of multinational corporations' supply chains also requires banks to be familiar with the laws of different economies such as laws on receivables, proper title documents and transfer or assignment of security interests, in order to assess risks in purchasing receivables through supply chain finance.[27] The practical difficulties of executing KYC for multiple suppliers in multiple economies, along with varied legal and regulatory environments surrounding A/R, help explain the slow SCF take-up by banks.

SMEs and specific geographical regions are the biggest casualties of banks' funding shrinkage due to high compliance (AML/KYC) costs. An ICC survey finds that small- and medium-sized trading enterprises, corporates and FIs are the most impacted by banks' stringent compliance requirements (ICC, 2014). Similarly, Africa and developing economies in Asia are among those reported by banks to be adversely affected. Developed economies are less affected. Much of this is also due to different governance arrangements in various jurisdictions and, since governance is usually weaker in developing economies, global banks are more cautious in extending credit in these places. For example, Figure 6.7 shows the AML index for APEC economies as developed by the Basel Institute on Governance. It is computed as a weighted average of various factors, such as the adequacy of the AML/KYC framework that is in place, the level of corruption and sanctions, financial and public transparency, and general political and legal risk. Two APEC economies are in the top 50 list with the highest AML index; whilst, as expected, the developed economies have lower AML indices.

27 Many of these associated legal issues related to asset-based lending have been discussed in the previous sections.

Figure 6.7: Basel AML Index for APEC economies

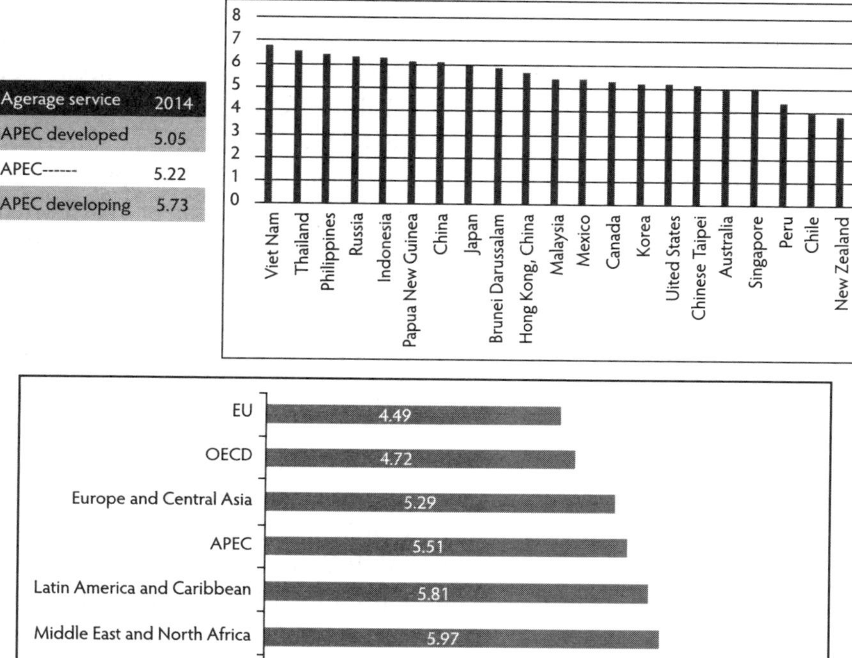

Source: PSU calculations based on Basel AML index information provided by Basel Institute on Governance[28]

What are possible solutions to the problem of high compliance burdens? On the one hand, the stringent KYC requirements are meant to protect the global financial system from being used for illegal activities by money launderers, criminals and terrorists. On the other hand, the behavioural effect of compliance on banks' appetite for risk is leading to financial exclusion, especially for SMEs that need financing the most. Given the highly publicized penalties on several banks, it is not difficult to understand their prevailing over-cautious approach.

Some suggest that banks should push for a 'KYC passport' model similar to

28 See http://index.baselgovernance.org/index/Index.html#ranking.

financial regulations in the European Union (EU) economies whereby 'approvals' by one competent authority in one jurisdiction can be used as a passport for approval in other economies without further review. How the KYC passport model could be applied to fulfill KYC requirements remains to be seen. Current KYC regulations do not allow for 'on-behalf-of' KYC procedures, which is precisely what the passport model advances. How could one guarantee that KYC procedures in one economy will be as stringent (and thus, acceptable) as in another economy? Should there be problems with a transaction of a passported bank, will one economy's legal framework excuse the bank located in another jurisdiction that accepted the illegal transaction?

Another possible solution to mitigate high compliance costs is to push for the harmonization of data requirements for KYC purposes.[29] At a minimum, what can be envisaged is a centralized and authorized database of registered companies' contact details, their board of directors, officers, and any other necessary and electronically-accessible information for KYC purposes.[30] Singapore already has such a facility managed by the Accounting and Corporate Regulatory Authority (ACRA), a statutory board established by the Singapore Government. Among ACRA's mission is 'To establish and administer a repository of documents and information relating to business entities … and to provide access to the public to such documents and information'.[31]

For KYC purposes, the central repository of company information should provide basic information about the company, its location, the names of major stockholders and officers of the company, as well as confirm the entity's legal existence. In Singapore, the fact that ACRA, the organization managing the registry, has some form of government backing (as a statutory board) gives assurance about the credibility and authenticity of the information contained in the registry. This service alone would provide significant support to both local and foreign banks undertaking KYC examination on any company registered in Singapore. If various economies in APEC can similarly adopt

29 Providing capacity building to economies, especially those that are lagging behind in their AML/Counter-Terrorist Financing (CTF) regulations is also another effective way to facilitate bank compliance.

30 SWIFT and the Wolfsberg Group (www.wolfsberg-principles.com) have also developed a KYC registry (sometimes called the 'due diligence registry'). The information contained in these registries, however, is those of FIs and not corporations. These registries are useful for doing KYC checks for correspondent banking relationships.

31 https://www.acra.gov.sg.

the same company registry to facilitate KYC procedures of companies from their respective economies, it would be an important contribution in alleviating KYC/CDD/AML-related concerns by banks; thus, preventing the exclusion of enterprises worthy of financing.

For clients, since companies often deal with multiple banks, each KYC check by each bank is also a company burden because it often means multiple, repetitive forms. Standardized forms available on a common platform, such as those used for the ACRA database, will also facilitate KYC procedures for companies more broadly. Though provision of an electronic central database of registered companies can also be provided by a private entity, some ways of establishing the authenticity of the information contained in such a database would be warranted for KYC procedures.

To check if a client carries a potential compliance risk, a KYC registry is a good but insufficient starting point. Additional information will still need to be obtained, usually based on fee-based specialized databases compiled by terrorism or AML experts.[32] Using data analytics, the nature of the transaction can also be monitored for patterns that reveal unusual behaviour. All in all, financial institutions already follow all of these steps to comply with AML/CTF regulations. Many of them have also hired additional staff solely to strengthen their compliance capabilities. However, unless something is done about the prevailing expectation that banks are 'financial policemen' who are slapped with heavy fines for every breach, they will remain over-cautious in lending. Sadly, adverse effects will neither be felt by developed economies nor by big corporations, but will fall heavily on less developed and developing economies and SMEs.[33]

Banks' voluntary withdrawal from certain financing business is leading to a restructuring of the financial services industry, in particular, to the growth of

32 An example is 'World Check', a product of Thomson Reuters Governance, a risk and compliance business unit that provides risk intelligence for KYC/AML/CTF purposes.

33 Though not directly related to trade financing, the adverse impact on worker remittance flows of global banks' withdrawal from some correspondent banking relationships should serve as a cautionary tale. This rupture in the global correspondent bank network is leaving some economies with absolutely no access to international finance. Foreign workers have to pay more for sending money home because banks have found it too expensive to do a KYC check on small local remittance firms. As *The Economist* points out: 'This can, in turn, exacerbate poverty and exclusion that fuel terrorism and crime these rules were designed to prevent' in the first place. See 'Forcing banks to police the financial system is causing nasty side effects'. *The Economist*, 14 June 2014.

less regulated shadow banking activities (or non-bank sector).[34,35] For example, commodity traders have become more active in doing their own trade financing, often going directly to the capital markets or hedge funds. The global cross-border factoring business[36] has also grown significantly, posting turnover growth of 33 per cent in 2012, and 15 per cent in 2013.[37] These activities were taking place even before, but now with banks reducing trade financing lines due to regulatory constraints non-banks have stepped more prominently to the frontlines. Yet, even non-banks concede that they need banks' participation, expertise and global footprint with their networks of subsidiaries or correspondent banking relationships in structuring complicated financing deals.

Basel III regulations

Basel III is another major regulatory issue that is impacting trade finance. In effect, Basel capital regulations initially demanded the same capital requirement for less risky trade finance products as for traditional corporate lending. By not differentiating trade finance products from other more risky assets, the Basel regulations required banks to incur the same capital costs for trade finance as other risky but highly profitable assets. Such regulation will realistically result in banks re-allocating less of their loan portfolios to trade finance and more to high-margin activities. In response to discussions with trade finance stakeholders and data-based illustrations of the low risk profile of trade finance[38] (see Table 6.1 below), the Basel Committee has since revised some of the rules applying to trade finance products. The changes are technical in nature, and mostly either impact the calculation of risk weights for trade finance products for capital or leverage ratio calculations, or the application of outflow or inflow rates on trade finance products for the purpose of liquidity ratio calculations,[39] all of which redound to provide trade finance at cheaper costs.

---

34 See 'Forcing banks to police the financial system is causing nasty side effects'. *The Economist*, 14 June 2014.

35 Ibid.; 'Big banks are cutting off customers and retreating from markets for fear of offending regulators', *The Economist*, 14 June 2014.

36 Factoring is where a business sells its invoices or accounts receivable to a third party (a factor) at a discount.

37 See Factors Chain International website, at https://www.fci.nl/en/home.

38 See, for example, the ADB/ICC Trade Register, http://www.iccwbo.org/products-and-services/trade-facilitation/icc-trade-register/.

39 See, for example, Wandhöfer (2012) for the technical details and explanation, and ICC (2014).

Table 6.1: Trade finance loss and default rates

2008–12	Trade finance	Other corporate lending
Default rate	0.003% to 0.043%	1.2% a/
Loss rate	0.008% to 0.029% c/	1.49% b/
Average tenor	~90 days	1-3 years
Diversification	Diversified – average US$454K transaction size	Less diversified; large corporate focus

Source: a/ Moody's Report, 2013 Q1; b/ Moody's Report 2011; c/ 2008-2011; ICC Trade Register (2013) and (2014) as cited in ICC Rethinking Trade and Finance (2014) and SCB (2013)

Whilst there has been progress in lowering bank costs for trade finance under the revised Basel III regulations, experts argue that a few issues remain to be resolved. For example, regulatory divergence across jurisdictions in the application of Basel rules can lead to regulatory arbitrage and competitive disadvantages. Without going into the technical details, such differences, whether in the applied credit conversion factor or inflow and outflow rate, can imply lower capital costs and greater comparative advantage for banks in some economies and not in others.

Regulations on cross-border data flows

Supply chain finance is highly dependent on an electronic platform that provides real-time data on physical and financial flows, relying on information about the buyer, suppliers and the different transactions that take place in the supply chain. This platform may be hosted in the funding institution's economy or elsewhere in the world. Likewise, data on A/R might be stored in the 'cloud', which makes it easy for any supplier, corporation, or SMEs anywhere in the world to access their own information, as well as the supply chain's finance flow data. This business model, therefore, cannot thrive if a jurisdiction imposes very strict restrictions on cross-border data transfers.[40]

Trade is inconceivable without data being transferred in some part of the transaction. If physical supply chains need efficient flows of information to function properly, it is even more critical for financial supply chains that require real-time information, both personal and otherwise. The system needs data to: identify customers, both those who are creditworthy and those who are not,

40 For example, some economies restrict the transfer abroad of data of their citizens.

determine when the transactions actually took place and when the financing of receivables can be done, and develop other possible financial instruments that can help customers and SME suppliers. Financial services also make use of credit bureaus to manage and underwrite risks, but credit bureaus need personal information that can be combined, processed, and analysed.

Efforts to prevent data from leaving national borders are motivated by various factors. One popular reason is to protect citizens' data from foreign surveillance, a concern that came to the fore after the 2013 Edward Snowden revelations of electronic spying. Another is to protect personal data privacy and data security. Still another issue around data relates to the extraterritorial application of laws leading to server localization requirements. Governments also often think that by keeping data within national borders, a good number of new jobs can be generated.

Regulations on cross-border data flows take a variety of forms. Some governments require prior consent for data transfers abroad, others require local servers to be established within the territory, others are contemplating imposing a tax on data transfers, whilst still others have enacted an outright ban of citizens' personal information flow out of the economy, or require copies of information sent abroad to be stored domestically as well (Kommerskollegium, 2014).

The economic argument of creating jobs through data localization requirements, such as mandating local server establishments, does not hold water.[41] First, because putting up data servers is too expensive, foreign businesses could just opt not to invest in the market, particularly in small economy markets. Hence, instead of generating new jobs, this form of localization requirement scares away investments. Second, data servers do not really require a lot of employees. What they really require is plentiful and reliable sources of energy. Requiring companies to establish domestic data servers will also increase a developing economy's capital imports and worsen its balance of payments deficit because most of the data server suppliers are from the US and other developed economies. Third, such regulations prevent the development of start-ups, especially relating to digital applications that need advanced applications from all over the world that run on the backs of advanced and sophisticated servers.

The objective of security and privacy of data, however, merits careful consideration because it is close to the heart of what the general population perceives the government should protect. Rightly, many governments have

41 Foregoing arguments are summarized from Chander and Le (2014) with detailed discussions of the various arguments for and against data localization.

privacy protection laws that respect the use of personal data, often requiring prior consent from concerned individuals in the use of personal information, whether stored domestically or abroad.

A more critical issue is the obligation to store data locally by requiring data servers to remain within country borders, or an outright ban on data transfer abroad.[42] Ironically, such localization requirements may actually undermine the economy's privacy protection and security objectives. First, by localizing data storage, domestic firms may not be able to take advantage of the distributed infrastructure of cloud technology where information is distributed across multiple servers in different locations, which helps to prevent the re-identification of the individual. Putting information in one place, as a data localization requirement attempts to do, makes data even more vulnerable to hackers. It is also doubtful whether the protected local data server provider has stronger security infrastructure and capacities than global companies.

Another problem with banning cross-border transfer of citizens' data is that it does not always make a clear distinction – presumably because it is difficult to implement in practice – between the different types of data, such as personal data, which may need some valid protection and other non-personal data. Since data is also increasingly linked to payment transactions and financial flows, strict data flow restrictions not only make platform-based supply chain finance unfeasible, they render any trade at all that uses the internet virtually impossible.

Conclusion

This chapter discussed supply chain finance as interpreted in two different but related ways. Supply chain finance can be understood as structured trade financing, which ensures that the financial institution's risks throughout the goods supply chain – from the factory to transport, warehousing and shipping, all the way to the buyer – are covered and mitigated. This form of financing can be used more widely to help fund SMEs because transactions financing and structuring relies more on the assets that are exported, rather than on

---

42 Other data transfer restrictions may mandate keeping a copy of data sent abroad in the domestic economy. Particularly for financial services, this restriction has been deemed necessary by some economies for the prudential regulation of the banking system because it allegedly provides supervisory authorities immediate access to financial information to enable them to formulate an appropriate response, especially in times of financial crisis. It is also a way of protecting data in case it gets destroyed due to some unfortunate events. Such restrictions do not prohibit cross-border transfer of data, *per se*, but they are variants of localization requirements.

balance sheets. This is important, since many SMEs have weak balance sheets but usable assets.

For growth in SCF and, in general, asset-based lending to happen, many economies in APEC need legal and regulatory framework reforms, especially to facilitate financing for movable assets. These reforms include:

- Development of laws that facilitate asset-based lending following international best practices, such as the UNCITRAL Model Law where the scope of assets considered as collateral are expanded to include, for example, A/R, invoices, or warehouse receipts
- Establishment of clear priority on secured transactions
- Development of a centralized electronic collateral registry that makes security interests transparent and prevents multiple and competing claims for priority over the same asset
- Improving enforcement and insolvency resolutions
- Strengthening the capacity of collateral management companies in APEC and developing the appropriate regulatory framework including possible licensing and regulation of collateral management companies

Supply chain finance can also be understood as a specific financing vehicle to support buyer-seller supply chains whereby sellers or suppliers, especially SMEs, are able to obtain cheaper financing on the back of the creditworthiness of the buyer, usually large corporations or multinationals. The need for improved legal and regulatory frameworks for asset-based lending remains important, even in this understanding of supply chain finance, especially because financial institutions provide supplier financing, mostly through purchase of A/R or extending credit lines based on suppliers' A/R from highly-rated companies. This form of supply chain finance helps improve buyer-seller relationships and, by ensuring that suppliers have access to funding, it also stabilizes the buyers' own supply chain. Supply chain finance has experienced rapid growth but for a wider adoption, attention should be directed to various regulatory issues that are hampering supply chain finance.

Major challenges to trade and SCF pertain to difficulties of onboarding suppliers in the supply chain finance platform, due to stringent KYC and CDD rules. At a minimum, each economy should have a central database where KYC-relevant company information is stored and can be accessed by financial institutions to ease the burden of executing KYC/CDD. This will prevent or minimize the financial exclusion that is resulting from an over-cautious stance of FIs due to concern over financial crimes and heavy penalties for supposed non-compliance.

The chapter also notes the adjustments to Basel III regulations on account of the low risk profiles of trade financing, but cautions about the potential adverse impact of regulatory arbitrage on competitiveness due to uneven implementation of Basel rules across economies. Another important inhibitor to the growth of supply chain finance is the growing consideration of laws that prohibit private data transfer cross-border in certain legislative assemblies and policy circles. Cross-border data transfer restrictions could prevent the adoption and implementation of new innovative instruments like SCF, acting as new non-tariff measures that will challenge the trade community in the foreseeable future.

References

Auboin, Marc and Martina Engemann. 2013. 'Trade Finance in Periods of Crisis: What Have We Learned in Recent Years?', *Staff Working Paper ERSD-2013-01*. World Trade Organization. Available at: http://www.wto.org/english/res_e/reser_e/ersd201301_e.pdf.

Cenzon, Bernadette. 2014. *Supply Chain Finance: Background Paper*. Unpublished. Singapore: APEC PSU.

Chander, Anupam and Uyen P. Le. 2014. 'Breaking the Web: Localization versus the Global Internet', *Research Paper 378*. Davis, California: UC Davis Legal Studies. Available at: http://papers.ssrn.com/sol3/papers.cfm?abstract_id=2407858.

Euromoney. 2012. 'Connecting the Value Chain', in *Insights on Transforming the Treasury*, edited by Philip Ayers, 25–28. London: Euromoney. Available at: http://www.euromoney.com/downloads/guides/RBS-Treasury-Guide-2012.pdf.

ICC. 2013. *Rethinking Trade and Finance 2013*. Paris: ICC. Available at : http://www.iccwbo.org/Products-and-Services/Trade-facilitation/ICC-Global-Survey-on-Trade-Finance.

———. 2014. *Rethinking Trade and Finance 2014*. Paris: ICC. Available at : http://www.iccwbo.org/Products-and-Services/Trade-facilitation/ICC-Global-Survey-on-Trade-Finance.

Kommerskollegium. 2014. *No Transfer, No Trade – The Importance of Cross-Border Data Transfers for Companies Based in Sweden*. Stockholm: Kommerskollegium. Available at: http://www.kommers.se/Documents/In_English/Publications/PDF/No_Transfer_No_Trade.pdf.

Lehman, Jeffrey and Shirelle Phelps. 2005. *West's Encyclopedia of American Law, 2nd Edition*. Detroit: Thomson/Gale.

Morgan, J. P. 2013. *Enabling Growth in an Uncertain Recovery – How Companies Chart a Path to Growth with Supply Chain Finance*. New York: J.P. Morgan. Available at: https://www.jpmorgan.com/cm/BlobServer/Enabling_Growth_in_Uncertain_Recovery_2013.pdf?blobkey=id&blobwhere=1320603654623&blobheader=application/pdf&blobheadername1=Cache-Control&blobheadervalue1=private&blobcol=urldata&blobtable=MungoBlobs.

Pasadilla, Gloria. 2014. 'Regulatory Issues Affecting Trade and Supply Chain Finance', *APEC PSU Issues Paper No. 8*, November. Singapore: APEC Secretariat. Available at: http://publications.apec.org/publication-detail.php?pub_id=1570.

Pricewaterhouse Coopers (PWC). 2009. *Demystifying Supply Chain Finance – Insights Into the What, Why, How, Where and Who*. New York: PWC. Available at: http://www.pwc.com/en_US/us/issues/surviving-the-financial-downturn/assets/supply_chain_finance.pdf.

Standard Chartered Bank (SCB). 2013. 'International Regulation and Treatment of Trade Finance', presentation at the APEC Workshop on 'Trade Finance', Lombok, 1 July.

Wandhöfer, Ruth. 2012. *Trade Finance – Protecting the Engine of Global Growth*. London and New York: Citibank. Available at: http://www.citibank.com/transactionservices/home/corporations/docs/tf_protecting_engine.pdf.

World Bank. Various Years. *Doing Business*. Washington: The World Bank and the International Finance Corporation. Available at: http://www.doingbusiness.org.

7

Services and Economic Integration in ASEAN

Julia Puspadewi Tijaja[1]

Introduction

Comprising 10 member states, the Association of Southeast Asian Nations (ASEAN) represents a dynamic region that is well integrated into GVCs, putting it squarely on the radar of many potential investors. Over the years, trade and investment flows in the region, including those that are intra-regional in nature, have continued to increase with the proliferation of GVCs.

Along with this phenomenon, there is growing recognition of the significant and potential role of services in the region's economies, not only in terms of their contribution to production, income and employment, but also as an enabler and driver of GVC participation and a new source of value and innovation (Low, 2013). There is also broad acknowledgement of the under-estimation and under-appreciation of services in trade data as conventionally measured, and the difficulty in measuring services activities to accurately assess their contribution.

The significant role of services is reflected in their growing contribution to the region's economy, as well as the intensification of trade, albeit from a low base. Services have also accounted for the largest share of direct investment inflows to the region in recent years. As a number of the region's economies seek to overcome the middle income trap and move up GVCs, others are seeking entry points into GVCs. In both these cases, services are likely to feature more prominently in national agendas.

Services have also been an important element of the region's economic integration agenda since the beginning. The region's goal to establish an ASEAN Economic Community (AEC) by 2015-end will necessarily entail

1 Dr Julia Tijaja was formerly Research Analyst at the Fung Global Institute (now the Asia Global Institute). She is currently Director of the ASEAN Integration Monitoring Directorate at the ASEAN Secretariat. The views expressed here are solely those of the author.

the integration of the services market. The AEC has four broad objectives, also called 'pillars'.[2] Free flow of services is a key element of the first AEC pillar, which is the establishment of a single market and production base. As the region's economies further develop, demand for high-value-added services – both as inputs to production and for direct consumption – will continue to increase, as will the need for the requisite skills and market environment to supply such services. Going forward, the challenge is to advance the region's understanding of and strategy on services, not only in the narrow terms of services integration, but also as an integral part of the region's development agenda.

Dynamic ASEAN: Opportunities and challenges in services

ASEAN's connection to and participation in GVCs has been growing in prominence as observed in its trade and investment performance. In terms of stock, ASEAN hosted over US$1.5 trillion of FDI in 2013. Though this came to just under 6 per cent of the global total, it accounted for 29 per cent of total FDI stock hosted in developing Asia, which includes some of the world's largest economies. The momentum has also continued to pick up for the ASEAN region. At US$125.4 billion, ASEAN accounted for 8.6 per cent of global total direct investment inflows in 2013, or 29 per cent of developing Asia's total (UNCTAD STATS, 2014). Total direct investment inflows to the region have in fact doubled the pre-crisis level. Two ASEAN Member States (AMS) were also in the top 20 FDI host economies in 2013, namely Singapore and Indonesia, and ranking eighth and twentieth respectively (UNCTAD, 2014).

ASEAN's appeal to foreign investors is partly attributed to its participation in international trade. Total merchandise trade in the region amounted to US$2.5 trillion in 2013 (ASEANstats, 2014). The importance of merchandise trade varies across AMS, from 41.6 per cent of GDP for Myanmar to a high of 262.9 per cent for Singapore. At only US$563 billion in 2012, services trade started from a much lower base, but overall has been growing at a faster pace. Between 2005 and 2012, services trade reported a higher average growth year on year at 12.31 per cent compared with 10.36 per cent for merchandise trade.

2 The first pillar of the AEC discusses the objectives of free flow of goods, services, investment, skilled labour and a freer flow of capital. There are four pillars altogether, and the other three address the creation of a competitive economic region, equitable economic development and integration into the global economy. For further information on ASEAN and the AEC objectives, see the ASEAN Secretariat website at www.asean.org.

Moreover, gross trade data vastly understates the importance of services due to their lower tangibility, the subsuming of services data into merchandise trade, and the prominence of in-house transaction of services. The actual significance of services in the region's trade is most likely higher than estimated.

Six out of 10 AMS – Singapore (fourth), Malaysia (ninth), Thailand (tenth), Indonesia (eleventh), Vietnam (sixteenth) and the Philippines (seventeenth) – were among the top 25 developing country exporters in 2010 (UNCTAD, 2014). The same economies were also among the developing country exporters with the highest GVC participation rates, with Singapore at 82 per cent (first), Malaysia at 68 per cent (third), the Philippines at 56 per cent (eighth), Thailand at 56 per cent (ninth), Vietnam at 48 per cent (fourteenth) and Indonesia at 44 per cent (fifteenth). These rates are comparable to those of advanced economies, such as Belgium at 79 per cent, the United Kingdom at 76 per cent, Germany at 64 per cent, South Korea at 63 per cent, Japan at 51 per cent and the United States at 45 per cent. The rate for China stood at 59 per cent.

The individual dynamism of AMS is complemented by the region's pursuit of economic integration through the AEC. Such regional integration efforts face significant challenges related to high variation in resource endowments, economic size and structure and levels of development among AMS. Some of these challenges are technical in nature, while others are political.

The size of AMS economies varies widely. The GDP of Lao People's Democratic Republic (PDR), a landlocked LDC, stood at only US$10 billion in 2013, the lowest among the 10 AMS. On the other hand, Indonesia is ranked as the sixteenth biggest economy by the World Bank with a GDP of US$868.35 billion[3] in 2013 (World Development Indicators).

A closer look at GDP per capita (in purchasing power parity or PPP terms), a common proxy for the level of economic development, reveals another layer of complexity. Levels of development vary widely amongst AMS. Three out of 10 AMS are LDCs (Cambodia, Lao PDR and Myanmar), while Brunei and Singapore are among the world's richest countries in GDP per capita terms. The biggest economy in the region, Indonesia, only came out sixth out of the 10 AMS when ranked in terms of income per capita, last among the ASEAN-6 subgroup.[4] This alone does not sufficiently illustrate the region's diversity. While

3 US$862.6 billion according to ASEAN statistics

4 The first six members of ASEAN, namely Brunei, Indonesia, Malaysia, the Philippines, Singapore and Thailand, are commonly called the ASEAN-6, while the newer members, including Cambodia, Lao PDR, Myanmar and Vietnam, are referred to as CLMV.

Brunei and Singapore have comparable high per capita incomes, their economies are vastly different. The former is highly oil-dependent and has continued to strive for economic diversification, while the latter, though resource-poor, is a dynamic knowledge-intensive economy that has long served as the region's entrepôt. In terms of geography, AMS range from mountainous, landlocked Lao PDR to the modern city-state of Singapore and an archipelago of 17,000 islands in the case of Indonesia.

This vast diversity both poses a challenge and gives a unique strength to the region's pursuit of becoming a single economic community. The challenge is amplified in a world of GVCs where interdependencies and competition among economies are intensified while the need for effective coordination and cooperation is emphasized.

Services contribute to the region's pursuit of economic integration, both internally as a region and externally to GVCs. They serve as the glue that enables fragmentation of production activities to take place in different locations. They are also integral to all value chains and are often bundled with final product offerings for increased consumer value. A competitive services market is therefore imperative for effective and gainful GVC participation. Services in themselves can also be a new source of value and innovation, as evidenced by growing 'servicification' – a phenomenon whereby manufacturing firms increasingly buy, produce, sell, and export services as an integrated or accompanying part of their primary offers (Kommerskollegium, 2013).

ASEAN in GVCs

ASEAN plays a key role in a region that is highly integrated into GVCs. From the late 1980s, growing intra-ASEAN trade and investment flows were observed together with the rise of production networks in East Asia. Trade in parts and components and final assembled products, the sum of which is also known as 'network trade', has been rising in importance. Over 70 per cent of intra-East Asian trade now comprises parts and components that are assembled into final goods and exported to the rest of the world, with the European Union (EU), China, Japan, and the United States as major markets (Chia, 2013). World network trade increased from US$1.21 trillion (about 23.8 per cent of total manufacturing exports) in 1992–93 to US$4.85 trillion (45.7 per cent) in 2006–08, accounting for nearly two-thirds of the total increase in world manufacturing exports in the same period. The share of developing countries in total network exports also increased from 22.0 per cent to 46.1

per cent over the same period, driven primarily by China.[5] In all countries in East Asia, except the People's Republic of China (PRC) and Thailand, parts and components accounted for well over half of total network exports (and imports) by 2007–08, and the share was particularly high among ASEAN countries. Exports within production networks accounted for over 60 per cent of total manufacturing trade in East Asia in 2007–08, as compared with the world average of 51 per cent. By 2007–08, network exports accounted for over two-thirds of total manufacturing exports in ASEAN, up from 57 per cent in the early 1990s. The patterns observed on the export and import sides of ASEAN are strikingly similar, reflecting growing cross-border trade within production networks (Athukorala, 2013).

The prominence of network trade, and within this trade in parts and components, is a reflection of vertical supply chain integration among AMS. However, intra-regional absorption of final products from these supply chains remains low – although growing – indicating externally-destined regional supply chains.

As previously highlighted, with such heterogeneity across their economic structures and levels of development, it is not surprising that the extent of AMS' GVC participation also varies. GVC participation rates reflect the role that an individual economy plays in GVCs and its reliance on GVC participation for economic growth and development. Participation in GVCs can be done either through backward or forward linkages.

Backward linkages refer to the connections of an economy to GVCs in terms of the sourcing of inputs. The more imported intermediates are used in the production of its exports, the stronger are the country's backward linkages. One indicator used to measure this phenomenon is foreign VA in gross exports. While the use of imported intermediates may lower the share of domestic VA, it could lead to higher domestic VA in nominal terms if imported intermediates enable the production of higher-value products.

Forward linkages refer to instances where a country provides intermediate inputs for the production of other countries' exports. They show how domestic industries export VA both through direct final exports and via indirect exports of intermediates through other countries to foreign final consumers. Forward linkages reflect how industries are connected to consumers in other countries, even where no direct trade relationship exists. The indicator used to measure this is the domestic VA embodied in foreign final demand.

5 The share of China increased from 2.1 per cent to 15.3 per cent.

GVC participation is the share of a country's backward and forward linkages in total global VA. In practice, obtaining these figures is nearly impossible due to the lack of data.[6] While it is intuitive to assume that a high GVC participation rate is good, the reality is more nuanced due to the complexity in its calculation. A higher GVC participation rate indicates deeper GVC integration, but may not guarantee higher accrued gains, at least not to all parts of the population. Participation through the importation of VA (backward linkages) will also generate gains different from those generated through the exportation of VA (forward linkages). The development outcomes of GVC participation should therefore be assessed carefully, by also looking at the impact on employment, income distribution, knowledge creation and skills building, economic diversification and resilience, and non-economic factors such as social and environmental implications.

The nature of GVC participation differs across AMS. Most members operate in the middle of the GVCs, with comparable backward and forward linkages. For commodity exporters such as Brunei and Indonesia, for example, backward linkages may be low as gross exports consist mostly of raw or minimally processed domestic commodities; using few imported intermediates thus leads to a low share of foreign VA (or alternatively a high share of domestic VA) in gross exports. However, a high share of domestic value added may equally be observed in countries with a well-developed and diverse production base that enables a larger share of VA to be domestically sourced. In an economy large enough to complete the processing and consumption process (i.e., ending the value chain within its territory), its backward linkages – however significant – may risk going unreported. GVC participation is therefore more nuanced than what these indicators can tell.

In sum, the difference between integration into GVCs and the accrual of gains from participation is not clearly delineated in GVC participation rates. Banga (2013) proposed an alternative way to measure the gains from participation by looking at the net (instead of the sum of) VA between forward and backward linkages, or the ratio of forward to backward linkages. Of course there is a risk

6 The GVC participation rate of certain individual countries could be calculated from the OECD-WTO TiVA database, but data is available only for 58 countries including 34 OECD members, the five BRICS (Brazil, Russia, India, China and South Africa) economies and eight newly industrialized countries (NICs). The data reveal a high concentration of countries involved in value-added trade. The six top OECD countries – US, Germany, the UK, Japan, Korea and France as well as China, together account for almost 45 per cent of global value added created by GVCs (Banga, 2013).

of reverting to the conventional assumption that export (of VA) is good and import (of VA) is bad, while the import of VA may be necessary for enhancing the overall participation in GVCs, including as inputs to value added exports. For this reason, Banga proposed that the ratio of forward to backward linkages be assessed together with the GVC participation rate.

GVCs matter to the AMS not only in terms of accessing export markets but also in terms of sourcing the most internationally competitive inputs, tangible or otherwise. A key aspect of ASEAN exports is their high reliance on imported parts and components. Excepting Brunei and Indonesia, the shares of foreign value added in AMS gross exports range from 34 per cent for Cambodia to just under 50 per cent for Singapore (Table 7.1). The sub-15-per cent shares of Brunei and Indonesia reflect the dominance of commodities in their export composition, but even this is compensated by stronger forward linkages in both cases.[7]

The high shares of re-exported intermediate imports in total intermediate imports amongst AMS, from 22 per cent for Indonesia to 77 per cent for Singapore, confirm the region's reliance on imported inputs for export production. The shares for other AMS range from 40 to 60 per cent (Table 7.1). Looking deeper into the sectoral level and taking Indonesia as an example, the shares of re-exported intermediate imports were notably higher for the manufacturing sectors such as textiles, leather and footwear (38 per cent), and machinery and equipment (33.3 per cent). Further, for 'transport and storage', 'post and telecommunications' and 'business services'– the services sub-sectors included in the breakdown – the shares were significant at 16.3 per cent and 10.8 per cent, respectively (OECD, 2014). The size of the contribution of services VA to gross exports is confirmed in Table 7.1.

Table 7.1: Key GVC indicators (2009) for select AMS, ASEAN FTA partners and EU

Country	Gross exports (USD million)	Foreign VA % gross exports*	Domestic VA in foreign final demand % GDP**	Re-exported intermediate imports % of total	Services VA as % gross exports
Brunei	7,683	11.3	63.1	46.5	20.6
Cambodia	5,932	34.1	37.6	44.0	41.0

Contd.

7 Note that the domestic VA as in foreign final demand as a share of GDP is also low in the case of Indonesia due to the size of its economy (but is much higher when measured as a share of gross exports).

Country	Gross exports (USD million)	Foreign VA % gross exports*	Domestic VA in foreign final demand % GDP**	Re-exported intermediate imports % of total	Services VA as % gross exports
Indonesia	125,692	14.4	19.8	21.9	21.0
Malaysia	179,790	37.9	57.3	72.6	36.0
Philippines	51,845	38.4	18.9	52.1	44.2
Singapore	212,449	49.9	57.5	76.6	56.5
Thailand	173,976	34.5	43.0	60.9	30.1
Vietnam	63,056	36.7	41.0	41.0	26.8
Australia	193,401	12.5	16.7	23.6	39.7
China	1,283,964	32.6	16.6	50.2	29.5
India	255,032	21.9	14.6	25.4	52.5
Japan	618,022	14.8	10.3	22.6	40.1
South Korea	401,162	40.6	28.1	55.2	37.7
New Zealand	31,573	18.4	21.9	31.0	45.7
EU27	2,228,065	13.6	11.1	N/A	54.1

*Indicator for backward linkages
***Indicator for forward linkages*
Source: WTO-OECD TiVA database

The regional (intra-ASEAN) market remains the biggest market for ASEAN's (merchandise) exports, accounting for 26 per cent of the total and placing it ahead of China (12 per cent), the EU (9.8 per cent), Japan (9.7 per cent) and the US (9 per cent) (ASEANstats, 2014). The same pattern is observed in imports. In today's world of GVCs, it is increasingly recognized that most GVCs are more regional than global in nature, as evident in the emergence of 'Factory Asia', 'Factory Europe' and so on. The share of intra-regional GVC flows in total GVC participation in East and Southeast Asia, which includes ASEAN, is 42 per cent, much higher than other developing regions. This emphasizes the contribution of, and the imperative to strengthen, regional economic integration among AMS to remain globally competitive.

Services in ASEAN economies

Services play a significant role in ASEAN economies. With the exception of commodity-dependent Brunei (28 per cent), services value added contributed to between 36 per cent and 73 per cent of AMS' GDP in 2012. The distribution of AMS share of services VA follows each country's level of development, with more advanced economies like Singapore and Malaysia having relatively higher shares of services value added in their GDP at 73 per cent and 49 per cent respectively, while the shares of Lao PDR and commodity-rich Indonesia stood at 36 per cent and 39 per cent respectively.

In addition to domestic production, the services sector also contributes significantly to employment. The services sector tends to be more labour-intensive; hence its development is likely to generate more jobs and involve the participation of more small and medium-sized enterprises. Further, as shown in Table 7.2, services are a major contributor to female employment, accounting for almost half of female employment in Indonesia in 2012 (as compared to just 16 per cent for industry), as well as a high 69 per cent in the Philippines, 72 per cent in Malaysia and 83 per cent in Singapore.

Table 7.2: The role of services in ASEAN: selected indicators (2012)

	Value added as % of GDP			**Trade as % of GDP**		**% in total female employment**	
	Agriculture	**Industry**	**Services**	**Merchandise**	**Services**	**Industry**	**Services**
Brunei	0.7	71.1	28.2	97.8	18.4		
Indonesia	14.5	46.8	38.7	43.2	6.6	16.0	49.5
Malaysia	10.0	40.8	49.2	138.9	26.3	20.3	71.5
Philippines	11.8	31.2	56.9	46.9	13.9	10.1	69.0
Singapore	0.0	26.7	73.3	274.7	87.1	*16.6*	*82.8*
Thailand	12.3	43.6	44.2	130.9	28.1	18.3	43.8
Cambodia	35.6	24.3	40.1	134.0	33.6	18.1	29.1
Lao PDR	28.1	36.2	35.9	56.9	9.8		
Myanmar							
Vietnam	19.7	38.6	41.7	146.5	14.2	16.8	33.7

Contd.

	Value added as % of GDP			Trade as % of GDP		% in total female employment	
	Agri-culture	**In-dustry**	**Ser-vices**	**Merchan-dise**	**Ser-vices**	**Indus-try**	**Ser-vices**
China	10.1	45.3	44.7	47.0	6.1		
India	17.5	26.2	56.3	42.3	14.8	20.7	19.5
East Asia Pacific Developing	10.9	44.5	44.7	54.2	7.9		
Low income	27.6	23.3	49.1	50.4	14.3		
Middle income	10.0	36.0	54.2	50.2	8.9		
OECD	1.6	24.2	74.2	45.6	11.9	11.4	84.3

Source: World Development Indicators

As elaborated earlier, though starting at a much lower base, services trade in the region has been picking up pace in recent years. ASEAN recorded a net deficit in services trade from 2005 to 2009, but as services exports were growing faster than imports (at 10.5 per cent per annum on average between 2007 and 2012, as compared with 9.7 per cent for imports), the deficit has been narrowing.

As shown in Table 7.3, the top three exported services were travel (35 per cent), transport (23 per cent) and other business services (23 per cent). The top three imported services were transport, other business services and travel at 36 per cent, 21 per cent and 21 per cent, respectively. Generally, there is a strong – albeit volatile – upward trend across sub-sectors in both exports and imports. Between 2007 and 2012, charges for the use of intellectual property, and to a lesser extent personal, cultural and recreational services, recorded the highest average annual growth among services exports at 25 per cent and 16 per cent, respectively. For imports, computer, information and communication services, and maintenance and repair services recorded the highest average annual growth in the same period at 17.4 per cent and 17.2 per cent respectively (Table 7.3).

Table 7.3: ASEAN selected services indicators (2012)

	Aggregate (US$ million)			**Intra-ASEAN as % of aggregate**		**Average annual growth (2007–12) (%)**	
Category	**Exports**	**Imports**	**Balance**	**Exports**	**Imports**	**Exports**	**Imports**
Maintenance and repair services n.i.e.*	8,590.2	1,597.9	6,992.2	12.0%	11.5%	13.4	17.2
Transport	62,299.3	103,268.0	(40,968.7)	13.7%	13.3%	6.1	8.5
Travel	95,357.5	58,644.9	36,712.6	32.3%	22.1%	12.3	11.9
Construction	4,294.2	4,619.9	(325.8)	24.7%	23.5%	6.7	3.6
Insurance and pension services	4,365.3	11,676.7	(7,311.4)	31.2%	14.4%	15.0	14.1
Financial services	17,619.7	5,008.8	12,610.9	7.2%	11.9%	9.5	7.7
Charges for the use of intellectual property n.i.e.	2,476.3	27,397.3	(24,921.0)	18.5%	2.3%	25.2	14.0
Telecom-munications, computer and information services	12,323.5	10,640.6	1,683.0	17.6%	19.2%	14.1	17.4
Other business services	61,907.1	59,057.6	2,849.5	14.2%	15.6%	12.8	7.7
Personal, cultural and recreational services	951.4	1,455.8	(504.4)	36.0%	13.5%	16.1	12.6
Government goods and services n.i.e	1,594.7	2,004.8	(410.1)	9.3%	6.5%	8.3	8.9
TOTAL	271,779.2	285,372.4	(13,593.2)	20.6%	14.9%	10.5	9.7

**not included elsewhere*

Source: ASEAN Statistics as of December 2014

In 2012, intra-ASEAN services trade accounted for 17.67 per cent of ASEAN's total services trade, a small decrease from 17.95 per cent in 2007. In recent years, intra-ASEAN services trade has nevertheless been growing slightly faster at 9.89 per cent per annum on average over the period of 2007–12 as compared with 9.19 per cent for total trade. In 2012, total intra-ASEAN services trade (imports + exports) stood at US$98.46 billion, a 55 per cent increase from the 2007 figure of US$63.59 billion, although it also shrunk more during the global financial crisis. A quick analysis of intra-ASEAN trade in services also showed that the pattern of regional services trade followed that of total trade, concentrating heavily in the three sub-sectors of travel, transport and other business services at 44 per cent, 23 per cent and 18 per cent, respectively in 2012. For intra-ASEAN exports, the highest average annual growth in the period of 2007–12 was observed for charges for the use of intellectual property and insurance and pension services at 21 per cent and 10 per cent, respectively. For intra-ASEAN imports, the highest average annual growth over the same period was observed for construction and insurance and pension services at 16 and 15.7 per cent.

How services enter ASEAN value chains

The discussion on services sector trade in ASEAN up to this point has been based on gross numbers. A closer examination of sector-level data, using the value-added statistics that are available, confirms the importance to ASEAN members of some services in GVCs. The use of value-added data reveals how services enter GVCs, which is impossible to do with gross flow data. Tables 7.4 and 7.5 look at business services and electrical and optical equipment services respectively, providing insights on the importance of services VA both in services and goods sectors. The latter is one of ASEAN's 12 Priority Integration Sectors (PIS).

Table 7.4 shows the significance of the business services sub-sector in AMS economies. For some AMS, the size of the sector is comparable to those of the dialogue partners (Japan, South Korea, China, India, Australia and New Zealand). The share of services VA in gross exports in this services value chain was dominant across the AMS (although note that some non-services value is also added). Of the services VA, domestic VA appears to dominate. Singapore is an exception, with a significant share of foreign VA at around 31 per cent. In all AMS other than Singapore, most of domestic services VA enters into the value chains directly, with the remaining share entering the value chains in an indirect manner (through services embedded in the intermediate inputs used in export production).

Table 7.4: Business services (2009)

	Gross exports	Services VA as % gross exports			Domestic services VA as % of gross exports		
	USD million	Total	Foreign	Domestic	Direct	Indirect	Re-imported
Brunei	85.2	92.1	10.1	82.0	74.8	7.3	0.0
Cambodia	13.5	85.2	11.1	74.1	66.7	7.4	0.0
Indonesia	1,639.4	85.8	7.2	78.6	56.2	22.4	0.0
Malaysia	2,975.1	84.5	12.7	71.8	59.6	12.2	0.0
Philippines	1,136.8	87.5	4.7	82.8	62.8	20.0	0.0
Singapore	11,531.4	87.3	30.6	56.6	40.0	14.6	0.1
Thailand	1,910.0	80.5	4.3	76.2	63.6	12.6	0.0
Vietnam	18.1	81.2	8.8	72.4	64.1	8.3	0.0
Australia	6,729.8	93.1	4.4	88.7	52.9	35.7	0.0
China	20,676.7	64.4	4.5	59.	38.8	21.0	0.1
India	51,537.0	94.3	10.5	83.9	69.1	14.7	0.0
Japan	8,018.2	92.7	2.0	90.7	61.8	28.8	0.0
South Korea	10,409.4	88.2	4.9	83.3	65.2	18.1	0.0
New Zealand	644.9	90.1	6.8	83.3	55.9	27.4	0.0
EU27	212,987.6	93.4	4.9	88.5	58.5	29.8	0.2

Source: WTO-OECD TiVA database

Table 7.5 provides an interesting insight into the significance of services in electrical and optical equipment, which is typically regarded as a 'goods' sub-sector. Electronics is a key industry in ASEAN. At 23–37 per cent of gross exports, the contribution of services value added is significant. The data also shows the relative significance of foreign services VA in gross exports. Being a typical goods sub-sector, domestic VA enters the value chain mostly in an indirect manner, through its embodiment in intermediate inputs used in export production.

Table 7.5: Electrical and optical equipment (2009)

	Gross exports	Services VA as % gross exports			Domestic services VA as % of gross exports		
	USD million	Total	Foreign	Domestic	Direct	Indirect	Re-imported
Brunei	10.0	37.0	22.0	15.0	0.0	15.0	0.0
Cambodia	158.5	31.6	27.5	4.0	0.0	4.0	0.0
Indonesia	9,676.4	26.3	10.8	15.5	0.0	15.5	0.0
Malaysia	41,587.3	23.2	17.0	5.3	0.0	5.2	0.2
Philippines	33,288.6	32.9	20.0	12.8	0.0	12.7	0.1
Singapore	44,866.7	35.9	28.7	7.2	0.0	6.9	0.2
Thailand	54,365.1	30.7	23.7	7.0	0.0	6.9	0.1
Vietnam	1,675.3	28.6	22.0	6.6	0.0	6.6	0.0
Australia	3,070.0	26.7	6.5	20.2	0.0	20.1	0.1
China	431,446.9	28.4	15.3	13.1	0.0	12.5	0.6
India	24,257.1	37.7	9.2	28.5	0.0	28.4	0.1
Japan	149,852.2	32.9	5.7	27.2	0.0	26.9	0.3
South Korea	117,489.0	33.0	17.7	15.3	0.0	14.9	0.4
New Zealand	857.2	35.9	10.3	25.6	0.0	25.6	0.0
EU27	180,028.4	36.7	7.1	29.6	0.0	29.0	0.6

Source: WTO-OECD TiVA database

Services in the context of ASEAN regional integration

ASEAN integration

ASEAN was formed in 1967. 20 years later, in 1987, members declared the objective of strengthening intra-ASEAN economic cooperation. This aspiration was institutionalized five years later in 1992 through the signing of the ASEAN Free Trade Area (AFTA), covering goods trade, by the ASEAN-6. The remaining ASEAN members became signatories to AFTA between 1995 and 1999.

ASEAN's goal for services integration was first institutionalized through the signing of the ASEAN Framework Agreement on Services (AFAS) in 1995, three years after signature of its goods counterpart, the AFTA. AFAS aims to substantially eliminate restrictions to trade in services among ASEAN countries and improve the efficiency and competitiveness of ASEAN service suppliers.

In 2003, leaders announced ASEAN Vision 2020 through the Bali Concord II, with the objective of seeking deeper regional integration by 2020. In 2007, the timeline was moved forward by five years to 2015. Three ASEAN community blueprints were also adopted, including the AEC Blueprint that sets out specific measures to be undertaken and the strategic schedule for the establishment of the AEC in 2015.

Broadly, the steps toward services integration in ASEAN involve market access liberalization among members. This effort is supported by provisions to facilitate open and transparent services trade through greater certainty in members' services regimes, mutual recognition agreements for selected professional occupations, and the negotiation of trade in services agreements with FTA partners.

AFAS

AFAS is ASEAN's key services integration instrument, evolving in its approach over time after starting with a requests-and-offers approach at its entry into force. Members have now conducted multiple rounds of negotiations, with each round resulting in packages of commitments from each ASEAN country in the agreed economic sector/sub-sectors and modes of supply. Eight packages of commitments under AFAS have been negotiated and concluded to date. The ninth package of commitments has also been concluded and is in the process of being signed. AMS aim to conclude 10 packages of services commitments by the end of 2015. All AFAS rules are consistent with international rules for trade in services as provided by the GATS, while aiming to achieve commitments beyond those under the GATS.

Although AFAS is the main framework for the region's services integration, it is not the only framework in which it is taking place. Since the Informal Meeting of ASEAN Economic Ministers in June 1999 in Auckland, the liberalization of air transport and that of financial services, which started off within the ambit of AFAS, were moved to the ASEAN Transport Ministry and Finance Ministry portfolios respectively.

AEC blueprint: A focus on services

The AEC blueprint sets out the specific measures required, and the strategic schedule for their implementation, for the establishment of the AEC by 2015. It was not until the adoption of the AEC blueprint in 2007 that the timeline for AFAS negotiations and other complementary measures relating to services integration were more firmly defined.

Element A3 of Pillar 1 of the AEC blueprint, namely the creation of a single market and production base, addresses the free flow of services and broadly comprises the following:

- The removal of substantially all restrictions on trade in services for the four priority services sectors, namely air transport, e-ASEAN, healthcare and tourism, by 2010, for the fifth priority services sector of logistics services by 2013 and in all other services sectors by 2015.
- Liberalization is to be undertaken through consecutive rounds every two years until 2015, targeting specific minimum numbers of new sub-sectors in each round within agreed parameters. These parameters include direct access of services products among AEC markets, investment conditions for AEC services suppliers, and terms on which labour can flow among member states.
- Timeline for conclusion of negotiations on mutual recognition arrangements (MRAs) on select professional services, namely architectural services, accountancy services, surveying qualifications and medical practitioners by 2008, dental practitioners by 2009 and other services sectors by 2015. These MRAs are key instruments for skilled labour mobility within ASEAN. Each MRA is to be expeditiously implemented with strengthened human resources and capacity building in the area of services.

- On the financial services sector progressive liberalization of restrictions in the sub-sectors or modes as identified by each AMS by 2015, and barriers to AMS firms in the remaining subsectors or modes that are not identified under 'pre-agreed flexibilities' are to be removed by 2020.

In addition to those under the first pillar of the AEC agenda, other measures that are relevant to the services sector are also found under the other pillars of the AEC. The fourth pillar of the AEC, for example, deals with ASEAN integration into the global economy and enhanced GVC participation. It foresees the region's pursuit of coherent external policies, including through FTAs with third parties, as integral to its economic integration agenda.

ASEAN is signatory to five 'plus 1' FTAs with China, Japan, South Korea, India and Australia and New Zealand. Apart from the ASEAN-Japan Comprehensive Economic Partnership (AJCEP), they include agreement on trade in services, while negotiations on the services component of the AJCEP are already at their conclusion stage. In September 2014, ASEAN commenced negotiations for the upgrading of the ASEAN-China FTA (ACFTA) (FTA – Free Trade Agreement) that includes a services component.

ASEAN is also currently participating in the negotiations for the Regional Comprehensive Economic Partnership (RCEP) with its six FTA partners, namely Australia, China, India, Japan, South Korea, and New Zealand. The RCEP negotiations are based on the agreed objective of achieving a modern, comprehensive, high-quality and mutually beneficial economic partnership agreement among the AMS and ASEAN's FTA partners. In the Guiding Principles and Objectives for Negotiating the RCEP, which were endorsed by leaders in 2012, the RCEP seeks to be comprehensive on trade in services, promoting high quality and substantially eliminating restrictions and/or discriminatory measures with respect to trade in services among RCEP participating countries. Further rules and obligations on trade in services under the RCEP will be consistent with the GATS and will be directed towards achieving liberalization commitments building on RCEP participating countries' commitments under the GATS and the ASEAN+1 FTAs. All sectors and modes of supply will be subject to negotiations. Like the establishment of the AEC, RCEP negotiations are also aimed at conclusion by the end of 2015.

There is also ongoing work to enhance the AFAS. AMS are currently discussing an ASEAN Trade in Services Agreement (ATISA), which will build upon the ASEAN+1 FTAs and RCEP.

Conclusion

ASEAN has put a negotiating framework in place for opening up services trade and has achieved some results. It will need to re-double efforts, however, to be able to fully embrace the potential of services to boost gainful GVC participation and to act as a driver of economic growth and development. The current framework focuses on liberalization. Improved efficiency in the services sector can also be achieved through more effective and efficient regulations, to which regulatory cooperation can also contribute while still preserving the space for bona fide public policy objectives and regulations. The services sector is complex and it intersects with many cross-cutting and often overlapping or inconsistent regulations. Addressing these will be no small feat. Having efficient services sectors will not only allow the region's industries to move to, or focus more on, higher value-added activities, it also will ensure better integration into GVCs. ASEAN can approach some of these challenges collectively as part of its regional integration agenda. However, efforts are also needed at local, national and even multilateral levels. Properly managed, services can serve as an effective tool for ASEAN to escape the middle-income trap and address distribution issues within and across individual economies.

While concerted efforts are needed to ensure the implementation of scheduled commitments, services integration can be further enhanced beyond just the removal of market access restrictions and discriminatory measures, including through cooperation and capacity building, as well as greater transparency. Beyond regional integration, ASEAN should also consider how to leverage regional cooperation and measures to contribute to services discussion at the multilateral level. This will be consistent with the vision in the fourth pillar of the AEC blueprint dealing with enhanced participation in global supply networks.

Last but not least, future efforts to enhance services integration must also be informed by forward-looking trends and the evolving frontiers of production and trade possibilities, including the growing importance of e-commerce, additive/digital manufacturing and data analytics. All these have considerable services components and will play a significant role in ensuring the continuous innovation needed for sustainable GVC participation.

References

ASEAN Secretariat. 2008. *ASEAN Economic Community Blueprint*. Jakarta: ASEAN Secretariat. Available at: http://www.asean.org/archive/5187-10.pdf.

ASEAN stats. 2014. Available at: http://aseanstats.asean.org/Menu.aspx?rxid=52e80179-1bb3-416d-959c-24abac592d2c&px_language=en&px_db=2-International+Merchandise+Trade+Statistics&px_type=PX.

Athukorala, Prema-Chandra. 2013. 'Global Production Sharing and Trade Patterns in East Asia', *Australian National University Working Papers in Trade and Development 2013/10*. Available at: https://crawford.anu.edu.au/acde/publications/publish/papers/wp2013/wp_econ_2013_10.pdf. Canberra: Australian National University.

Banga, Rashmi. 2013. 'Measuring Value in Global Value Chains', *Unit of Economic Cooperation and Integration amongst Developing Countries (ECIDC) UNCTAD Background Paper RVC-8*. Available at: http://unctad.org/en/PublicationsLibrary/ecidc2013misc1_bp8.pdf. Geneva: United Nations Conference on Trade and Development.

Chia, SiowYue. 2013. 'The ASEAN Economic Community: Progress, Challenges, and Prospects', *ADBI Working Paper 440*. Available at: http://www.adbi.org/sites/default/files/publication/156295/adbi-wp440.pdf. Tokyo: Asian Development Bank Institute.

Kommerskollegium. 2013. *Global Value Chains and Services – An Introduction*. Stockholm: Kommerskollegium. Available at: http://www.kommers.se/Documents/dokumentarkiv/publikationer/2013/rapporter/GVC_and_Developing_Countries_webb.pdf.

Low, Patrick. June 2013. 'The Role of Services in Global Value Chains', *Fung Global Institute Real Sector Working Paper*. Available at: http://www.fungglobalinstitute.org/en/wp-content/uploads/The%20Role%20of%20Services%20in%20Global%20Value%20Chains_1.pdf. Hong Kong: Fung Global Institute.

OECD. 2014. *OECD Factbook 2014: Economic, Environmental, and Social Statistics*. Paris: OECD.

———. 2014. 'OECD-WTO TiVA Database'. Available at: http://www.oecd.org/sti/ind/measuringtradeinvalue-addedanoecd-wtojointinitiative.htm

UNCTAD. 2013. *World Investment Report 2013: Global Value Chains: Investment and Trade for Development*. New York and Geneva: United Nations. Available at: http://unctad.org/en/PublicationsLibrary/wir2013_en.pdf.

UNCTAD STATS. 2013. *Manual on FDI Statistics*. Available at: http://unctad.org/en/pages/PublicationArchive.aspx?publicationid=393

UNCTAD. 2014. *Global Investment Trends Monitor* 15. Available at: http://unctad.org/en/PublicationsLibrary/webdiaeia2014d1_en.pdf. Geneva: United Nations Conference on Trade and Development.

World Bank. 2014. *World Development Indicators*. Available at: http://data.worldbank.org/sites/default/files/wdi-2014-book.pdf.

8

Indian IT Firms

The Push for Innovation

Dev Nathan, Sandip Sarkar and Balwant Singh Mehta

Introduction

This chapter deals with the development trajectory of the major Indian information technology (IT) software service companies. They have established themselves through their initial innovation of the global delivery model (GDM), where they combined high-cost, on-site work with low-cost, off-site work in India in order to cheapen the cost of providing IT services. Whilst they started out at the low complexity end of programming in IT services, they have faced increased competition as the GDM has been copied by other IT service providers, including the global majors such as IBM and Accenture. The end-to-end service provision capabilities of these global majors have enabled them to take up the important managed service function, where they provide an entire IT service to a client. At the same time as the Indian IT majors failed to move into managed services, higher salaries have also eroded their margins. This decline in margins has forced some of them to change their business models, so far based largely on labour arbitrage. In dealing with declining margins, they have the options of either developing as IT product companies, such as SAP or, as in a recent development of Infosys, moving to innovate and automate the service delivery function.

The next section lays out the global IT value chain. We then locate Indian IT firms within the IT GVC. The limitations of this location are discussed in the context of the Airtel outsourcing decision. This is followed by a brief discussion of the trends in earnings. Ways of responding to the declining trends are also discussed. The next section discusses the upgrading strategy and its link with employment strategy. The concluding section tries to draw broader lessons on the nature of upgrading and the role of the state.

IT Services GVC

IT services production has its own production network or value chain, which does not vary with the type of client. Its production stages can be summarized as in Figure 8.1.

Figure 8.1: The Software GPN

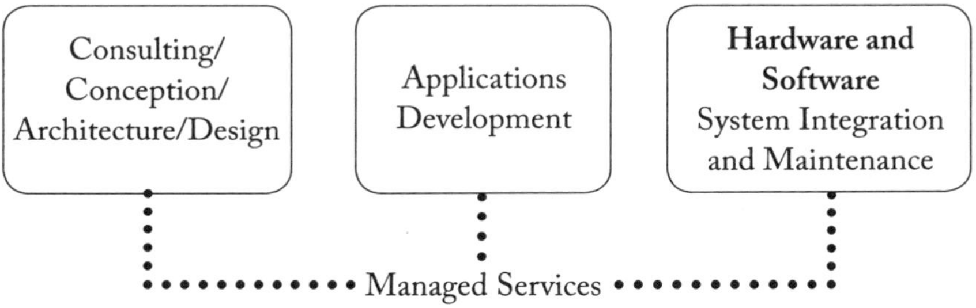

Source: Authors' adaptation from various sources.

The high-end of IT services production is that of consulting, conception, and architecture and design. This is the beginning of the process. Whilst customers have a role to play in setting the requirements, this first step in IT services is increasingly outsourced. But there is substantial interaction between customer and service provider in setting up and designing the service, which is why IT services, as such, falls within what Gereffi *et al.* (2005) call relational governance. Once the IT service requirements have been established, programming and development can begin. This is where Indian IT firms have excelled and captured a major portion of the world market. Once deployed, the hardware and software are supported with maintenance provisions. In the managed services system, all of the IT service requirements are outsourced to an IT company, which is expected to conceive, execute (including the provision of both hardware and software) and maintain the system, in order to provide the required IT services.

The above illustrates the feedback loops that exist among the different stages of the IT service provision process. Problems dealing with, for example, programming or systems integration can occur at any stage, requiring backtracking into the system's architecture. The advantage is that the inherent modularity of IT service provision makes it possible to outsource the provisions by piecemeal.

In the early period of outsourcing, these IT services were managed by customers themselves. However, in-house management of IT services, especially in the banking and insurance industries, has been changing. The need to cut costs during the global financial crisis led Citibank and others to outsource entire segments of IT requirements in terms of managed services. In the telecom sector, India's Airtel pioneered the complete outsourcing model, not only of all IT services it required, but even of other services, such as tower installation and network management.

When Airtel decided to outsource its entire IT services requirement, it gave the contract, worth more than US$1 billion, to IBM. Given the strong position of Indian IT majors in global outsourced IT services, it is important to ask why the contract was not granted to an Indian major instead. Answering this question entails a closer look at the role of Indian IT majors in different segments of the IT services production network.

Position of Indian IT majors

Indian IT service providers established themselves in the global market by carrying out a process innovation of the so-called GDM. The GDM was a process innovation of the Indian IT majors, in which they combined on-shore with off-shore staff in more than one location to reduce both the lead time and the cost of providing services. When working, staff could 'follow the sun', thus reducing lead time. Off-shore facilities in India or other developing country locations took advantage of the international segmentation of the workforce to pay lower salaries to off-shore staff than to on-shore employees. This labour arbitrage reduced costs, while 'follow the sun' work reduced lead time in providing a service.

This process innovation disrupted the market for software services, not only allowing Indian companies to acquire 40 per cent of the global programming development market (Dossani, 2010), but also forcing established international majors such as IBM and Accenture to adopt the same model. In a sense, it could be said that if China perfected the low-cost manufacturing model, India perfected the low-cost IT service delivery model.

But while IT service provision as a whole is a complex task, within it are segments of differing complexity. Following Dossani (2013), the tasks involved in providing IT service can be divided into three levels of complexity. The highest complexity is that of design and consulting. This is followed by system integration as a medium complexity task. Applications development or programming and testing are low complexity tasks.

Table 8.1: Indian IT firms' share of complex work

2010	Design and consulting	System integration	Applications development and testing
Complexity	High	Medium	Low
Global spending (%)	29	51	20
Indian exports (%)	4	19	77 (2000 = 88%)

Source: Dossani, 2013, 174

The share of low complexity tasks, applications development and testing has gone down from 88 per cent in 2000 to 77 per cent in 2010. Nevertheless, it still accounts for the bulk of Indian IT exports. But in order to provide a managed service an IT service provider must have capabilities in all three complexity levels. In particular, it must be able to carry out the design and consulting functions. This, however, requires knowledge not just of IT but also of the domain or sector in which the service is to be provided. Thus, along with IT experts, it is also necessary to have domain experts who know the sector and its requirements.

Global majors' response to the Indian challenge

Business models, whether the Japanese just-in-time manufacturing system or the Indian GDM cannot be patented and thus can be easily copied, and as they are, first movers lose their competitive advantage. IBM, much like Accenture, had been strong in providing both high-end consulting (conception, design and architecture of software services) and end-to-end managed services, often with parts or all of programming being outsourced. But to stave off the threat of Indian majors developing capabilities to take up managed service provision, IBM and Accenture also adopted lower-end activities based on the Indian companies' GDM. The US majors IBM and Accenture moved downstream to set up off-shore programming and call centre facilities in India. IBM took this step earlier than Accenture, which started to adopt the GDM in the mid-2000s.

In adopting the GDM, they were pushed by large customers, such as the major banks and insurance companies, who were increasingly asking for managed services and not just high-end consulting from IT service providers. To avoid having to outsource middle and lower-end services to Indian companies, the US majors developed their own middle and lower-end capabilities.

Accenture, for instance, increased its off-shore presence, increasing its staff in India from 27,000 in 2005 to 124,000 in 2011 (Morgan Stanley, 2011, 26). With India-based staff providing the lower-end services; Accenture, like IBM, moved from high-end consulting to providing end-to-end services.

The Airtel outsourcing decision

As pointed out in Table 8.1, Indian companies usually operate in the lower and middle segment of the IT services value chain, i.e., after the design conceptualization and design has been done, they carry out the programming and related work. This also means that they did not develop end-to-end capability, which requires knowledge of the domain, whether in telecom or manufacturing. Lacking proven capability in the managed services segment, it is no surprise that the Indian IT majors did not win the end-to-end IT service contract from Airtel. Vodafone and IDEA followed suit, and outsourced their IT services as well. All US$3 billion in contracts went to IBM.

A number of factors seem to be at play in securing such managed services contracts. First is the experience of already having provided such end-to-end services, which the Indian majors did not have. Furthermore, the Indian IT majors were organized horizontally by different types of services (programming, systems integration, call centres, etc.) rather than vertically, or end-to-end. For instance, three Wipro departments dealt with Citibank separately –' Its banking vertical would be selling a banking software, the sales team might be making a pitch for the bank's back-office work and its software division would be offering its testing services' (Mishra, 2011).

The Indian majors had some experience working with telecommunications companies, such as Tata Consultancy Services (TCS) with Nortel or British Telecommunications (BT). This experience, however, was in providing specific services, not end-to-end services covering an entire domain, which requires high-end capabilities to conceive, design and put together a whole package that integrates an entire spectrum of IT service requirements. As the Chairman of Airtel, Sunil Mittal, explained the choice of IBM:

> Western companies ... have proven ability to work for large mobile providers and can render services locally through their Indian subsidiaries. IBM has thousands of people in India who work on my job. Indians run it, but they're governed by the IBM structure, under the command and control of IBM's global experts (Subramanyam, 2011, 404).

It was the high-end knowledge of those whom Mittal refers to as 'IBM's global experts' that seems to have been a key difference between the western and Indian IT majors.

Indian majors' response

Along with the weakness of Indian majors in providing end-to-end services, their own business model, based on labour arbitrage, was facing the challenge of increasing salaries.

Average salaries in the IT sector rose by more than 80 per cent over the decade from 1999 to 2009 (Mehta, 2013). In addition, barriers to entry in the lower end of programming or applications development are quite low. Many mid-sized firms have sprung up, employing a few hundred workers. Their competition itself could reduce margins. However, given the brand value of the Indian IT majors, which mid-sized companies do not have, the erosion of margins may be due more to rising salary costs than competition.[1]

Revenue per employee peaked in 2003. In the period from 2003 until 2011, revenues per employee declined by 10.5 per cent, translating into a -1.4 per cent compound annual growth rate (Morgan Stanley, 2011). This decline in margins signaled the need to improve the nature of growth. Continued horizontal expansion required a greater number of employees, which did not help to boost these ratios. Even offering more commoditized IT programming services could not change this trend.

Cost reductions could reduce the effect of deterioration in revenues per employee. The Indian IT majors did carry out cost reductions, TCS more successfully than others. However, as the Morgan Stanley (2011) report points out, these steps would not improve the quality of growth. In terms of economic upgrading and downgrading, the strategy of cost cutting would be a strategy of downgrading, while that of moving to higher-paying segments of IT services would be a strategy of upgrading.

Reducing costs could always be copied and spread throughout the industry, recreating the same problems after a while. Movements into higher-value services and products, where barriers to entry are high (i.e., requiring specialized,

1 The decline of margins in IT services has been frequently reported and commented on in the Indian press. *The Economic Times*, 19 February 2013, headlined: 'IT margins headed inexorably downwards, may fall below 20%' (Nandakumar and Prasad, 2013). Analysts pointed out that wage inflation is likely to be the most important pressure point for Indian IT services companies.

high-level knowledge and the ability to conceptualize and design), such as end-to-end consulting, or products that obtain intellectual property rights protection, could result in higher returns.

Indian IT majors' move to upgrade

End-to-end consulting or providing a managed service, requires an organization of the service provider along industry verticals. As pointed out earlier, the Indian companies were initially organized along horizontal lines, i.e., with departments for programming, system integration, call centres and so on. But an end-to-end service requires that all the services that make up a managed service be organized in an industry line.

To meet this requirement, Indian majors have been re-organizing along industry verticals. TCS, a Tata company which provides managed services to the telecom company Tata Docomo, made the first steps in this direction, followed by Wipro, which has secured managed services contracts from relatively smaller telecommunications companies, namely Aircel and Telenor. Infosys has also jumped on the bandwagon, but for the time being, Indian companies are having difficulty matching IBM's combination of conceptualization and design capabilities, along with hardware, software, services and research.

In an attempt to move into higher value-added services, Infosys took what might be the more difficult, but potentially highly lucrative route of developing software products. It developed Flypp as a mobile platform and m-Connect as a mobile middleware. More recently, it has come out with m-Wallet, which is now being used by Airtel in its mobile money transfer system. The well-established banking software, Finnacle, has been modified for mobile banking as well. TCS, too, has its software products, most notably TCSBancS for banking. However, TCS does not seem to have put the same emphasis on developing products as Infosys.

In services, although the Indian IT firms started at the lower end, they did not remain confined there. Working with customers and learning their requirements allowed them to move into managed services, although on a smaller scale. Some of the learning in providing managed services was through Indian contracts, for instance, TCS for the National Stock Exchange. Indian companies took great strides to enter into higher-end consultancy and end-to-end services by: (1) hiring entire teams of enterprise solution consultants on-shore, who had a much better understanding of the realities in developed countries; and (2) acquiring independent consultancy firms (Chari, 2010).

More recently, Infosys has decided to meet the challenge of increasing revenue per employee by moving towards automation and innovation in its production of services. As the CEO of Infosys put it, it is necessary to move from labour arbitrage and the drudgery of programming to automation and innovation. With this change, he targets revenue per employee to go up from the current (2015) $50,000 per employee to $85,000 per employee (2020). Wipro, too, has decided to go the automation route to increase revenue per employee and to allow a 35 per cent fall in the workforce, to be achieved not through lay-offs, but through the attrition route.

In beginning to make this move, it is interesting to note that Infosys has abandoned the 'bell curve' method of removing employees at the bottom tail of assessment, a practice that reduced employment security. Other IT companies, such as Cisco and Adobe, and even the originator of the bell curve method of employee removal, General Electric (GE), have also abandoned the bell curve. Can one expect innovative ideas about the automation of programming from employees whose jobs are at stake?

Conclusion

Social upgrading in the form of increased remuneration has introduced a new dynamic into the telecom and other IT services markets. Increasing salaries, diminishing margins, increasing competition among suppliers and deterioration in the quality of growth have been pushing Indian IT firms to move up the value chain. In an attempt to undertake economic upgrading, Indian IT firms are now offering high-end consulting and managed services. At least one is even moving to automation and innovation. From having been stuck in the middle-to-lower end of programming but facing both increased competition and higher costs through increased salaries, it seems likely that business models might change to stress new innovations in service delivery. Process innovations clearly can be copied, and are, forcing suppliers to adapt yet newer process innovations.

But upgrading is not just a matter of cost dynamics. Other factors come into the picture. First is the availability of the necessary skills. But these can also be acquired, not only through buying up firms that have the capabilities, but also through international hiring. Thus, the supply of skills does not seem a binding constraint.

The second factor is the business strategies of firms. Will a firm continue on the same lines and add employee strength, whilst not trying to increase revenue per employee? Some of the Indian firms are clearly on this path of trying more of the same or horizontal expansion. But even where horizontal expansion is successful, a threat always looming on the horizon is that some firm comes up with a process innovation that drastically alters the cost equation. The Indian IT firms themselves disrupted the market by developing the GDM, and that innovation enabled them to establish a major presence in the global IT services market. But there is the new threat of automation of much of the routine programming work that still accounts for the bulk of Indian IT firms' revenues. In the manner that 3-D printing is a threat to the outsourcing of low-end manufacturing, the automation of routine programming is a threat to its outsourcing in IT services.

This is a threat that Indian IT firms ignore at their peril. A way of meeting this threat would be for Indian firms themselves to go this route, as Infosys promises to do. This will surely have implications for employment; but since the threat of programming automation is real, the negative implications for employment will materialize in one way or the other. Capturing a higher share of world IT services output would be a way of dealing with the employment threat of automation. But that will happen only if Indian companies, or companies based in India, undertake this innovation.

This step of automation is possibly something that the IT firms could manage on their own. What is needed here is for firms to accept the strategic necessity of automation, in order to retain their position in the market.

But the difficulties that Indian IT firms are facing in developing the capabilities for providing end-to-end or fully managed services in various domains points to one more problem – the lack of a policy of the Indian state to develop IT services to the next level. US IT service companies, for instance, have the advantage of being able to work on relatively protected home markets for defence services. Such experience in providing end to-end services is important in being able to carry out the same in commercial fields. In the Indian case too, we saw earlier that TCS acquired some experience in providing end-to-end services by supplying the National Stock Exchange. But the level of digitization of Indian Government and military services has, so far, been too low to provide Indian firms the necessary experience in end-to-end services. A clear policy on digitization of government and its military services, where a measure of domestic preference has been acceptable, is necessary for Indian firms to develop the necessary domain and managed service capabilities. In fact, as strongly argued by Maria Mazzucato (2012), state support is an important part of any innovation strategy.

In the Indian case, such state support for innovation is quite lacking. On the contrary, Indian firms point to the various difficulties and corruption issues they face in handling Indian Government contracts. In newspaper reports, it is often pointed out that the Indian IT majors prefer not to handle Indian Government contracts, because of corruption issues. Improving the business atmosphere by reducing both corruption and related bureaucratic hassles would seem to be necessary for IT firms to secure the needed experience in providing managed services through government contracts.

Indian IT firms have been able to utilize market situations and the global segmentation of workers to establish a strong position in the global market for IT services. But their position is still mainly confined to the lower-to-middle levels of complexity and returns. To move to the next level, whether of end-to-end capabilities or of IT software products, would seem to require a state policy that supports innovation, in addition to firms' own moves to automate and innovate.

References

Chari, S. K. 2010. 'We are Recruiting More and More in Local Markets', *Livemint*, 19 October.

Dossani, Rafiq. 2010. 'Software Production: Globalization and its Implications', in *The Service Revolution in South Asia*, edited by E. Ghani. New York: OUP and the World Bank.

———. 2013. 'A Decade After the Y2K Problem: Has Indian IT Emerged?', in *The Third Globalization: Can Wealthy Nations Stay Rich In The Twenty-First Century?*, edited by Dan Breznitz and John Zysman. New York: Oxford University Press.

Gereffi, Gary, John Humphrey and Timothy Sturgeon. 2005. 'The Governance of Global Value Chains', *Review of International Political Economy* 12 (1): 78–104.

IAMAI (Internet and Mobile Association of India). 2009. *IAMAI-MA FOI Compensation and Benefits Benchmarking Survey Reports*. New Delhi: IAMAI.

Mazuccatto, Maria, 2012. *The State as Entrepreneur*. London: Anthem Press.

Mehta, Balwant S. 2012.'Employment in the Information and Communication Technology Sector', *Indian Journal* of *Labour Economics* 55 (4): 687–96.

———. 2013. *Workers in IT and Telecom*. Mimeo.

Mishra, Bibhu R. 2010. 'Building Smarter Strategy for India, the IBM Way', *Business Standard*, 26 August.

Mishra, Pankaj. 2011. 'Infosys, Wipro Increase Focus on Verticals to Overcome Growth Challenges', *The Economic Times*, 19 April.

Morgan Stanley. 2011. 'Global IT Services: "Per-Employee' Metrics are Key to Quality of Growth".' Available at: http://www.morganstanleychina.com/conferences/apsummit2011/research/30GlobalITServices.pdf.

Nandakumar, Indu and Akanksha Prasad. 2013. 'IT Margins Headed Inexorably Downwards', *The Economic Times*, 19 February.

Sarkar, Sandip, and Balwant S. Mehta. 2010. 'Labour Market Patterns and Trends in India's ICT Sector', in *Labour in Global Production Networks in India*, edited by Anne Posthuma and Dev Nathan. Delhi: Oxford University Press..

Silicon India News. 2010. 'Knowledge Faber', 13 May.

Subramanyam, Raghunath. 2011. 'Managing Core Outsourcing to Address Fast Market Growth: A Case Study of an Indian Mobile Telecom Service Provider', in *Global Outsourcing and Offshoring: An Integrated Approach to Theory and Corporate Strategy*, edited by Farok J. Contractor, Vikas Kumar, Sumit K. Kundu and Torben Pedersen. Cambridge: Cambridge University Press.

Wadhwa, Naresh. 2012. 'Quote from CISCO's President and Country Manager', India, *Daily News and Analysis*, 24 January.

9

Leveraging Business Process Outsourcing for Growth

Pradeep Mukherji and Chirag Rawat

Introduction

The outsourcing of business processes, also referred to as business process outsourcing (BPO), has enabled businesses to make their operations more scalable, flexible, resilient and cost effective, while delivering better service and value to their customers. Globally, the BPO industry has also created millions of jobs in low-cost countries, propelling economic development. The sector has also contributed to job creation for underprivileged youth, catalyzing social empowerment and poverty reduction. Providing a channel into the global services market, governments around the world have realized the potential of the sector for growth and socio-economic development.

Governments across Asia, Africa and Latin America have adopted innovative strategies to become significant players in the BPO value chain. This chapter tries to unravel the BPO value chain and analyse the approaches some of the countries have taken to become leaders in the sector by assessing their inherent strengths and best practices. In conclusion, this chapter provides insights and an evolutionary analysis into making an emerging BPO location attractive vis-à-vis the dynamics at play in the sector.

BPO value chain

BPO is defined as the procurement of services that are non-core to the organization but improve efficiency, reduce costs and enable focus on key business operations (Parikh and Mukherjee, 2013). The services are procured mainly from a third-party firm that operates from a low-cost country. BPO involves outsourcing of back-office functions such as finance and accounting

(F&A) and human resource management (HRM) (NASSCOM, 2012). Front-office functions, such as customer interactive services (CIS) that require regular interaction with customers through multiple channels, are also a part of the BPO value chain (NASSCOM, 2012).

While most BPO processes, like F&A and human resource organization (HRO), are transaction-oriented, outsourcing of knowledge-intensive processes like business analytics and legal services involves processes that demand strong domain knowledge and reasoning abilities (NASSCOM, 2013). CIS processes require multichannel interaction with a large component of voice interaction through call centres. Industry vertical-specific BPO, such as services for the insurance industry, are tailored for the industry's requirements and demands. Business value delivered by BPO services has a direct correlation with the human knowledge and capital required to execute the process (Gereffi and Stark, 2010). This means that a more complex task has a higher strategic value and contributes more to the business' revenue and success. A snapshot of a BPO knowledge value chain is illustrated in Figure 9.1.

Figure 9.1: BPO knowledge value chain

Incresing Human Knowledge & Capital	Customer Interaction Services	Finance & Accounting	Human Resources	Procurement	Industry Specific Services and KPO
Strategic	• CRM Plafform • Privacy & Security • Campaign Management	• Tax Planning & Reporting • Treasury Management • M &A Management	• HR Strategy • Labor Relations Strategy • HR Policy	• Sourcing Strategy Management • Spend Analysis • Sourcing Plan	• Automation Research • Research & Development • Clinical Research
Operational	• Technical Support • Warranty Management • IVR & Voice Services	• Credit Management • Order Management • Budgeting	• Vendor Management • Benefits Administration	• E-Procurement • Compliance Management • Contract Administration	• Big Data & Analytics • Engineering Services • Clinical Trials
Transactional	• Customer Service • Chat Support	• Payroll Processing • Accounts Payable • Collections	• Employee Recordkeeping • Payroll Administration	• Reconcile Returns • Order Management • Payment Authorization	• Claims Processing • Billing Generation and Payment Analysis

Source: Avasant research

BPO services – climbing the value chain

Since the turn of the century, the BPO industry has continuously evolved and experienced significant growth. As per Gereffi and Stark (2010),

The scope of the BPO industry has evolved over time and increasingly sophisticated activities are being outsourced. What began with the outsourcing of basic information technology (IT) services to external firms now includes a wide array of activities known as business process outsourcing (BPO), knowledge process outsourcing (KPO), and other advanced activities in the value chain such as research and development (R&D), which were previously considered core functions of the firm.

In addition, demand for higher financial efficiency has put pressure on firms to reduce their operating costs. Technological advancements in the ICT infrastructure have encouraged many firms to seek out innovative solutions, including executing business processes from low-cost countries, where quality skilled resources are available. In the early 1990s, outsourcing of low-skill tasks, such as data entry for digitization of processes was most popular. Outsourcing of voice-based processes for customer care by setting up contact centres in off-shore locations like India and the Philippines came next. Later, after the turn of the century, offshoring transaction-oriented tasks, such as F&A, human resources and specialized back-office processes for industry verticals like the insurance and healthcare sectors, have seen significant growth. Today, BPO has become strategic for organizations, delivering significant business value by servicing core processes and facilitating business decisions by leveraging tools and services like consumer analytics. Figure 9.2 depicts the development of outsourced BPO activities over time.

Figure 9.2: BPO industry evolution

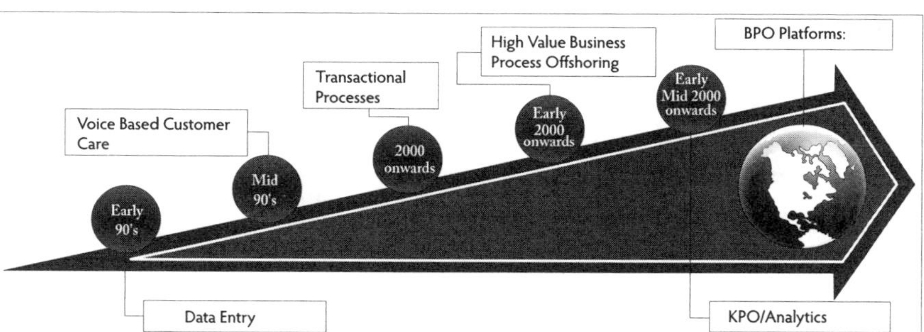

Source: Avasant research

With the growth in the BPO industry, the number of off-shore service delivery locations in low-cost countries has been steadily increasing. Mature service delivery locations, such as India and the Philippines, have been re-shuffling the portfolio of their services to focus on delivery of higher value-added processes. The segment being vacated by these countries is being seen as a strategic opportunity by other countries considering a play in the BPO industry. Figure 9.3 shows the historical evolution of involvement in BPO in various economies.

Figure 9.3: Transformation of the BPO global landscape

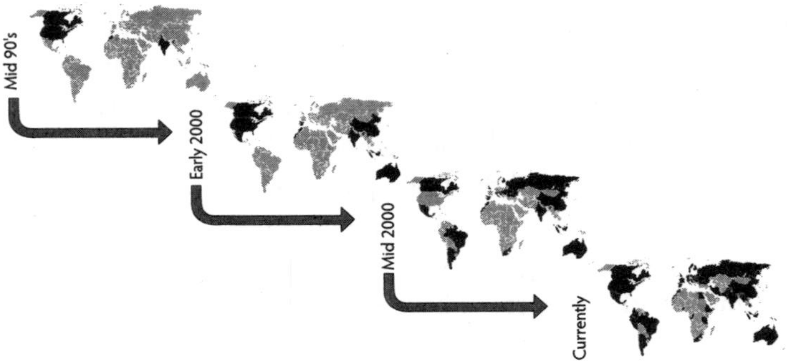

Mid 90's
Early 2000
Mid 2000
Currently

Source: Avasant research

The largest amount of spending on BPO services is from advanced economies such as the US, the UK, Western Europe, Japan and Australia. The geography of the BPO landscape is illustrated in Figure 9.4 below.

Figure 9.4: BPO buyers and service delivery destinations

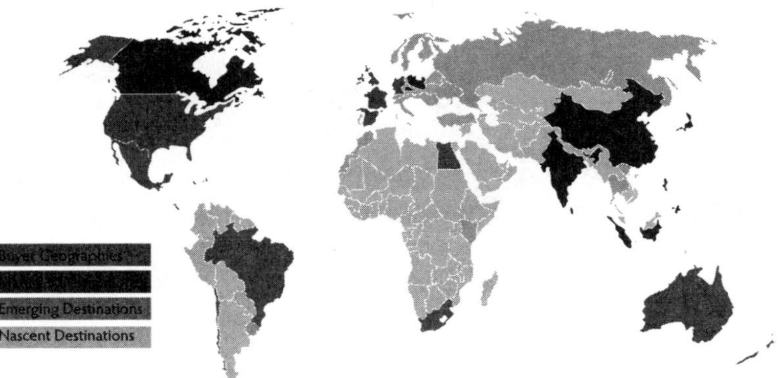

Source: Avasant research

BPO spending, which includes domestic outsourcing (the outsourcing of business processes within a buyer country) and offshoring, reached US$168 billion in 2013. It is expected to reach US$190 billion in 2015, growing at a cumulative annual growth rate (CAGR) of about 6.5 per cent. Procurement of BPO services from offshoring is expected to grow faster at a 9.5 per cent CAGR, reaching US$55 billion in 2015. In 2013, the largest global providers of BPO services were India and the Philippines, contributing to 55 per cent of the entire offshore service delivery market (Figure 9.5).

Figure 9.5: BPO market size

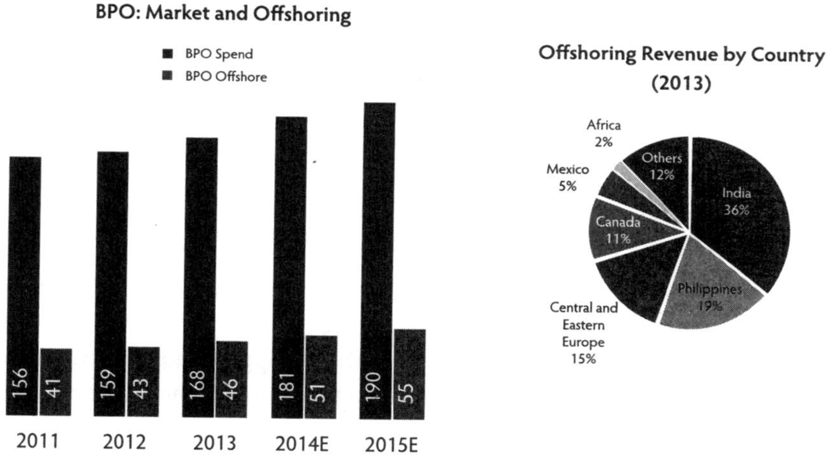

Source: Avasant research, NASSCOM

Besides these two countries, Canada, Mexico and certain Central and Eastern European countries (such as Poland and Russia) contributed 11 per cent, 5 per cent and 15 per cent, respectively, to the global BPO offshore service delivery market.

Global trends catalyzing growth of emerging and nascent destinations

the growth in offshoring of BPO services over the last decade has provided an opportunity to low-cost countries, also referred to as emerging or nascent destinations, to transform their socio-economic environment and catalyze economic growth (Low, 2013). More specifically, the trend has allowed emerging countries to significantly increase trade in these services, enhance export earnings, reduce youth unemployment, create a large number of jobs, catalyze foreign investments and increase the rate of GDP growth.

The governments of many emerging destinations have accorded priority status to the BPO sector, treating it as a strategic pillar of economic growth over the next decade. For countries like India and the Philippines, which have large educated workforces and low operating costs, the sector has become a significant contributor to export earnings, improving their balance of trade.

Between 2000 and 2004, the initial years of the BPO industry in India, the revenue from IT and BPO services grew threefold and service exports grew by 60 per cent. The offshoring industry accounted for a major part of the foreign exchange inflows in the country, directly providing employment to 700,000 people and indirectly to 2.5 million people. In 2013, the sector contributed 8 per cent to national GDP (Mitra, 2013) and became the largest private sector employer with 3.1 million employees. Further, the sector attracted US$2.4 billion in early stage start-up investments and contributed 38 per cent to service exports, the largest contribution by any sector (NASSCOM, 2014).

The Philippines, known for the availability of quality English voice capabilities, employed 400,000 people in its CIS industry in 2013 (Oxford Business Group, 2014). The CIS industry in the Philippines now contributes to 80 per cent of the BPO industry's earnings in the country. The sector exported US$13.2 billion in 2013, becoming the largest exporting sector. It is expected to achieve annual growth steadily at about 4.5 per cent until 2030, transforming the country to a one trillion-dollar economy.

Noting the significant socio-economic progress made by these leading destinations, many countries around the world are putting in place strategies to facilitate BPO sector growth. Global trends are also encouraging new pockets of offshore destinations to sprout.

- *Increasing direct costs in mature destinations:* Due to wage inflation and high employee attrition rates in more mature destinations, such as India and the Philippines, buyers and service providers are seeking new offshore locations. Wage inflation in mature offshore destinations is expected to rise annually between 7 and 11 per cent. In India, the attrition rate is expected to vary annually between 8 and 20 per cent (Figure 9.6).

Figure 9.6: Employee turnover rates in Indian companies

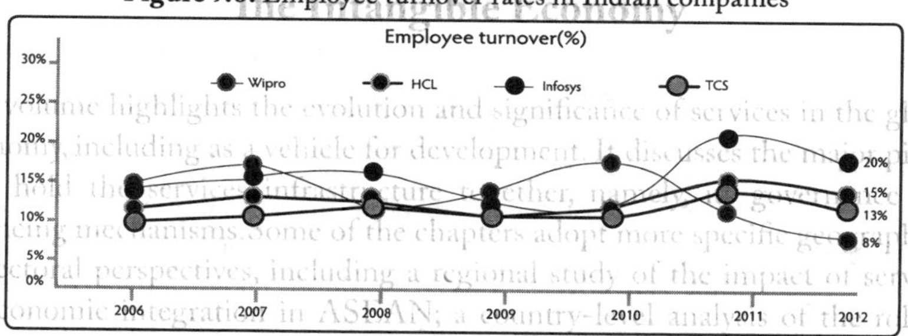

Source: The Economist

- *Mature locations are climbing the knowledge curve:* With experience and knowledge gained by firms in mature locations, service providers are focusing on climbing up the value chain and specializing in higher value-added processes. Small and medium-sized BPO buyers, who cannot afford the value-added services or the costs of more mature locations, increasingly prefer service providers from niche low-cost destinations.
- *Attempt to reduce separation costs:* Global BPO service providers are looking at increasing their near-shore presence (closer to the BPO buyer) to reduce business travel time, provide service in the same time zone and create a closer cultural match with buyer firms. This move is seen as an opportunity by many countries close to buyer geographies, like the Caribbean countries, to host such delivery centres.
- *Risk diversification:* BPO buyers are now more wary of putting all of their eggs in a single basket. Due to recent global political unrest, economic instability and terrorist threats, BPO buyers are exploring newer geographies to mitigate their service delivery risks. This is providing a window of opportunity to newer economies to compete effectively in the BPO market.
- *Increasing focus on specialization:* Buyers now prefer locations that have specialized talent pools. This increases their chances of being assured of a higher quality of service when compared to a country that has a more commoditized talent pool. For example, the Philippines is preferred for voice-based CIS processes because of its language and cultural similarities with US businesses. Similarly, other locations, such as Sri Lanka, Tunisia, South Africa and Argentina, are becoming increasingly respectively known for their capabilities in F&A and languages such as French, UK English and Portuguese.

Opportunities for emerging and nascent destinations

As mature destinations move up the BPO knowledge value chain, nascent and emerging destinations gain an opportunity to tap into the lower end of knowledge value chains (Figure 9.7). For a new location considering a strategic play in the BPO sector, it is more viable and effective to strengthen a select number of offerings rather than targeting a variety of transactional, operational or strategic processes of the knowledge value chain. This allows the country to effectively invest in skill development initiatives and better align the available talent pool to the needs of a particular business process. The following illustration depicts the adoption level and relative demand of BPO services from buyers.

Figure 9.7: BPO maturity curve

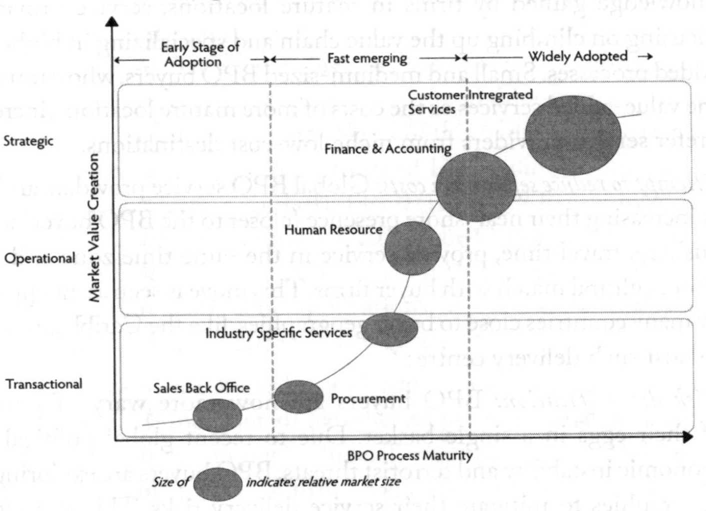

Source: Avasant research

The horizontal scale in Figure 9.7 represents the maturity of providers in delivering services, while the vertical scale reflects the maturity of the market as perceived by buyers. A mature process would imply that its sub-processes, especially at the operational and transactional levels, could be more easily procured from a delivery location with lower maturity.

A more mature BPO destination is expected to have capabilities across the value chain and is more likely to introduce newer processes than emerging destinations. A new delivery destination with limited service delivery capabilities is more likely to enter the market with services that focus on transactional and operational processes, as illustrated in Figure 9.8.

Figure 9.8: Entry point for nascent and emerging BPO destinations

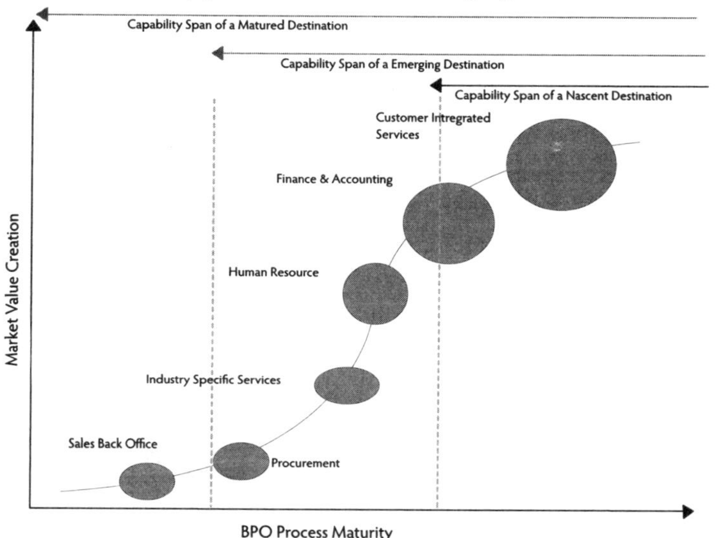

Source: Avasant research

Many countries in, for example, Africa and Latin America, that have strategic interests in the BPO sector, are actively looking at increasing their capabilities in selected niche and mature processes (Table 9.1).

Table 9.1: BPO process abilities of countries

Country	Maturity level	Processes targeted	Enabling factors	Number of BPO employees
South Africa	Emerging	CIS	Large pool of English speaking youth that need less accent neutralization	120,000
Ghana	Nascent	CIS, HRO, content development	Government support and policies to enable job creation for youth; enhancement of ICT infrastructure	3,500–5,000
Kenya	Nascent	CIS, F&A, CAD/CAM, transcription	Large pool of specialized professional services in the region, government support and policies to enable job creation for youth; enhancement of ICT infrastructure	4,000–6,000

Contd.

Country	Maturity level	Processes targeted	Enabling factors	Number of BPO employees
Egypt	Emerging	CIS, KPO	Large pool of educated youth and government support and policies to enable job creation for youth; enhancement of ICT infrastructure	43,000
Tunisia	Emerging	CIS, KPO	Large pool of French speaking population, closeness to Europe	25,000
Morocco	Emerging	CIS, F&A, HRO	Large pool of French speaking population, closeness to Europe	46,000
Mauritius	Nascent-Emerging	CIS, BFSI, specific services, legal process outsourcing (LPO), graphic design	Reputation as a financial hub and the best place to do business in Africa. Government support and policies to enable job creation for youth; enhancement of ICT infrastructure	7,600
Brazil	Emerging-Matured	KPO, back office, IT-BPO, integrated services, procurement	Large domestic market and closeness to the US	100,000
Mexico	Matured	CIS, F&A, HRO, procurement, sales, back office, creative services	Multilingual capabilities and large pool of educated youth. Government support and policies to enable job creation for youth; enhancement of ICT infrastructure	300,000
Colombia	Emerging	Back office, CIS, F&A, tech support, logistics, specific services	Multilingual capabilities and large pool of educated youth; government support and policies to enable job creation for youth; enhancement of ICT infrastructure	75,000

Source: Avasant research

Factors that make a delivery location attractive

Before a buyer decides to move to or explore new offshore BPO service delivery locations, a detailed assessment of the following factors is undertaken:

Operating costs: The attraction of a location is primarily associated with the cost advantages it offers in wages, training and recruitment, real estate, utilities, telecommunications, etc. Although wages form a large part of the operating costs, other costs can also impact the cost advantages of a particular location. For example, telecommunications costs form a large part of BPO operating costs in Trinidad and Tobago, whereas real estate makes up a large part of operating costs in South Africa. Although the affordability of operating costs is an important element of the BPO buyers' decision making processes, BPO buyers increasingly prefer service quality and reliability to direct cost advantages.

Talent Pool: The educational profile and scalability of a talent pool reflect a location's ability to offer and scale a particular set of business process services. The scalability of a location is assessed by the number of technical and non-technical school and university graduates. For certain low value-added tasks, even dropouts and unemployed youth can be considered. It is also important for a location to showcase an increase in annual graduate enrollment and demonstrate sufficient future scalability. The mix of the type of universities also dictates the type of services that can be offered from that location. For example, Sri Lanka has a high proportion of universities and training institutes offering accounting courses that are affiliated with the Chartered Institute of Management Accountants-UK. This enables Sri Lanka to be perceived as having a ready pool of graduates trained for F&A processes for UK firms. Similarly, India has 854,000 engineers and technical graduates, 900,000 science graduates and 3.3 million graduates in the arts, commerce and other disciplines. This is one of the reasons why India is seen as a location that can offer multiple scalable business process services.

Infrastructure: The infrastructure readiness of an offshore destination denotes a location's ability to provide high telecommunications bandwidth, flight connectivity with buyer locations, speed and comfort of travel within the location, the ability to adopt more advanced technologies and an overall positive experience in doing business in the country. Many leading destinations have sprawling business parks and technology campuses that house global service providers. Larger BPO service providers such as TCS and Infosys also have large campuses for training their employees. Emerging off-shoring destinations also offer incubation facilities with seating for 25 to 50 employees and communications bandwidth conforming to international standards.

Business Environment: The BPO industry ecosystem includes all external and internal factors that influence the daily operation of a business. These include:

- Political factors, such as government laws, regulations, tariffs and political stability
- Macroeconomic factors, such as interest rates, unemployment rates, currency exchange rates and inflation
- *Microeconomic factors*, such as market size, domestic demand and existence of global service providers
- *Technological factors*, such as mobile and smartphone penetration, ICT adoption in other sectors and usage of outsourcing by local industries, which are important factors that reduce the time needed for BPO awareness raising and marketing

Box 9.1: The Philippines – tackling unemployment through BPO

The Philippines has been able to reduce the BPO learning curve and create substantial employment and revenue through effective government intervention. The growth of the BPO industry has been phenomenal, and is currently employing over 700,000 people with over 350,000 in the call centre industry itself. The government is aiming to create 1.6 million jobs by 2016.

The government has played a key role in developing the sector:

Infrastructure – Next Wave Cities: Various government bodies have identified key cities based on comprehensive scoring mechanisms and have started developing the supporting infrastructure.

TOOL: An initiative to increase the number of capable managers in the BPO industry.

National Competency Assessment and Certification Program: Certification programme for entry-level talent in the BPO industry.

Scholarship programmes: The 'Training for Work Scholarship Program' (TWSP) has earmarked funds for the IT industry to provide educational and training grants for BPO applicants.

The Advance English Proficiency Training (AdEPT) program: It aims to improve English proficiency of the Filipino labour force.

BPO investment missions and conferences: Intensive marketing activities.

Lucrative investment environment: The government has been able to create a very healthy incentive policy.

Impact over five years

Contribution to GDP **4% – 5% of Annual GDP**

Employment generation

Growth of Next Wave Cities

Catalyzed growth of related industries in the service value chain

Source: Remulla and Medina (2012)

- Risk factors, such as social unrest, terrorism, climatic conditions and civil uprising

Government Support: This is a key element that impacts all of the above factors. Government supports international businesses by offering them incentives for setting up operations in the country. Government initiatives, such as skill and infrastructure development, also help enhance the supply capacity of an off-shore location. Policies, such as according the sector priority status, allocating budgets for development of the sector, putting in place legislation to protect intellectual property (IP) and having proactive telecommunications and infrastructure development policies, determine the attraction of a location. Buyers tend to be positively disposed towards a location if the government in the country ensures long-term support for the BPO sector. As an example, even though India and the Philippines had poor 'Ease of Doing Business'[1] rankings in the last decade (India's average was 131 in 2004-08 and 134 in 2009-13; the Philippines' average was 133 in 2004-08 and 108 in 2009-13), the BPO sector in both of these countries was among the largest and fastest growing throughout the world, mainly due to government support.

Strategizing government efforts

To make a country an attractive BPO service delivery destination, governments must focus on strengthening the factors that are important for the industry's growth (Sudan *et al.*, 2011). This requires competitive benchmarking of the country's capabilities in targeted areas with international best practices. A significant initiative should be undertaken to articulate and showcase the country's value proposition through a communications plan. A strategic roadmap should demonstrate a progressive advancement up the services value chain. Some of the initiatives that can be pursued are detailed below.

Reduction of capital and operational costs

Governments typically conduct a cost benchmarking exercise with other competing countries to identify opportunities for financial incentives (Figure 9.9 and Figure 9.10). In essence, the country assesses its operating costs for BPO services, including salary, training, infrastructure facilities, telecommunications and utilities costs.

As an example, assume the government belonging to Country 4 wants to

1 The World Bank's 'Ease of Doing Business' is an index that ranks some 185 economies in terms of requirements for setting up a business and a range of policy and institutional factors in the operating environment. Lower rankings indicate less business friendliness.

identify opportunities for fiscal incentives that will help its service providers gain further cost advantages. During assessment, it will compare its country's operating costs to its competitors' for three types of processes:

- Near-shore: to compare the cost effectiveness of offering more commoditized transactional services.
- Vertical focus: to compare the cost effectiveness of offering vertical-specific BPO services, like in the Banking, Financial Services and Insurance (BFSI) sector, with more specialized destinations.
- Horizontal focus: to compare the cost effectiveness of offering operational processes like F&A with destinations that have a scalable talent base in the particular process.

Figure 9.9: Benchmarking annual operating cost

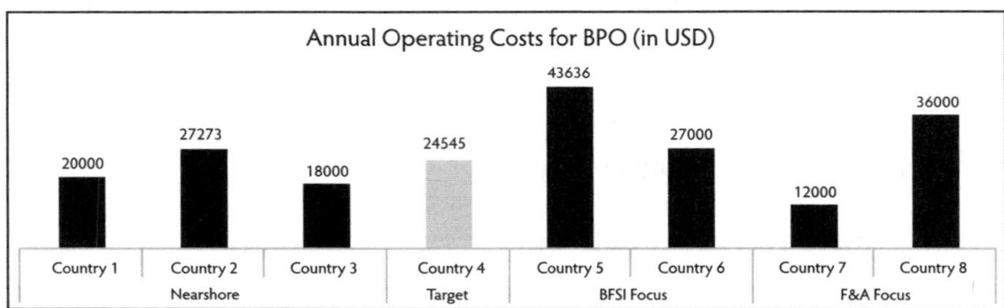

Source: Avasant research

As can be seen from the illustration, the target country in the study is about 10 per cent cheaper than the least economical near-shore competitor, about 10 per cent cheaper than the most economical vertical-specific services competitor and about 200 per cent costlier than the most economical horizontal (F&A) services competitor. As shown in Figure 9.10, the cost factors contributing to such differential are analysed in detail to identify cost reduction opportunities.

As can be seen in Figure 9.10, electricity costs are least competitive for Country 4. In order to circumvent that, the country's government will focus primarily on offering fiscal incentives for electricity costs. Detailed analyses of capital and operational costs help in identifying factors that need more targeted fiscal incentives.

Typically, fiscal incentives fall into the following categories:

- Skills: Reduction of taxable income based on the number of people trained by the BPO service provider. Sometimes, this incentive also considers the hiring costs.

Figure 9.10: Benchmarking annual operating costs (sub-components)

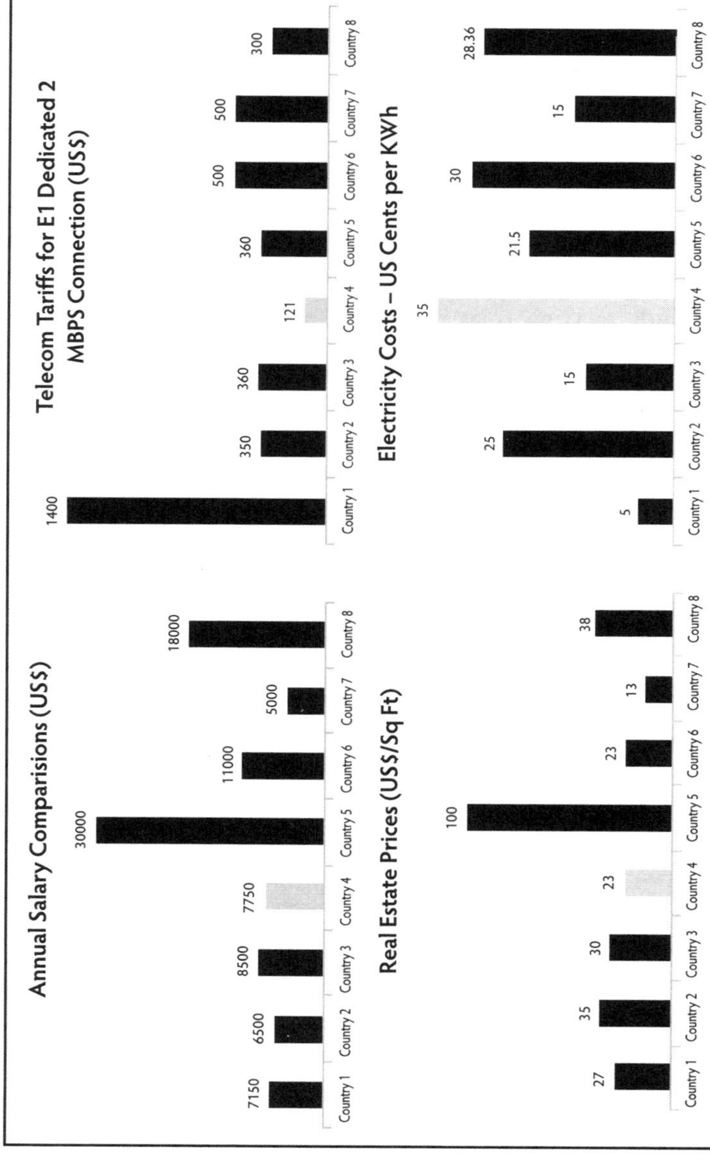

Source: Avasant research

- Taxes: Tax holidays for an initial period of 10 to 15 years of operation if the company is set up in an export zone. Other tax benefits include those on R&D expenditures and waiving withheld taxes. Box 9.2 provides an example in the case of India, where financial incentives play a significant role.
- Infrastructure: Taxes deducted based on a certain depreciation rate provided by the government on new construction or on computer hardware. There are also lease reductions in export units/economic zones.
- Telecommunications: Bandwidth and voice charges pre-negotiated with the utilities or telecommunications service providers at lower rates.

Others include relaxing rules regarding foreign shareholders, reducing interest rates on loans, easing venture capital availability and decreasing taxes on foreign currency.

Box 9.2: Financial incentives play a key role in growth of BPO industry in India

India's BPO industry has played a key role in putting the country on the world map. As one of the most significant contributors to growth, the BPO industry has played a significant role in transforming India's image from a slow-moving bureaucratic economy to a land of innovative entrepreneurs and a global player in providing excellent technology solutions and business services. The industry has helped India transform from a rural and agriculture-based economy to a knowledge-based economy.

Government initiatives:
After the economic reforms of 1991–92, the Government of India and the state governments provided major fiscal incentives, including the liberalization of external trade, elimination of duties on imports of IT products, relaxation of controls on both inward and outward investments and foreign exchange, setting up of export oriented units (EOU), Software Technology Parks (STP) and Special Economic Zones (SEZs), which enabled the country to flourish and acquire a dominant position in the worldwide BPO industry. In line with international practices, norms for the operations of venture capital funds have become liberalized to boost the industry. The Government of India is also actively providing fiscal incentives, liberalizing norms for FDI and raising capital abroad.

Financial assistance:
SEZs: They entitle domestic suppliers to duty entitlement pass book (DEPB) benefits for exports, central sales tax (CST), and service tax exemptions. Certain exemptions, like the income tax exemption on export profits, are available to SEZ units for the

Contd.

first five years, 50 per cent for the next two years and 50 per cent of ploughed-back profits for three years thereafter.

The Government of Karnataka provides capital investment subsidies of up to INR 20 lakh for a 100-seater BPO unit. Recurring financial support occurs in the form of an INR 5000 per employee subsidy to meet rent and internet connectivity costs. In addition to slashing internet charges by 50 per cent for BPO companies, the government also provides INR 10,000 per candidate for training.

The Government of Tamil Nadu has authorized a 15 per cent capital subsidy up to a maximum of INR 300,000 for BPO companies employing more than 100 people and operating for over three years. It has committed to contributing INR 1,500 per month for three months as part of its training subsidy for BPO companies.

R&D: A weighted deduction of 150 per cent of the expenditure on in-house R&D is exempted from income taxes.

Source: FICCI-India

Mapping skills and infrastructure initiatives to the BPO service

Maturity of a location

For a buyer of BPO services interested in off-shoring to a location, government support and initiatives aimed at enhancing the location decreasing taxes on foreign curremportant. Firstly, this encourages a buyer to invest in the location for the long term and develop it into a regional 'center of excellence', delivering business-critical services. In addition, with the advent of robotics, many lower-skill BPO processes are expected to be automated. Thus, upward mobility of a location through maturity is vital for the buyer to consider a long-term BPO investment.

A comparative analysis of talent and infrastructure readiness versus the BPO process maturity offers insight into the type of initiatives and incentives required to transform a country into a preferable delivery location, moving it to the next phase of maturity. This is illustrated in Figure 9.11 below:

Figure 9.11: BPO readiness and process maturity of countries

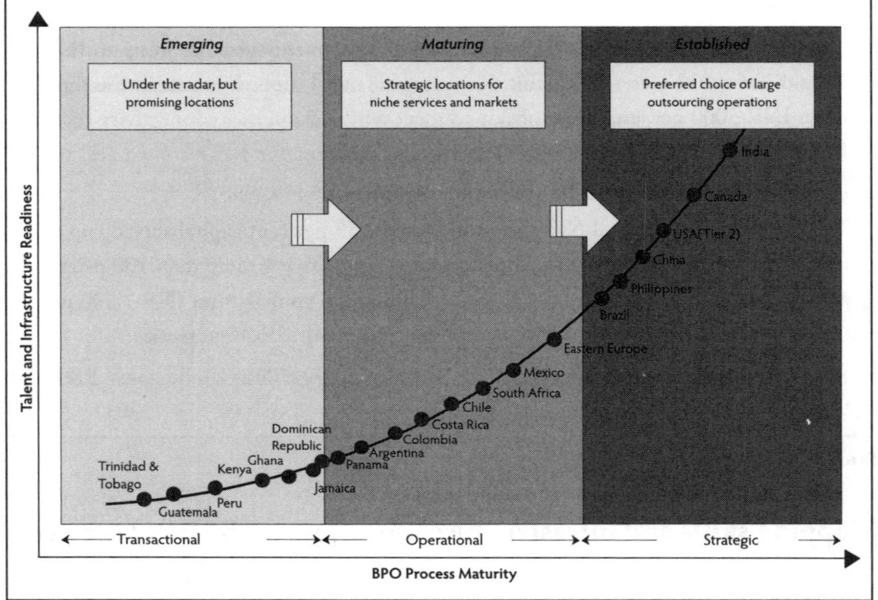

Source: Avasant research

Experts assess the talent and infrastructure readiness and BPO process maturity based on factors such as the graduate and non-graduate talent pool, youth population, language capability, availability of business and technology parks, and air travel connectivity. BPO process maturity is assessed on the number and type of service providers providing services to international clients from a particular location. There is a direct correlation between the BPO process maturity index and the talent and infrastructure index. If infrastructure in a country such as telecommunications bandwidth improves, it allows the country to service CIS and computer-aided design/computer-aided manufacturing (CAD/CAM) work that requires higher bandwidth. Similarly, when talent pool capabilities in a country develop, they enable locations to handle higher-end processes, thus allowing them to move up the value chain. These points are illustrated in Table 9.2 and Box 9.3 below.

Table 9.2: Sample talent pool and infrastructure initiatives for countries

	Transactional	Operational	Strategic
Talent pool initiatives	Skill training initiatives at a country-level that focus on teaching school and college students basic BPO competencies Ingrain basic school-level computer skills Launch train-the-trainer programmes and encourage entrepreneurship in the BPO training sector through public-private partnerships	Encourage certification courses that are widely accepted in the client's country (e.g., Chartered Institute of Management Accountants (CIMA) in the UK or Chartered Financial Analysts (CFA) in the US) Facilitate industry-university linkages	Facilitate university-industry linkages at higher level universities, specifically focused on R&D and subjects such as economics, business, and statistics Include courses on particular streams of business functions and technology, such as analytics and social media, in business schools
Infrastructure initiatives	Improve the affordability and bandwidth of international telecommunications networks Provide incubator facilities for international service providers to assess the location at the nascent stage of operations Enhance air travel connectivity and road infrastructure	Provide last-mile optical fibre access to service providers Set up export-oriented units/ business parks with an aim to house a number of BPO firms Enhance reliability of broadband Enhance road and air infrastructure	Further focus on increasing bandwidth availability Establish dedicated optical fibre ports for business parks Create public-private partnerships to encourage foreign investors and construction firms to invest

Source: Avasant research

Balancing capacity development and investment promotion

Striking a balance between supply-side service delivery capabilities and demand-side drivers for services is crucial in the effective implementation of a BPO sector growth strategy (Baldwin, 2013). The principal elements on the supply and demand sides are listed in Figure 9.12.

Figure 9.12: Balancing demand and supply-side initiatives

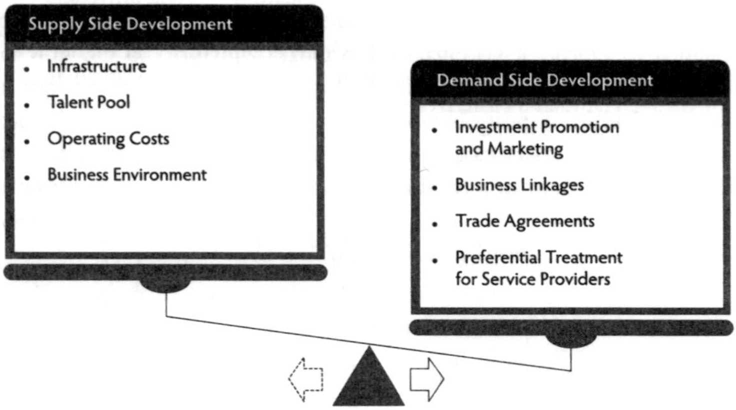

Supply Side Development
- Infrastructure
- Talent Pool
- Operating Costs
- Business Environment

Demand Side Development
- Investment Promotion and Marketing
- Business Linkages
- Trade Agreements
- Preferential Treatment for Service Providers

Source: Baldwin (2013) and Avasant research

Along with developing internal drivers, such as infrastructure and skills, it is important for a government to establish favourable business linkages with buyer countries to grow the BPO industry. Based on bilateral relationships, government should negotiate trade agreements that would provide service providers an impetus to market their services. The balance between capacity development and investment promotion is essential to ensure that a situation of under-utilized infrastructure, an over-supply of talent or disinterested investors does not occur.

Often, governments of emerging service delivery locations invite potential investors to consider their BPO sector before preparing a suitable business park or infrastructure that can house a scalable BPO operation. Such uncoordinated actions breed investors' disillusionment, which lead them to abort their evaluation processes.

Similarly, in order for capacity development initiatives to succeed, it is important to identify potential investors who would be keen to leverage the built capacity. In China, for example, there is a proliferation of ghost cities (or towns) that house many buildings constructed in anticipation of BPO sector growth that still remain unoccupied because of uncoordinated promotion and capacity building initiatives.

Figure 9.13 below provides a framework for implementing a synchronized investment and marketing platform:

Figure 9.13: A framework for investment promotion and marketing

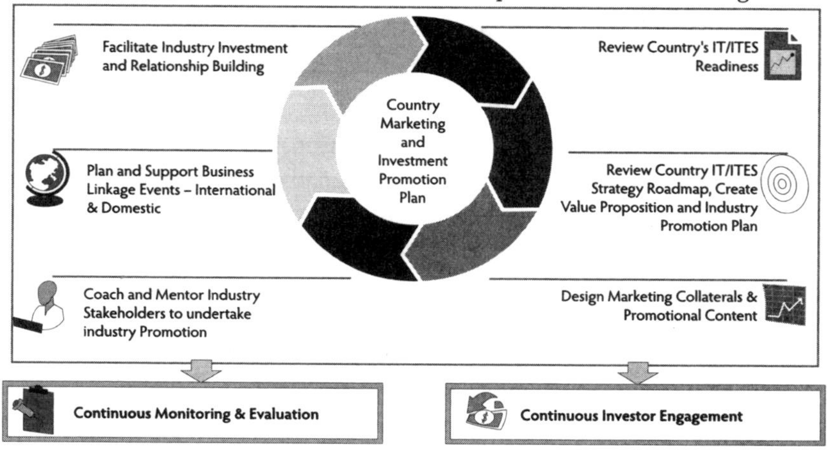

Facilitate Industry Investment and Relationship Building

Review Country's IT/ITES Readiness

Country Marketing and Investment Promotion Plan

Plan and Support Business Linkage Events – International & Domestic

Review Country IT/ITES Strategy Roadmap, Create Value Proposition and Industry Promotion Plan

Coach and Mentor Industry Stakeholders to undertake industry Promotion

Design Marketing Collaterals & Promotional Content

Continuous Monitoring & Evaluation

Continuous Investor Engagement

Source: Avasant research

- Review BPO readiness: It is of the utmost importance that a country's BPO readiness, both in terms of exporting services and attracting investments, is carefully assessed. This is helpful in identifying areas that can deliver quick results that enhance readiness while the promotion plan is created and implemented.
- Clearly identify the location's advantages and differentiators: The industry promotion plan must include the careful selection of target geographies, branding, public relations efforts, outreach initiatives and events.
- Design marketing collateral and promotional content: Marketing and branding activities in recent years have undergone drastic transformation. Digital marketing, social media, blogs, portals, interactive sites and newsletters have replaced some of the more traditional means of branding and marketing. It is critical to identify the optimal communication channel for each stakeholder group.
- Coach and mentor industry stakeholders to undertake industry promotion: With a long-term strategic perspective, it is important to continuously coach and mentor the government and industry stakeholders responsible for promoting the sector. This helps ensure that messaging is consistent while interacting with potential investors.

- Plan and support business linkage events: Business linkage events have been an integral part of industry promotion. They have shown high impact if executed properly with the right stakeholders at the right time. These events should be very structured with clearly stated objectives. Meticulous planning and preparation in terms of identifying the right invitees, timing (to maximize participation rates), planning for site visits, presentations and speakers play a very important role.
- Facilitate industry investment and relationship building: A successful investment promotion platform is developed on the foundation of strong relationships. Building and nurturing trust relationships is essential as large investments hinge on relatively long decision making cycles. It is also very important to continuously engage key industry influencers, such as rating and ranking agencies, so that they are aware of positive industry developments occurring in the country.

Investment promotion activities are medium to long-term engagements that require continuous market information and trends to align with market dynamics. The promotion plan needs to be a working document that is continually updated during the actual execution phase with ongoing monitoring and evaluation efforts that provide the essential pointers for effective governance and course correction.

Conclusion

The BPO industry has been growing globally at a tremendous pace and has a great potential to create jobs. The growth of the BPO sector in India and the Philippines has resulted in 1.3 million direct jobs and about four million indirect jobs. The sector has employed people ranging from the minimally educated to PhD holders having specialized domain or industry knowledge. As mature service delivery destinations become less economically viable due to escalating costs or focus on higher-value services, opportunities are created for countries in emerging locations to increase their share of trade in BPO services.

Realizing this opportunity, governments of many low-cost countries have identified the BPO sector as one of the key economic growth engines driving the socio-economic development. To ensure that a country's limited resources are effectively deployed to realize these goals, a planned approach to develop capacity in the country and marketing its value proposition is essential. Government must proactively support the growth of the industry through various policy initiatives and incentives, including the following initiatives:

- Enhance and mature its service delivery capacities and competitiveness
- Reduce capital and operational costs and
- Create business linkages with buyers of BPO services from target countries

References

ABS-News. 2014. 'Linkages with Buyers of BPO Shouldn't Get Complacent'. Available at: http://www.abs-cbnnews.com/business/05/26/14/why-philippines-bpo-industry-shouldnt-get-complacent.

Avasant. 2012. cbnnews.com/business/05/26/14/why-philippines-bpo-industry-shouldnt-get. Available at: http://www.avasant.com/press-release/Avasant-releases-Impact-Sourcing-Report.

Baldwin, Richard. 2013. 'Global Supply Chains: Why They Emerged, Why They Matter and Where They are Going', in *Global Value Chains in a Changing World*, edited by Deborah K. Elms and Patrick Low. Geneva: World Trade Organization.

Cyber Media Publications. 2008. 'Outsourcing to Africa'.

Federation of Indian Chambers of Commerce and Industry. 2013. 'Information Technology Sector Overview', Federation of Indian Chambers of Commerce and Industry working paper on Information Technology Sector Status. Available at: http://www.ficci.com/sector/21/project_docs/ficci_website_content_-it.pdf.

Gereffi, Gary and Karina Fernadez-Stark. 2010. *The Offshore Services Global Value Chain*.Mimeo. Durham, North Carolina: Center on Globalization, Governance and Competitiveness, Duke University.

Low, Patrick. 2013. 'The Role of Services in Global Value Chains', in *Global Value Chains in a Changing World*, edited by Deborah K. Elms and Patrick Low. Geneva: World Trade Organization.

Mitra, Raja Mikael. 2013. 'The Information Technology and Business Process Outsourcing Industry: Diversity and Challenges in Asia', *Asian Development Bank Economics Working Paper Series*. Manila: Asian Development Bank.

NASSCOM (The National Association of Software and Services Companies). 2013. *The IT-BPM Sector in India –Strategic Review*. Available at: http://www.nasscom.in/itbpm-sector-india-strategic-review-2013.

NASSCOM. 2014. *The IT-BPM Sector in India Strategic Review*. Available at: http://www.nasscom.in/itbpm-sector-india-strategic-review-2014.

NASSCOM-EVEREST India BPO Study. 2012. *Roadmap 2012 - Capitalizing on the*

Expanding BPO Landscape. Available at: http://www.everestgrp.com/wp-content/uploads/2012/08/.

Oxford Business Group. 2014. content/uploads/2012/08/d Available at: http://www.oxfordbusinessgroup.com/news/philippines%E2%80%99-revenues-bpo-set-rise-15-2014.

Parikh, Kevin (Esq.) and Pradeep Kumar Mukherjee. 2013. 'New Horizons of Business Process Out-sourcing in Africa, Latin America & Caribbean'. Available at: http://www.amazon.com/Horizons-Business-Process-Outsourcing-Caribbean/dp/1492183423.

Remulla, Marriel M. and Grace M. Medina. 2012. 'Measuring the Contribution to the Philippine Economy of Information Technology-Business Process Outsourcing (IT-BPO) Services'. Available at: http://www.bsp.gov.ph/downloads/publications/2012/bs12_a1.pdf

SLASSCOM (Sri Lanka Association for Software and Services Companies) and PWC. 2012. *Finance and Accounting Outsourcing Sector of Sri Lanka*. SLASSCOM Publications.

Sudan, Randeep, Seth Ayers, Philippe Dongier, Siou Chew Kuek, Arturo Muente Kunigami, Christine Zhen-Wei Qiang and Sandra Sargent. 2011. *The Global Opportunity in IT-Based Services: Increasing Country Competitiveness*. The World Bank. Available at: http://siteresources.worldbank.org/EXTINFORMATIONANDCOMMUNICATIONANDTECHNOLOGIES/Resources/282822-1208273252769/The_Global_Opportunity_in_IT-Based_Services.pdf.

UNCTAD. 2008. *Globalization for Development: The International Trade Perspective*. New York: United Nations.

10

Services in Global Value Chains and the Impact of Policy

Denise Cheung and David Sit

Introduction

The growing importance of services has been one of the most significant trends in the global economy in the last few decades. In high-income countries,[1] the value-added service sector accounted for 74 per cent of GDP in 2011. The dominance of the service sector is not unique to developed economies. Its shares in middle-income, low-income and least developed countries are also significant, amounting respectively to 53 per cent, 49 per cent and 43 per cent. Services are similarly important to employment. Approximately 45 per cent of jobs in the world in 2010 were in the service sector. In high-income countries, this figure reaches 74 per cent.

The importance of the service sector to the world economy has been reinforced by the rise of GVCs. With advances in telecommunications, transportation and IT, services can now be imported from distant locations with cost advantages. Service suppliers in developing countries, such as call centre service providers, can now access the world market by taking part in GVCs. Moreover, services are consumed by manufacturing firms as intermediate inputs to goods, contributing significant value to final goods. According to TiVA statistics jointly compiled by the OECD and the WTO, service inputs account for 47.7 per cent of the value of gross exports in goods of OECD countries. Even this figure likely underestimates the value of services in trade because services provided in-house in manufacturing firms that are not supplied on an arms-length basis, will not be separately identified in the statistics.

1 Source of data: World Development Indicators, World Bank. Classification of income level follows World Bank definitions.

In this chapter, we intend to further our understanding of the linkage between services and manufacturing in a GVC context by analysing the experiences of Singapore and Thailand, drawing on insights from value chain level case studies conducted by the authors and their colleagues.

The next section discusses current literature on the relationship between the services and manufacturing sectors. The subsequent section sets out the various ways through which policy may influence services in manufacturing value chains, making reference to illustrations from case studies conducted by the authors and their colleagues. The last section explores policies in Singapore and Thailand, which have different economic structures and policy backdrops, in an attempt to set out government best practices for enhancing value addition of services in manufacturing GVCs.

Tracing the relationship between services and manufacturing

the majority of the existing literature focuses on the quantitative relationship between the services and manufacturing sectors. Multi-national datasets, national data and firm-level data are used to evaluate how services are associated with growth, productivity, and employment in manufacturing sectors, as well as national economies as a whole.

With an OECD panel dataset of 78 countries spanning 1994 to 2004, Francois and Woerz (2008) examined the effect of service inputs into manufacturing sectors in countries across income levels. In particular, they studied the service value embedded in manufacturing exports, and how policy in service sectors may affect manufacturing exports. Through panel data regressions, they confirmed the growing importance of producer services in the manufacturing sector since the 1990s. Pilat and Wolfl (2005) worked with international input-output tables and found strong evidence pointing to services as manufacturing inputs. They also found that 50 per cent of employment in manufacturing sectors can be classified as services. Guerrieri and Meliciani (2005) discovered that industrial composition may help to shape a country's service sector portfolio, and thus, its international specialization and competitiveness, confirming the mutual influence between manufacturing and services. Through regression analysis, Azad (1999) found a statistically strong linkage between services and goods production sectors in Bangladesh, suggesting a strong linkage between the two sectors, even in the least developed countries.

Changing policy regimes in services may affect manufacturing sectors in different ways. Using national firm surveys in the Czech Republic and India, Arnold et al. (2011, 2012) examined the effects of changes in government policy regimes for manufacturing-related service sectors. Firm-level datasets in both countries suggest that service sector reforms benefit productivity in manufacturing firms. In the Czech Republic, service sector liberalization was the key contributor to productivity in manufacturing firms. In India, one standard deviation improvement in policy reform in the banking, telecommunications, and transportation sectors was found to improve the productivity of manufacturing sectors respectively by 6.6 per cent, 8.4 per cent, and 18.8 per cent. Banga and Goldar (2007) also found that Indian trade reform in the 1990s allowed the service sector to contribute more significantly to growth and productivity in the manufacturing sector, as well as boosting the overall use of services in Indian manufacturing. Francois and Woerz (2008) found producer services liberalization contributed to exports, value addition, and employment in manufacturing, notably in technology-intensive sectors. Clemes, Gani and Arifa (2003) studied the linkage between the manufacturing and service sectors in Asia, and found positive spillover effects in both directions. Fernandes and Panuov (2011) and Okeyo *et al.* (2014) found similar results respectively in Chile and Kenya. Policymakers and business leaders need to adopt a holistic view on both sectors when examining alternatives and contemplating decisions.

A relatively neglected issue in existing literature is how policy – its existence or non-existence, its design, and its efficiency in implementation – may impact services in manufacturing GVCs. This chapter aims to contribute towards filling this gap. The country and value chain case studies reported below provide examples of what governments can do to increase the value addition of the manufacturing sector by improving the provision of services, or will provide examples of how poorly conceived policies or neglected options may adversely affect value in the manufacturing sector.

Policies affecting services along the value chain

Policy interventions affecting services in value chains are usually imposed by government authorities in pursuit of public policy objectives. Public policy is essential in catering to various kinds of socially desirable outcomes that individual firms or unfettered markets cannot supply by themselves. In this sense, they may be conceived as a source of value addition. If government services are efficiently supplied, they represent pure social benefit. If the services (regulations) are imposed in an unnecessarily costly manner or are inessential, they can impart negative value. The following analysis of these issues is drawn from a series of case studies conducted by the authors and their colleagues at the Fung Global Institute.[2] These case studies illustrate the key role played by governments, with respect to services entering manufacturing value chains.

Services and public policy in value chains

a case study on a simple value chain – for a loaf of bread – highlights both the role of services in manufacturing and the impact of policy on operations. The loaf of bread in question is manufactured in Shenzhen and sold in Hong Kong, beginning with the procurement of ingredients and ending with the sale of the bread loaf to the consumer. The bread produced in the lead firm's Shenzhen factory is trucked across the border daily to the firm's Hong Kong warehouse, and then distributed to the lead firm's shops across Hong Kong several times a day.

No less than 30 services are required in this operation, accounting for more than 72 per cent of the final cost of the loaf of bread. Service inputs are required at all stages of the production and marketing stages of the value chain, including the importation of ingredients, in-factory operations, transport and related services, distribution and retail services, and business processes (back-office services). This intensity and range of service inputs is commonplace in manufacturing value chains. Each of the services involved will be affected in some way or another by an interface with policy. Policy can, therefore, affect the configuration, location, and operation of value chains in numerous ways. Often, however, relatively few policies impose a significant impact in particular cases.

In the bakery value chain, much of the public policy service input involved in compliance is attributable to China's safety standards on food production. The Guangdong Entry-Exit Inspection and Quarantine Bureau (GDCIQ) inspects the factory once a month (inspection service), and requires that the company regularly send food samples to GDCIQ (back-office service) for laboratory tests (testing and certification service). Moreover, every batch of exported bread is tested by GDCIQ officials at the border (quality assurance service). There is also management involved in relationship building with the officials (management service). Finally, apart from services directly employed or paid for by the firm, excessive compliance procedures also lead to the use of additional government services, such as inspection and document approval.

2 The Fung Global Institute was renamed the Asia Global Institute on 1 July 2015 and became a Centre at the University of Hong Kong.

The firm in this case study had mixed feelings about China's stringent food safety standards. Although compliance with the standards significantly increased production costs, the firm deemed stringent standards to be essential for the reputation of its products, and hence, a source of value.

Another major policy area that comes with expensive compliance costs is environmental policy in China. Being one of the designated companies for Shenzhen's pilot Carbon Emissions Trading Scheme, the bakery firm was subject to annual emission caps. The firm was required to keep detailed records (accounting and bookkeeping services) of its energy use for government inspection (auditing service). If the firm exceeded its designated cap, it could purchase surplus permits on the China Emissions Exchange (financial service).

Overall, the firm estimated that compliance costs associated with activities in China added some 10 to 20 per cent to production costs. This figure is large and it suggests that there is likely to be potential for efficiency improvements on the policy side that would feed through into increased productivity.

In addition to inefficiencies arising from poor design, excessive administrative costs, or poor governance, an unnecessary 'multi-layering' of policy-induced services inputs can also can be a source of unwarranted additional cost. The way customs services are operated in some jurisdictions exemplifies this problem. In several value chains that the authors had studied, the appointment of customs agencies specified by local customs officials was a mandatory requirement. Deficiencies in the organization of customs services mean that these agents become essential for the smooth and timely clearance of goods. These agencies are often handpicked by local customs officials with little transparency, potentially imposing yet further unjustified costs upon import and export transactions.

Moreover, the quality of customs services can vary among different checkpoints within a country. To alleviate the risk of delay arising from customs clearance procedures, one of the firms interviewed chose to route its goods through a distant customs checkpoint rather than the local one. The rerouting led to the use of extra services, such as inland transport and logistics services.

Duplicative public policy requirement

as GVCs cross borders, firms have to comply with requirements from the different countries that are included in the value chains. This multiplies the impact of red tape. One obvious example is the need for the bread value chain to comply with food safety regulations of both China and Hong Kong. Fortunately for the bakery firm, Hong Kong's food safety regulations are relatively simple. Under its regular surveillance programme, the Centre for Food Safety takes random samples of food at both the border and retail outlets in Hong Kong for laboratory testing.

Overlapping standards regimes, as imposed by different countries and different levels of government within these countries, are particularly costly for the toy and infant product industry. An infant feeding bottle value chain, where products were manufactured in China and sold overseas, illustrates the situation. As the products were mainly sold in the US, Canadian, EU, Australian and New Zealand markets, they had to conform to standards and labelling requirements in these markets. They also had to comply with standards in China, including National Standards (Guobiao, known as GB in short) and China Compulsory Certification (CCC),[3] both of which are mandatory for products manufactured in China. When a company wants to sell their products in China to test the waters of the Chinese market, they are also subject to the National Industrial Product Manufacturing License (Quality Safety (QS))[4] regulations. A long list of services including laboratory testing, factory inspection, and the auditing and filing of documentation are involved in complying with the regulations. In this case study, standard conformity procedures for a new product typically required four months or more to complete, and considerable additional spending on testing and certification services.

Policy supporting services innovation

if it is designed with the right targets and incentive structure, policy can provide incentives for innovation. An example is the Carbon Emissions Trading

3 CCC applies to 23 product categories covering more than 400 harmonized system (HS) codes regulating both locally manufactured products (intended for domestic and export markets), and imported goods that are intended to be sold in Chinese markets. It makes reference to GB standards, but comes with much stricter enforcement.

4 The rules of QS implementation were published by the General Administration of Quality Supervision, Inspection and Quarantine (AQSIQ) of the People's Republic of China in 2014. The rules regulate production of 62 categories of products, including products that would come in direct contact with food and, therefore, apply to toddler bottles, which the company sold in China. For goods in the covered categories, the rules required manufacturers to comply with official requirements in staff qualification, manufacturing procedures, quality standards, environmental protection, and other relevant rules and regulations that apply to each of the categories, as long as they are manufactured for domestic sale in China. A qualified product was awarded a 'QS' label and a 12 digit product code in the national database that is available to consumers online.

Scheme, as discussed above. In order to stay within its emission cap, the firm had to improve its equipment and processes in the first year. These included simple manoeuvres, such as improving the insulation of ovens to reduce air-conditioning costs. However, if the caps are tightened every year, it is unclear whether the firm would have enough room to improve energy efficiency. If not, it may resort to buying emission permits from the carbon exchange in the future.

Government incentives

Governments often provide incentives for engaging in high value-added services. For example, a high-tech manufacturing firm in Thailand enjoyed the exemption of import duty on machinery and raw materials, as well as a time-limited corporate income tax exemption upon establishment. The incentives are part of Thailand's activity-based incentives programme, which grants additional corporate income tax exemptions to manufacturing firms that undertake projects on a number of high value-added activities, including R&D in technology and innovation, advanced technology training, intellectual property acquisition/ licensing fees for commercializing technology developed in Thailand, and product packaging and design. Such incentives may induce firms to engage in high value services, which they would otherwise outsource or undertake in other countries.

Investment in infrastructure

The availability of certain services may be dictated by the existence or quality of infrastructure in the area. IT and transportation services are obvious examples. To an apparel firm that has its manufacturing facilities in Indonesia, road and airfreight were the only feasible freight transportation options. The firm was forced to use trucking, which was extremely slow, as the primary means to transport its goods. In the case of an urgent order, the firm had no choice but to employ airfreight transport, which is extremely expensive.

Policy leading to the outsourcing of services

cost minimization has long been a reason for outsourcing. Whilst this is the case for most of the outsourced services in the bakery value chain discussed above, the outsourcing of certain services is also necessitated by policy. Case studies conducted by the authors and their colleagues revealed that whilst efficiency or cost routinely accounted for half of the outsourcing decisions, a non-negligible proportion of services in the value chains were outsourced for policy reasons. The case studies illustrated five different ways through which government policy necessitates outsourcing.

First, policy may mandate outsourcing because the service provider is required to be independent in order to fulfill the policy intent. Examples are independent financial auditing, as well as auditing with respect to International Organization for Standardization (ISO) and standards for Hazard Analysis Critical Control Point (HACCP). Second, governments may require that certain mandatory services be obtained from a list of government-approved firms. This is usually the case for testing and certification services, for which strict licensing may be required in order to ensure the capability and integrity of the service provider. This can be a problem if the licensing criteria are arbitrary, or when the bar is set too high so that otherwise qualified service providers are shut out. Third, governments may be the most appropriate provider of certain services. An example from this value chain is social insurance, which includes worker's compensation, medical insurance, and pensions.

Fourth, constraints on trade in services, such as through restrictions on foreign investment or labour mobility, often compel firms to outsource to foreign firms. In a Chinese solar panel manufacturing value chain, the company had to commission a local contractor in the UK to build the power plant and install the modules there, due to difficulties in obtaining work permits for its own engineers. The company estimated that outsourcing to a UK firm had doubled its cost of building the power plant.

Finally, firms may be compelled to outsource because established relationships with government officials are crucial to getting things done. In the case of the bakery value chain, an external agent is hired to handle transactions with customs to smoothen out the procedures and process overall.

Government best practises

The discussion above has briefly documented various ways in which policy can exert influence on GVCs, in particular through services activities. This section takes a closer look at two Asian economies in an attempt to extract government best practices that facilitate the value addition of services in manufacturing GVCs.

First, we look at how the Singaporean Government has built an ecosystem in which its services and manufacturing sectors can form symbiotic relationships, how world-class business services facilitate the operation of manufacturing firms, and how a thriving manufacturing sector generates demand for services. Next, we discuss how Thailand has upgraded its manufacturing sector towards higher value-added manufacturing activities by enhancing its service components.

Singapore: Building an ecosystem for co-development of services and manufacturing sectors

singapore's economy is supported by both its services and manufacturing sectors. Value addition of services accounts for 73 per cent of GDP, with 70 per cent of jobs attributed to services in 2013. The same numbers for manufacturing respectively account for 19 per cent and 15 per cent. For the past five decades, the Singaporean Government has maintained a supportive role in the development of business and manufacturing services, with various industrial policies including subsidies, tax benefits, or direct provision of such services through government departments, statutory bodies, and government-linked companies (GLCs).[5] The result is a robust services sector and a manufacturing sector focusing on high value-added industries.

As a market economy with significant government intervention, Singapore has achieved its policy targets through various measures. Active government policy is central to its economic strategy. An example of these policies is the 'headquarters programme', which offers tax deductions for companies that establish global or regional headquarters in Singapore. The Economic Development Board (EDB) drafted the list of requirements, including specific headquarter services, that companies are required to meet in order to relocate to Singapore. These include the operation scale of the business, as well as a corporate annual income requirement that qualifies them for an annual concessionary tax rate of 15 per cent for a maximum of five years (EDB, 2014).

The linkage between the services and manufacturing sectors is strong. First, a rough estimate on the services that are most directly related to manufacturing projection[6] jointly account for approximately 58 per cent of the value-added of all of the services produced in Singapore and 42 per cent of GDP in 2013.[7]

---

5 GLCs in Singapore are government controlled companies, where the Singaporean Government owns the majority shares. However, the operation of these companies is left in the hands of professional managers who run the companies on a profit basis. Hence, inefficiency in state owned enterprises (SOEs) is seldom found in Singapore GLCs.

6 Includes business services, transportation and storage, information and communications, finance and insurance, utilities and constructions.

7 GDP by industry, Singapore statistics.

Second, input-output (I-O) tables estimate how outputs of sectors are used as inputs by other sectors. The 2010 I-O table prepared by the Singaporean Government estimated that services account for 36 per cent of all domestic intermediate inputs consumed by the city-state's manufacturing sector.

In 2007, total domestics and imported services inputs represented 23 per cent of all inputs consumed in Singapore's manufacturing sector. The proportion of services inputs, as exhibited in Figure 10.1, is along the lines of other OECD countries which ranged from 18 to 57 per cent, with a median of 29 per cent in the mid-2000s.[8] The linkage of Singapore's services and manufacturing sector is comparable to other OECD industrial economies.

Figure 10.1: Total input consumed in manufacturing sectors, Singapore and selected OECD countries

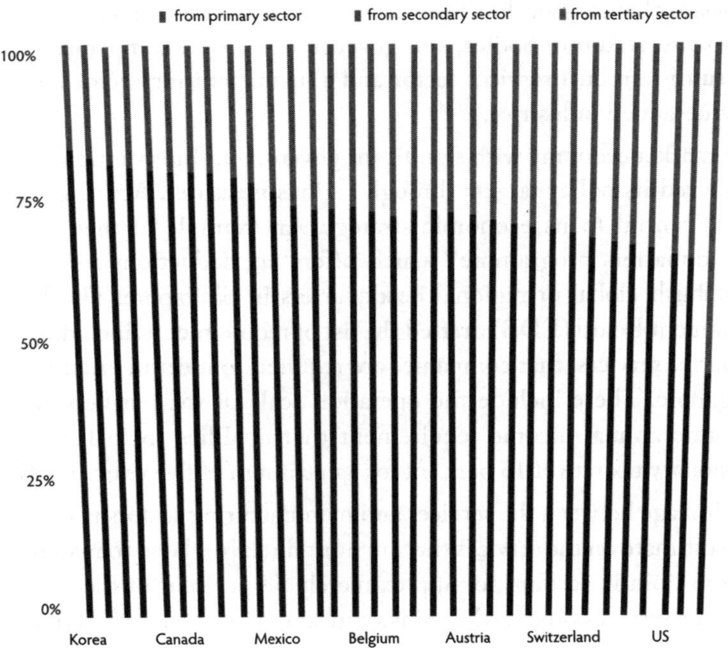

Source: OECD countries' data extracted from OECD STAN Input-Output Database; Singapore data compiled from Singapore Input-Output table 2007 by SingStat. Diagram compiled by authors.

8 OECD countries' data extracted from OECD Structural Analysis Database (STAN) I-O database; Singapore data compiled from Singapore Input-Output table 2007 by SingStat. Data compiled by authors.

Development of human capital in Singapore has been one of the key factors to the success of Singapore's manufacturing and service sectors. Ever since its independence, the Singaporean Government has been devoting resources on nurturing quality labour to support economic development. Early in the 1960s, the Singaporean Government expanded primary and secondary education to support the rising manufacturing sector in the city-state. Large scale expansion of technical colleges and universities in the 1960s and 1970s provided skilled labour required by the city for development of higher value-added manufacturing sectors. University programmes expanded heavily, particularly in the 1980s. The number of university graduates tripled between 1980 and 1989. In particular, the number of engineer graduates grew eightfold between 1978 and 1988. MNCs were also invited in partnership with government agencies to set up training centres for workers (Tan, 1997). Since the 1990s, the Singaporean government had taken a holistic approach to human capital development in the country. The arrangement involves different stakeholders, including employers, labour, and government in national human capital development strategies. Government agencies work with the private sector to provide government-funded programmes to develop the skills of their workers. The multi-departmental approach consolidates resources and planning in different government departments to achieve national human capital development goals, headed by the Ministry of Manpower. This goal, highlighted in Manpower 21 blueprints, aims to develop Singapore's human capital to meet the needs of a knowledge economy with upgraded skills and knowledge (Osman-Gani, 2004). In 2014, over 50 per cent of labour in Singapore held diploma or professional qualifications/degrees, or above.[9] Human capital development policies evolve with the changing economy.

The Singaporean government also subsidizes R&D activities, which are pivotal both for the country as a whole, and for the enterprises settling there. The government has committed more than 16.1 billion Singapore dollars (SGD) to R&D between 2011 and 2015, which amounts to 1 per cent of the expected GDP ((Research Innovation Enterprise (RIE) Secretariat, 2011). Money is granted to universities, research institutes, and enterprises through various funding or co-investment schemes. The results have been successful and can be measured by patent applications per million of the population. Singapore ranked thirteenth out of 144 countries in the World Economic

9 Ministry of Manpower, Singapore. http://stats.mom.gov.sg/Pages/Labour-Force-Summary-Table.aspx.

Forum global competitiveness report of 2014–15. An example of a successful sector which benefits from the national R&D policy is the biomedical industry, whose contribution to GDP grew from 3.6 per cent in 2008 to 4.9 per cent in 2012.[10]

A fundamental element to the success of Singapore's economy is a fair legal system for commercial transactions. The common law system permits Singapore to remain at par with other nations in attracting MNCs. Singapore is ranked consistently high in terms of its legal system in the World Economic Forum Global Competitiveness Reports. In the 2014–15 edition, Singapore ranked top in terms of the efficiency of its legal framework in settling disputes and fairly high in judicial independence (twenty out of 144 countries/territories). Legal services are key to Singapore's economic success.

Singapore has a robust and effective legal system for the protection of IP. Established in 2001, the Intellectual Property Office of Singapore (IPOS),, under the Ministry of Law, provides advice and administers the country's IP framework, with the aim of maintaining a solid ecosystem to support IP (IPOS, 2014). As a result, Singapore ranks high internationally in IP protection. In a recent index by the U.S. Chamber of Commerce that ranks international IP, Singapore scored fifth place out of 30 major economies, and first in Asia. Protection of IP rights, itself a service, helps Singapore develop a high value-added manufacturing sector.

The provision of key infrastructure is essential to the development of industries. Jurong Town Corporation (JTC) plans, constructs, and operates industrial facilities for targeted manufacturing and services sectors. For example, three logistic parks with ready-made facilities were constructed and provided by JTC to third-party logistics operators to support the development of the logistics industry.

The Singaporean Government also operates directly in industries that are considered strategic to national security or stability, as well as those with good economic prospects. The former industries include telecommunications (SingTel), mass media (MediaCorp) and transportation (Singapore Airlines). For the latter group, the government usually serves as a pioneering investor to develop the necessary industrial foundations, such as shipbuilding and repairs in the 1960s, electronics and wafer fabrication factories in the 1970s to the 1980s; and, more recently, in the biomedical industry (Wong and Ng, 1997).

10 SPRING Singapore and Economic Development Board. http://www.spring.gov.sg/developing-industries/bhs/pages/statistics-biomedical-and-healthcare-services.aspx.

Thailand: Upgrading of the manufacturing sector by enhancing service provisions

in Thailand, the service sector dominates the economy. In 2012, the services, manufacturing, agriculture, and quarrying and mining sectors respectively made up 56 per cent, 28 per cent, 12 per cent and 3 per cent of GDP.[11] The importance of the manufacturing sector gradually climbed from 25 per cent of GDP in 1992 to 28 per cent in 2012.[12]

Thailand's manufacturing sector has shifted from lower value-added products, such as textiles, apparel, and furniture; to higher value-added products, including motor vehicles, computers, and machinery and equipment. The top product categories, by value-added, in 1992 and 2012 are shown in Table 10.1. Of all of the top product categories in 1992, only food products and beverages were still in the top five by 2012.

Industrial policy has played an important role in the upgrading of the Thai manufacturing sector along and between value chains (Humphrey and Schmitz, 2000). The Thai Government started adopting industrial policy in the 1960s with the use of tariff barriers to promote the manufacturing sector. In the 1970s through the early 2000s, focus turned to preferential policies for inward FDI in export-oriented industries. Partly attracted by the policy incentives, and partly forced by increasing production costs in established regional manufacturing hubs, multinational enterprises relocated many production lines to Thailand, resulting in the rapid development of higher value-added industries, including motor vehicles, chemicals, electronics, and electrical appliances (Hiratsuka, 2011).

Table 10.1: Top product categories in 1992 and 2012

	1992		**2012**	
	Rank	**% of total value-added of the Thai manufacturing sector**	**Rank**	**% of total value-added of the Thai manufacturing sector**
Food products and beverages	1	23	1	20
Textiles	2	11	(Not in top 5)	

Contd.

11 Office of the National Economic and Social Development Board.

12 Ibid.

	1992		2012	
	Rank	**% of total value-added of the Thai manufacturing sector**	**Rank**	**% of total value-added of the Thai manufacturing sector**
Furniture; manufacturing n.e.c.	3	7	(Not in top 5)	
Apparel	4	6	(Not in top 5)	
Other non-metallic mineral products	5	6	(Not in top 5)	
Motor vehicles	(Not in top 5)		2	11
Office, accounting and computing machinery	(Not in top 5)		3	7
Chemicals and chemical products	(Not in top 5)		4	7
Machinery and equipment	(Not in top 5)		5	7

Source: Office of the National Economic and Social Development Board

Furthermore, there is evidence that Thailand's manufacturing sector has been undergoing functional upgrading—moving toward higher value-added functions. Elementary occupations account for only 9 per cent of employment in the manufacturing sector (Table 10.2). Labour productivity in manufacturing achieved real average growth of 3.1 per cent per annum since 2000. Figure 10.2 shows the productivity indices of all sectors ('integrated index'), as well as those of selected industries that are leaders in productivity growth. Among those, we shall discuss the food and beverage industry in more detail below.

Figure 10.2: Labour productivity of selected leading industries

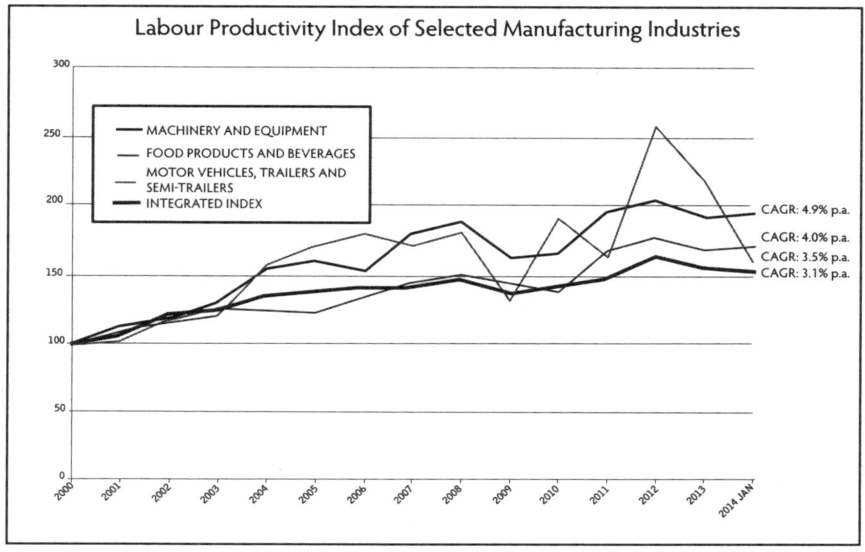

Source: Office of Industrial Economics, authors' calculation.

Another indication of the role of services in Thailand's manufacturing sector is from the employment data (Table 10.2). Many of the semi-skilled and virtually all of the high-skilled jobs in the manufacturing sector are service-oriented. This implies that services account for much of the cost, and therefore, much of the value-added in the manufacturing sector.

Table 10.2: Employed persons by occupation in Thailand's manufacturing sector (Q4, 2013)

		thousand persons	**percentage**
High-skilled (tertiary education or equivalent)		705	13%
Of which:	Professionals	183	3%
	Technicians and associate professionals	339	6%
	Legislators, senior officials and managers	182	3%
Semi-skilled (first or second stage of secondary education)		4,117	78%
Of which:	Craft and related trades workers	1,986	38%

Contd.

		thousand persons	percentage
	Plant and machine operators and assemblers	1,734	33%
	Clerks	237	4%
	Service workers and shop and market sales workers	148	3%
	Skilled agricultural and fishery workers	11	0%
Elementary occupations (primary education)		466	9%
Workers not classifiable by occupation		4	0%
Total		5,291	100%

Source: National Statistical Office of Thailand, authors' calculation

In 2013, Thailand's food and beverage exports ranked eleventh in the world, and second in Asia.[13] Thailand is now among the top exporters of many processed foods, including canned pineapple, shrimp, and canned tuna. In 2013, 84 per cent of Thailand's food and beverages exports were processed food, compared to 63 per cent two decades ago.[14]

Policy and government services have played a significant role in establishing Thailand as a major food producer. Since the 2000s, the Board of Investment, which operates under the Ministry of Industry, has introduced incentives to promote the entire value chain, as opposed to earlier policies that mainly targeted the production process (UNCTAD, 2005). A wide range of government services are involved in the food processing industry in order to promote Thailand as the 'Kitchen of the World'.

Food safety and quality standards

To enhance the competitiveness of Thai food products in the world market, the Thai Government has made conscious efforts to strengthen its standards regime. Realizing the importance of safety and hygiene standards, the Thai government opted to adopt mostly international standards, thus focusing its efforts on robust implementation rather than designing its own regime.

The Thai Government, working together with industry associations, helped

13 UN Comtradedatabase.

14 Ibid.

Thailand's processed food industry to upgrade its procedures and technologies, so that its products meet international quality and sanitation standards (BOI, 2003). Implementation of production standards was gradual and supported by relevant training. The Thailand Food and Drug Administration (FDA) has implemented the Good Manufacturing Practices (GMP) programme for food manufacturers on a voluntary basis for more than 10 years prior to making the GMP mandatory for 54 types of food products in 2001.[15] The government also provides technical and advisory services to assist companies in meeting these standards. The National Food Institute (NFI), for example, provides consultancy services in the implementation of various standards, disseminates information related to food safety laws and standards, and undertakes chemical and microbiological testing of food samples against international standards.

Being a major player in the international food trade, Thailand is also actively participating in international standards negotiations and standards harmonization discussions. In this connection, the Ministry of Agriculture and Cooperatives has been negotiating with ASEAN economies to harmonise agricultural and food standards.

Market development

The Thai Government has been promoting Thai restaurants worldwide, with a view towards increasing demand for Thai food ingredients. Under the Kitchen of the World project, the government provides funding to assist Thai entrepreneurs to open Thai restaurants overseas, as well as holding road shows to promote Thai cuisine overseas (Varanyanond, 2013). In addition, the government sponsors market research to help Thai food processors develop new food products to keep up with shifting tastes in their overseas markets.

Research and development

Working with university research centres and the private sector, the Thai Government has supported applied research to enhance the quality of food production (Poapongsakorn, 2011). These include aspects such as product development, shelf-life stability, and food safety.

To improve the quality of Thai cuisine served in restaurants, the government has funded university research to develop a set of voluntary quality standards on 'authentic' Thai cuisine tastes. Robots were also developed to assess the tastes

15 FDA website: http://www.fda.moph.go.th/eng/food/pre.stm.

and scents of the dishes against these standards. Through such research, the government aims to raise the brand image of Thai cuisine, thus expanding the market for Thai food ingredients.

The latest research-related initiative is the Thailand Food Valley project, which was inspired by the Netherlands' Food Valley NL and launched in 2012. Under this project, the Ministry of Industry aims to strengthen linkages between the private sector and research institutes to 'increase the number of products with added value on the market, improving productivity and achieving 10 per cent annual growth in exports'.[16]

Conclusion

Recent research has demonstrated the linkages between the services and manufacturing sectors. It is unsurprising that policies targeting one sector will affect the other, as several firm-level surveys in various countries have suggested. This chapter has looked at existing literature on the linkages between services and manufacturing sectors, and the overall impact of policies on manufacturing sectors. We have presented findings from case studies, which have shed light on the ways through which policies affect services in manufacturing value chains and, by extension, affect manufacturing as well. We have reviewed the experience of Singapore and Thailand on how governments can enhance the value addition of services in the manufacturing sector.

Whilst policy plays an important role in this process, it can destroy value through poor design or inefficient delivery. On the positive side, well-designed and mandated government policy can help establish profitable linkages between the manufacturing and service sectors, as demonstrated in Singapore's case. Moreover, carefully designed and implemented regulations can promote process innovation, enhancing the efficient use of services in value chains. Despite the compliance costs involved, a robust standards regime can increase the potential for value creation in the domestic economy on the basis of a good reputation for reliability and quality.

The value chain case studies also provide insights on the ways policy can adversely impact value addition of services in value chains. Overlapping or overly complicated regulations can impose significant deadweight losses in the form of excessive compliance burdens. Poorly designed or outdated policies

16 Food Valley NL website: http://www.foodvalleyupdate.com/news/food-valley-nl-piques-thai-interest/.

can increase uncertainty. Inefficiency in regulatory provision will reduce the productivity of value chains.

Manufacturing and services provision are highly interdependent. The functioning of a manufacturing GVC – even one as simple as the bread value chain – involves a considerable number of services. To raise value addition in the manufacturing sector, governments should not focus on sectoral policies alone, but also make a broader effort to improve markets for services. Singapore stands as an example to countries looking to develop their manufacturing sectors beyond low-end assembly activities.

A fine line exists between effective and excessive regulation, as illustrated through various examples relating to standards regimes. The experience of Thailand's food processing industry is an illustration of how the value of exports can be enhanced through strengthened regulation. For food safety, Thailand opted for international standards and focused on strengthening implementation, rather than attempting to design its own standards. However, without other supportive measures, imposing stringent standards alone may not be sufficient to increase value addition in an industry. Government services that help manufacturers cope with conformity assessment will lessen firm costs. Government efforts to develop overseas markets by informing potential foreign customers about the country's industries can help to drive export demand. Taken together, these government services ensure that businesses can reap benefits from an enhanced reputation underpinned by a robust regulatory regime.

References

Akkemil K. Ali. 2008. *Industrial Development in East Asia: A Comparative Look at Japan, Korea, Taiwan, and Singapore*. Singapore: World Scientific.

Ali-Yrkkö, Jyrki, Petri Rouvinen, Timo Seppälä, Pekka Ylä-Anttila. 2011.'Who Captures Value in Global Supply Chains? Case Nokia N95 Smartphone', *Journal of Industry, Competition and Trade* 11 (3): 263–78. Berlin: Springer.

Ang, James S. and David K. Ding. 2006. 'Government Ownership and the Performance of Government-Linked Companies: The Case of Singapore', *Journal of Multinational Financial Management* 16: 64–88, accessed 25 April, 2013. Doi: http://10.1016/j.mulfin.2005.04.010.

Arnold, Jens M., Beata S. Javorcik and Aaditya Mattoo. 2011. 'Does Services Liberalization Benefit Manufacturing Firms?: Evidence from the Czech Republic', *Journal of International Economics* 85 (1): 136–146. Washington DC: World Bank. Doi: http://10.1016/j.jinteco.2011.05.002.

Arnold , Jens Matthias, Beata Javorcik , M. Lipscomb and Aaditya Mattoo. 2012. 'Services Reform and Manufacturing Performance: Evidence from India January', *World Bank Policy Research working paper*. Doi: http://dx.doi.org/10.1596/1813-9450-5948.

Azad, A. K. 1999. 'Inter-Industry Linkages of Services in the Bangladesh Economy (With a Case Study of the Ready-Made Garments Industry) and Potential Service Trade', paper prepared for presentation at WTO2000 South Asia Workshop, organized by the National Council of Applied Economic Research (NCAER) and the World Bank, held in New Delhi, India, 20–21 December, 1999. Available at: http://siteresources.worldbank.org/INTRANETTRADE/Resources/Azad-text.pdf.

Banga, Rashmi and Bishwanath Goldar. 2007. 'Contribution of Services to Output Growth and Productivity in Indian Manufacturing: Pre- and Post-Reforms', *Economic and Political Weekly* 42 (26) (30 June): 2769–777. Available at: http://www.jstor.org/stable/4419765.

Clemes, Michael D., Ali Arifa and Azmat Gani. 2003. 'An Empirical Investigation of the Spillover Effects of Services and Manufacturing Sectors in ASEAN Countries', *Asia-Pacific Development Journal* 10 (2): 29–40. Doi: http://10.1111/ecoj.12206.

EDB. 2014. 'Headquarters Award'. Economic Development Board Singapore. Available at: https://www.edb.gov.sg/content/dam/edb/en/resources/pdfs/financing-and-incentives/International%20or%20Regional%20Headquarters%20(HQ)%20Leaflet.pdf.

Feng, F., Sun, Q. and W. H. S. Tong. 2004. 'Do Government-linked Companies Underperform'?, *Journal of Banking & Finance* 28: 2461–92.

Fernandes, Ana M. and Caroline Paunov. 2008. 'Foreign Direct Investment in Services and Manufacturing Productivity Growth: Evidence for Chile', *World Bank Policy research working paper 4730*. Available at: http://elibrary.worldbank.org/doi/pdf/10.1596/1813-9450-4730.

Francois, Joseph F. and Julia Woerz. 2008. 'Producer Services, Manufacturing Linkages, and Trade', *Journal of Industry, Competition and Trade* 8 (3–4): 199–229. Doi: http://dx.doi.org/10.1007/s10842-008-0043-0.

Guerrieri, Paolo and Valentina Meliciani. 2005.'Technology and International Competitiveness: The Interdependence between Manufacturing and Producer Services Structural Change and Economic Dynamics', *Structural Change and Economic Dynamics* 16 (4):489–502. Doi: http://dx.doi.org/10.1016/j.strueco.2005.02.002.

Hiratsuka, Daisuke. 2011. 'Production Networks in Asia: A Case Study from the Hard Disk Drive Industry', *ADBI working paper No. 301*. Asian Development Bank Institute.Available at: http://www.adbi.org/working-paper/2011/07/28/4669.production.networks.asia.hard.disk.case/.

Humphrey, John and Hubert Schmitz. 2000. 'Governance and Upgrading: Linking Industrial Cluster and Global Value Chain Research', *IDS working paper 120*. Institute of Development Studies.

Kommerskollegium. 2010. 'At Your Service: The Importance of Services for Manufacturing Companies and Possible Trade Policy Implications'. Available at: http://www.kommers.se/Documents/dokumentarkiv/publikationer/2010/skriftserien/report-2010-2-at-your-service.pdf.

MTI.1991. 'The Strategic Economic Plan: Towards A Developed Nation—Executive Summary'. Singapore: Ministry of Trade and Investment. Available at: http://www.mti.gov.sg/ResearchRoom/Documents/app.mti.gov.sg/data/pages/885/doc/NWS_plan.pdf.

Okeyo, Washington Oduor, James Gathungu and Peter K'Obonyo. 2014. 'The Effect of Business Development Services on Performance of Small and Medium Manufacturing Enterprises in Kenya', *International Journal of Business and Social Research* 4 (6): 12–26. Available at: http://thejournalofbusiness.org/index.php/site/article/view/536.

Osman-Gani, AAhad M. 2004. 'Human Capital Development in Singapore: An Analysis of National Policy Perspectives', *Advances in Developing Human Resources* 6 (3): 276–87. Doi:10.1177/1523422304266074.

Pilat, D. and A. Wölfl. 2005. 'Measuring the Interaction between Manufacturing and Services', *OECD Science, Technology and Industry Working Papers, No. 2005/05*. Paris: OECD Publishing. Doi: http://dx.doi.org/10.1787/882376471514.

Poapongsakorn, Nipon. 2011. 'R&D and Performance of the Thai Agriculture and Food Processing Industry: The Role of Government, Agribusiness Firms, and Farmers', in *Agricultural Development, Trade and Regional Cooperation in Developing East Asia*, edited by *Intal, Ponciano S. Jr., Sothea Oum and Mercy J.O. Simorangkir*. Jakarta: Economic Research Institute for ASEAN and East Asia.

RIE Secretariat. 2011. *Research, Innovation and Enterprise 2015*. RIE Secretariat of Ministry of Trade and Investment Singapore. Available at: http://www.mti.gov.sg/ResearchRoom/Documents/app.mti.gov.sg/data/pages/885/doc/RIE2015.pdf.

Tan, Peng Boo. 1997. 'Human Resource Development for Continued Economic Growth—The Singapore Experience', paper presented at the ILO Workshop on Employers' Organizations in Asia-Pacific in the Twenty-First Century. Turin, Italy, 5–13 May, 1997. Retrieved from: http://www.ilo.org/public/english/dialogue/actemp/downloads/publications/tanhrd1.pdf.

Thailand Board of Investment (BOI). 2015. 'Thailand's Food Industry'. Available at: http://www.boi.go.th/upload/content/BOI_edit_9-8-58_19610.pdf.

UNCTAD (United Nations Conference on Trade and Development). 2005. 'A Case Study of the Electronics Industry in Thailand', *Transfer of Technology for Successful Integration Into the Global Economy Series*. Available at: http://www.

eria.org/publications/key_reports/agricultural-development-trade-and-regional-cooperation-in-developing-east-asia.html.

Varanyanond, Warunee. 2013. 'Fostering Food Culture With Innovation: OTOP and Thai Kitchen to the World', presentation at the Japan International Research Center for Agricultural Sciences (JIRCAS) International Symposium on New Direction of Sustainable Technology Development in Asia, Tokyo, 20–21 Nov, 2013. Retrieved from: http://jircas-d.job.affrc.go.jp/Ver-1/english/files/2014/03/2013-session-42.pdf.

Wong, P. K. and C. Y. Ng. 1997.'Singapore's Industrial Policy to the Year 2000', *in Industrial Policies in East Asia*, edited by S. Masuyama, D. Vandenbrink and C. S. Yue. Singapore and Japan: Institute of Southeast Asian Studies & Nomura Research Institute.

Yeoh, Caroline. 1995. 'Challenges of Global Economic Competition, the Singapore Response', First Annual AAM Conference (Creating Management Synergy in Asian Economies), UniversitiSains Malaysia, 355–64. Avialbale at: http://works.bepress.com/caroline_yeoh/35.

Yue, Chia Siow and James Jeremy Lim. 2003. 'Singapore: A Regional Hub in ICT', in *Towards a Knowledge-based Economy: East Asia's Changing Industrial Geography,* edited by Seiichi Masuyama and Ding Choo Ming. Singapore: Institute of Asian Studies. Available at: http://www.jamus.name/research/ISEASpub2.pdf.

Yue, Chia Siow. 2005. 'The Singapore Model of Industrial Policy: Past Evolution and Current Thinking', paper for presentation at the Second Latin America/Caribbean and Asia/Pacific Economics and Business Association (LAEBA) Annual Conference, Buenos Aires, 28–29 Novemeber, 2005. Retrieved from: http://www.adbi.org/files/2005.11.28.cpp.singapore.industrial.policy.pdf.

Contributors

Anne-Katrin Pfister is a Consultant with the Trade and Competitiveness Global Practice of the World Bank Group. She is interested in the nexus between trade, investment, and development. Her research and advisory roles focus on investment policy, trade in services, global value chains, and the depth of services and investment commitments of regional trade agreements.

Arian Hassani is a Vice President at J. P. Morgan's Global Philanthropy group in Hong Kong. Her career in international development has spanned positions at the United Nations, think tanks and foundations in the U.S., Europe and Asia, focusing on job creation, small business development and broadening economic opportunity.

Balwant Singh Mehta is working as Associate Fellow at the Institute for Human Development, New Delhi. He has worked extensively in the areas of information and communication technology for development, labour market and child well-being.

Chirag Rawat is a management consultant and has advised several developmental institutions and transitional economies on IT-BPO industry and innovation ecosystem development. He holds a MSc in Management of Information Systems from the London School of Economics and Political Science.

Christopher Findlay is Executive Dean of the Faculty of the Professions at the University of Adelaide. His research interests include the drivers of the growth of the service sector and the nature of barriers to trade in services and their consequences. He is also interested in Australia's economic relations with Asia.

David K. N. Sit is a Senior Research Analyst at the Fung Business Intelligence, Hong Kong. His research interests are in global value chains, cross border e-commerce and public policies. David was a member of Fung Global Institute in Hong Kong from 2013 to 2015.

Deborah Elms is Executive Director at Asian Trade Centre, Singapore. She helps companies and governments collaborate to create better trade policy outcomes for Asia. Her work includes research, training and advocacy across a wide range of trade topics including trade agreements, global value chains and e-commerce.

Denise Cheung is Senior Research Manager at Fung Business Intelligence in Hong Kong. Prior to joining Fung Business Intelligence, Denise conducted research on global value chains at the Fung Global Institute under Dr Patrick Low. Her research interests are in trade policy, regional economic integration and global value chains.

Dev Nathan is Visiting Professor at the Institute for Human Development, New Delhi, and Visiting Research Fellow at the Center on Globalization, Governance and Competitiveness at Duke University, USA.

Gloria O. Pasadilla is Senior Analyst at the APEC Policy Support Unit (PSU) in Singapore and a former research fellow at the ADB Institute in Tokyo. Her research has focused on services trade, free trade areas, supply chains, non-tariff measures, and more recently on the digital economy. She also has experience as an FTA negotiator.

Julia Tijaja is Director at the ASEAN Integration Monitoring Directorate of the ASEAN Secretariat. Her areas of specialization include global value chains, regional economic integration, FTA negotiations as well as trade and industrial policy.

Maria Joy Abrenica is Professor at the School of Economics, University of the Philippines Diliman and Research Fellow at the Center for the Advancement of Trade Integration and Facilitation. Her research interests are in energy, telecommunications, competition policy and trade.

Patrick Low is Visiting Professor and Director of the Asia Global Institute's Asia Global Fellows Programme at Hong Kong University. From 1997–2013, he was Chief Economist at the World Trade Organization and a senior research economist at the World Bank from 1990–94, where he worked on trade issues, trade and environment, fiscal policy and governance in customs administrations.

Pradeep Kumar Mukherji is a globally renowned management consultant and expert on ICT for economic development and is consulted regularly by multilateral development institutions such as the World Bank, Africa Development Bank, USAID, Commonwealth secretariat and UNCTAD. He holds a PhD in management sciences and expert systems from IIT, Kharagpur.

Sandip Sarkar is Professor at the Institute for Human Development, New Delhi. He has previous research experience with research institutes like Institute of Economic Growth and Institute for Studies in Industrial Development. His areas of research interest are industry, poverty, labour and employment, on which he has experience of more than two decades.

Sherry Stephenson is a Senior Fellow with the International Centre for Trade and Sustainable Development (ICTSD) in Geneva, Switzerland. She is an international trade policy analyst specializing in the areas of services trade, global value chains and regional trade integration. She has long been supportive of APEC's work in the area of services, has worked with the OECD and the GATT, and was an Advisor to the Minister of Trade in Indonesia in the early 1990s.

Index

Development Trajectories in Global Value Chains

Other titles in the series

1. *Labour in Global Value Chains in Asia*
   Edited by Dev Nathan, MeenuTewari and Sandip Sarkar
2. *The Sweatshop Regime: Labouring Bodies, Exploitation, and Garments* Made in India
   By Alessandra Mezzadri